Childhoods of the
American Presidents

Childhoods of the American Presidents

WILLIAM O. FOSS

McFarland & Company, Inc., Publishers
Jefferson, North Carolina, and London

LIBRARY OF CONGRESS CATALOGUING-IN-PUBLICATION DATA

Foss, William O.
Childhoods of the American presidents / William O. Foss.
p.   cm.
Includes bibliographical references and index.

ISBN 0-7864-2382-X (softcover : 50# alkaline paper)

1. Presidents—United States—Biography.
2. Children—United States—Biography.
I. Title.
E176.1.F765   2005   973.09'9—dc22   2005026325

British Library cataloguing data are available

On the cover: Franklin D. Roosevelt, 1895
(Franklin D. Roosevelt Library);
Seal of the President of the United States

Manufactured in the United States of America

McFarland & Company, Inc., Publishers
Box 611, Jefferson, North Carolina 28640
www.mcfarlandpub.com

To Wilma

I've always believed in the truth of the old saying that "America is great because anyone can grow up to be President."

Bob Dole, former U.S. Senator
and Republican presidential
nominee in 1996.

Table of Contents

Table of Contents

Preface

The idea for a book about the childhoods of American presidents began many years ago after I read several biographies of presidents Herbert Hoover and Franklin Delano Roosevelt. In my younger days, FDR was the dominant political figure in the United States. After all, he was the first and only president to be elected to a third term. And then to a fourth.

Franklin D. Roosevelt's boyhood was one of privilege. He enjoyed a good life; he attended prestigious Harvard University. Perhaps his only problem was a domineering mother. Herbert Hoover, on the other hand, was orphaned in his childhood; he lost his father when he was six years old, and his mother passed away when he was nine.

Sometime after I read their biographies, I had an opportunity to visit the birthplaces of the two presidents. Roosevelt's home at Hyde Park, New York, overlooking the Hudson River was a palace compared to the small, two-room cottage that was Hoover's home in West Branch, Iowa.

The visits to those two presidential homes piqued my interest in the childhoods of American presidents. I wanted to know about their home life, their education, and the qualities that led them to the path of the presidency.

Growing up is hard to do. Most children are guided through the process period by caring parents, but some are forced to struggle. American presidents have come from both groups.

A great number of books are written about our presidents; most of them deal with their adult life. Those interested in their childhoods must usually turn to books written for children. Myriad books of that sort are available to interested readers, but some may be more legend than fact. For example, serious researchers should avoid anything written about George Washington by a parson named Mason Locke Weems. In the mid–1800s, Parson Weems fictionalized the life of George Washington to include the famed legend of little George not being able to lie and admitting to cutting the cherry tree.

In my quest for information about the childhoods of American presidents, I sought out the help of the able librarians at the Virginia Beach public libraries. Another source was the presidential libraries operated by the U.S. National Archives and Records Administration. Presidential libraries and museums that predate Herbert Hoover's presidency are administered by state and private institutions. For more information about the presidents, go to www.archives.gov on the World Wide Web.

In my search for previously published books on the childhoods of American presidents, I found a chapbook entitled *When the Presidents Were Boys*, written by Winifred Estabrook, published in 1925 by the Statler Press in Johnstown, Pennsylvania. The 63-page book devoted two pages—one of text and one a drawing—to each president from George Washington to Calvin Coolidge.

The reader will note that in this book the presidents are all given their official numerical designation, which means that the chapter on Grover Cleveland is numbered "22 and 24." The chapters for the 23rd president (Benjamin Harrison) and the 25th (Theodore Roosevelt) follow the chapter on Cleveland. Each chapter throughout the book thus gives the correct numerical designation to the president.

Researching this book has been a lot of fun. I love the excitement of discovering new information. Nevertheless, there comes a time when the writer has to stop researching and write. Here is what I have learned and written about the presidents. I hope you enjoy it.

W.O.F.

★ 1 ★

George Washington

First President
1789–1797

George Washington did not cry and confess to his father that he was the one who cut the cherry tree. That story was made up by Mason Locke Weems, an eccentric preacher who wrote a fanciful biography of our first president. But what is true is that George Washington tried to enlist in the British Royal Navy when he was 14. His stern mother issued a flat no, and that ended George's dream of becoming a midshipman in the Royal Navy.

What if George Washington had been allowed to enter the British Navy? Would the course of the American Revolution have been different? Would it have transformed America into a different nation from what it is today? One can only wonder.

George Washington was born in a four-room brick house located along the banks of Pope's Creek in Westmoreland County, Virginia. The date was February 11, based upon the Julian calendar then in use throughout the world. In 1582, Pope Gregory XIII ordained that ten days should be added to the tally of all past time since the birth of Jesus, to make up some fractional deficiencies in the calendar. The British government did not impose the calendar change on all its possessions, including the American colonies, until 1752. The British decreed that the day following September 2, 1752, should be September 14, a loss of 11 days. All dates preceding were marked O.S. for

Old Style. George Washington was born on February 11, 1732, O.S., and after 1752 his birthday fell on February 22.

George was the first child of Mary Ball who married Augustine Washington in 1731. Gus, as he was known to intimates, was a widower with three children—Lawrence, age 13 at the time of his father's remarriage; Augustine "Austin," 12, and Jane, nine years old.

Mary Ball was an orphan who had been brought up by George Eskridge, a respected lawyer and land speculator in Westmoreland. Her first child was probably named after her benefactor. The marriage of Mary Ball and Augustine Washington was to produce five more children—Samuel, John Augustine, Charles, Elizabeth and Mildred, who died in infancy.

George Washington's grandfather, John Washington, had come to Virginia from England in 1657 as a seaman on a British merchant vessel. Although arriving in Virginia almost penniless, he worked hard and soon acquired land of a modest fortune.

Augustine Washington was a hardworking man. Educated in England, he became a planter, cultivating land he had inherited or purchased along Bridges Creek, Pope's Creek, and Little Hunting Creek up the Potomac River. The Hunting Creek land was then called Epsewasson. Today we know the property as Mount Vernon. He performed his public service as vestryman, county justice, militia captain and sheriff. Augustine also operated a fairly profitable iron mill. When Augustine Washington died in 1743 he left his sons and daughters 10,000 acres of land and at least 48 slaves.

When George was three years old, his father moved the family from Pope's Creek to their new home on the Epsewasson plantation. It was at Epsewasson in 1736 that six-year-old George first met his half brother Lawrence, who was to play an important part in George's life. Lawrence, then 21, returned to Virginia from England, where he had attended school. Lawrence fascinated the younger boy with his knowledge and tales of adventure in distant England.

The same year that George made his acquaintance with Lawrence, his father purchased and rented additional property near Fredericksburg. By December, Augustine Washington had moved his family into a two-story house located on Ferry Farm, abutting the Rappahannock River. Lawrence was entrusted with the important duties of managing the Epsewasson plantation.

George's third home, Ferry Farm, was aptly named, because a ferry operated from the Washington property across the river to Fredericksburg. For George, growing up at Ferry Farm would offer much excitement; he could fish and swim in the river, ride the ferry, watch ships sail on the river, or visit a real town with a courthouse, a prison, a church, tobacco warehouses, and other structures, including a school.

School was held in a one-room log house and conducted by the Reverend James Marye. Here George learned to read, write and to do arithmetic, a subject in which he excelled. George was also tutored by one Hobby, an indentured servant—a former teacher whom Augustine Washington had brought over from England. Under Hobby's guidance, George learned about geography, logarithms, geometry, and a bit of astronomy, subjects in which he took a special interest and which prepared him for his first job as a surveyor.

George's teachers had him copy many of his lessons. Among his copy books that remain are morality edicts laid out in the *Rules of Civility and Decent Behaviour in Company and Conversation*, and rules of conduct in *Youth Behaviour*. Among the gems copied by young George Washington were:

> Honor and obey your natural parents although they be poor.
> Let you recreation be manful, not sinful.
> Use no reproachful language against any one, neither curse nor revile.
> Strive not with your superiors in argument, but always subject your judgment to others with modesty.
> Cleanse not your teeth with the tablecloth.
> Keep to the fashion of your equals.
> Be not curious to know the affairs of others, neither approach those that speak in private.
> Every action done in company ought to be with same sign of respect to those that are present.
> Labour to keep alive in your breast that little spark of celestial fire called conscience.

George would find these lessons to be beneficial in his future career. He always displayed courteous behavior toward others and was the consummate man of honesty and truthfulness.

In the summer of 1740 Lawrence joined a Virginia colonial military force that sailed to the Caribbean to take part in British Admiral Vernon's expedition against the Spanish at Cartagena. Lawrence, who had been commissioned a captain in the Marines, served aboard the flagship of Admiral Vernon and fought bravely in a successful attack against a Spanish battery at Baraderas. When Lawrence came home safely from the war to Ferry Farm, his tales of soldiering greatly impressed young George. The stories Lawrence told about military life and war was to have strong influence on George's decision to volunteer for the military when he reached maturity.

In June 1742, George met for the first time his other half brother, Augustine, Jr., called Austin, who had returned to Virginia after completing his studies in England.

In the spring of 1743, George was visiting some of his cousins in the Chotank district of the Potomac when he was called home because his father was seriously ill. Augustine Washington died April 17, 1743. George was 11.

Lawrence, the eldest son, received the largest share of his father's estate. Among the property he received was Epsewasson, which he later named Mount Vernon, after his honored admiral. George received the Ferry Farm, half a tract of 4,360 acres, ten slaves, and three lots his father had acquired in Fredericksburg. George's inheritance was to be under the control of his mother, Mary Washington, until he reached the age of 21.

The death of his father ended any opportunity for George to further his education by attending English schools as his elder half brothers had done. With Lawrence and Austin building their own lives, George became the man of the house at Ferry Farm, but under the strict control of his mother, a headstrong and short-tempered woman. She would retain control of George's inheritance until almost 30 years had passed. Whatever her character, George remained a considerate son.

George dutifully performed his chores on the Ferry Farm, but he also had time to ride horses, shoot and fish. He was a tall and strong lad, who, as an adult, measured six feet two inches and weighed 175 pounds. His bones and joints were large, as were his hands and feet; he wore a size 13 shoe.

While Mary Washington kept a close rein on George, she allowed him to visit the homes of his half brothers, Lawrence, who lived at Mount Vernon, and Austin, who resided at Pope's Creek. George was tremendously fond of Lawrence, who became a substitute father to the boy.

In 1746, when George was 14, Lawrence encouraged him to seek appointment as a midshipmen in the British Royal Navy. George was not averse to this, but his mother squashed the idea after seeking out advice from a relative in England. She would rather have her eldest son become a gentleman farmer in Virginia than live the uncertain life of a sailor. In this instance she acted sensibly rather than simply possessively.

Riding the neighboring area of Ferry Farm, George would see surveyors measuring acres of land for dividing and selling. He became interested in their work, and decided that he wanted to learn the trade. Since he had a flair for mathematics, with good knowledge of logarithms and geometry, he already possessed the basic academic talents to become a surveyor. In the storehouse at Ferry Farm were some surveying instruments that had belonged to his father, and George began to work with these. Then he got some of the professional surveyors in the Fredericksburg area to teach him the basics of surveying. Soon he was assisting the surveyors, and by the middle of his fifteenth year George was earning money from his own surveys.

George had begun to spend more time with Lawrence at Mount Vernon. Lawrence had married Anne Fairfax, daughter of Colonel William Fairfax, a cousin of Lord Thomas Fairfax, owner of an almost boundless tract of land in northern Virginia. The wealthy and influential Fairfaxes lived at Belvoir, a magnificent estate located near Mount Vernon.

In the spring of 1748, Lord Fairfax decided to send an expedition to map his vast western lands, and through the influence of Lawrence Washington, young George was invited to go along as an assistant surveyor. Although he would be going into the wilderness for an extended period, George's mother made no objection to his new adventure.

He had just reached his sixteenth birthday, and the surveying trip was an important step in George's life. It marked his farthest journey away from home and brought him in contact with the new frontier, the wilderness of the Blue Ridge in the Shenandoah Valley.

Though he was a good horseman and knew how to work on the farm, George Washington was unfamiliar with life in the wilderness. Fascinated with frontier living, George wrote about his new experiences in a daily journal—a habit he was to continue for a lifetime.

Admitting that he was "not a good woodsman" as were his companions, George wrote about his new experiences of swimming his horse across a snow-filled river and meeting a war party of 30 Indians who were carrying a human scalp and who performed a war dance for the white men. He also recorded how he cooked his food on a forked stick over a fire, and used a large chip of wood from a tree as a plate. While George was accustomed to sleeping in his own bed at Ferry Farm, he quickly learned how to sleep in a small tent or in the open beside a fire.

Almost every day George did some surveying work, often under difficult circumstances, in muddy, partly flooded lands or heavily wooded areas. When the surveying party ended its work in April, George had surveyed 400 acres of land for future settlers in the Virginia wilderness.

George Washington learned a lot about surveying from the Fairfax expedition and soon he was doing survey jobs on his own and making money. A year later, in 1749, George Washington helped lay out the new town of Belhaven, later to be called Alexandria. Then he obtained a commission as a surveyor of Culpeper from the College of William and Mary. As a qualified county surveyor, George could now work anywhere he was engaged. Later that year, he was in charge of a surveying expedition in Frederick, Maryland. Surveying became profitable. It enabled George to make his first land purchase—1,489 acres at Bullskin Creek, a tributary of the Shenandoah River.

George Washington spent much of his time with his older half brother Lawrence at Mount Vernon. Through Lawrence, who socialized with the influential and well-to-do Fairfaxes at Belvoir, George had his first close view of British upper-class life. He learned how to play billiards, whist and lo, a game of cards in which forfeits are paid into a pool.

In the acquisition of social graces, George became increasingly concerned over his clothes and appearance. In the future George Washington would always dress fashionably. He enjoyed social pleasures such as attending dinner dances and amateur plays.

Young George Washington also began to take an interest in girls, but he did not have much success with them. George was quite awkward in encounters with girls. Very tall and masculine for his age, and lacking humor, George was more often than not given the cold shoulder by the affluent Virginia girls he tried to date. He took his defeats hard, translating some of them into atrocious poetry. To a girl named Frances Alexander, lovesick George wrote a poem which began:

> From your bright sparking Eyes, I was undone;
> Rays you have more transparent than the Sun.
> Amidst its glory in the rising Day,
> None can you equal in your bright array....

While living at Mount Vernon, 16-year-old George Washington met and fell in love with Sally Fairfax, the 18-year-old wife of George Fairfax, Washington's good friend and son of Lord Fairfax, the man who gave him the opportunity to become a surveyor. While the attractive young woman was amused and flattered by the young man's attention, she never gave him an opportunity to openly express his affection. They corresponded over the years, and just before he married Martha Dandrige Custis, at the age of 27, he wrote his last letter to Sally Fairfax, then living in England.

In his letter, Washington wrote, "Misconstrue not my meaning; doubt it not, or expose it. The world has no business to know the object of my love declared in this manner to you, when I want to conceal it." Sally never answered his letter.

In the fall of 1751, Lawrence, who had developed a cough that turned into a lingering illness, decided to seek a cure in a milder climate. His wife could not go with him as she had just had a baby, so George volunteered to go along and help his beloved half brother. They sailed for the island of Barbados in the West Indies. While there George contracted the smallpox that pockmarked his face permanently, but fortunately left him immune to the disease that later ravaged the country during the American Revolution.

Lawrence decided to stay in Bermuda in search of more warmth and sunshine. George then sailed home to Virginia where he landed in January 1752. Upon his return George resumed his surveying work, earning enough money to increase his land holdings. Lawrence came home six months later to die of turberculosis. His will provided that his widow was to hold Mount Vernon in trust for their child. If the child died, however, the estate would pass to George. This event came to pass two years later.

Lawrence had held the position of adjutant of the Virginia volunteer militia company. On Lawrence's death, George sought the office. On February 1, 1753, George was sworn in as an adjutant with the rank of major for the southern part of the Virginia colony. At the age of 20, the military career of George Washington had begun.

Commissioned a lieutenant colonel in 1754, Washington fought the first skirmishes of what grew into the French and Indian War. Later, as an aide to General Edward Braddock, he escaped injury although four bullets ripped his coat and two horses were shot from under him.

From 1759 to the outbreak of the American Revolution, Washington settled down as a gentleman farmer at Mount Vernon and served in the Virginia House of Burgesses. As a delegate to the Second Continental Congress assembled in Philadelphia in 1775, Washington was selected as commander in chief of the Continental Army and took command at Cambridge, Massachusetts, on July 3, 1775.

Washington conducted the war on the policy of avoiding major engagements with the British and wearing them down by harassment tactics. Eventually, with French aid, he forced the British to surrender at Yorktown, Virginia, on October 19, 1781.

In 1787 he presided over the Constitutional Convention meeting in Philadelphia. He was elected the first president of the United States and inaugurated in New York on April 30, 1789. He was reelected in 1792. George Washington died at Mount Vernon on December 14, 1799.

Bibliography

Alden, John R. *George Washington: A Biography.* Baton Rouge: Louisiana State University, 1984.

Clark, Harrison. *The Life of George Washington: From Youth to Yorktown.* Washington, DC: Regnery, 1995.

Flexner, James Thomas. *George Washington: The Forge of Experience (1732–1775).* Boston: Little, Brown, 1965.

Freeman, Douglas Southall. *Washington* (an abridgment in one volume by Richard Harwell). New York: Scribner's, 1968.

Lewis, Thomas. *For King and Country: George Washington, the Early Years.* New York: John Wiley, 1993.

Randall, Willard Sterne. *George Washington: A Life.* New York: Henry Holt, 1997.

★ 2 ★

John Adams

Second President
1797–1801

John Adams was a shiftless boy. He had little ambition; he preferred playing, hunting and fishing to attending school. When he did attend school he daydreamed, because he felt that the classes were boring.

That is how John Adams, the second president of the United States, described his youthful behavior in his diaries. Fortunately, his father, also named John Adams, had other ideas; he insisted that his first-born son complete his education.

John Adams, the son, was born in the village of Braintree (now Quincy), Massachusetts, a small town about 12 miles from Boston, on October 3, 1735. His father was a deacon in the local church, a militia officer, and a selectman (one of the town's elected administrative officers). He worked a small farm and was also the town's shoemaker.

John's mother, Susanna Boylston, came from a prominent family in Muddy River, now called Brookline. She was 20 years younger than her husband. She was industrious, talkative and hot-tempered. John recalled in his memoirs that his parents were often bickering. "Reason" prevailed in most of the homes of his friends, he wrote, but "passion" ruled the Adams household. He thought his mother won most arguments.

The strong-willed parents tried to educate John, Jr., and his younger brothers, Peter Boylston and Elihu, at home. The boys learned how to read and write. However, Deacon Adams was determined that his first-born son would get a college education.

According to custom of those days, the oldest son was destined to receive the best education that the family could provide. Younger sons were expected to help their father, such as working in the fields. Daughters were expected to help their mothers with house chores and care for the younger children.

John's formal education began when he was about six years old, when he attended an academy for boys and girls conducted at the home of the teacher, Mrs. Belcher, who lived across the street from the Adamses. Here he studied reading, writing, and arithmetic. Mrs. Belcher, addressed as Dame Belcher, was a pleasant woman who enjoyed teaching children. While they spent much time reading and reciting their study books, Mrs. Belcher would at times offer her students cookies. She also taught the children how to sing.

After a couple of years of studying with Mrs. Belcher, John was enrolled in the Latin School at Braintree. That school was operated by Joseph Cleverly, a Harvard College graduate.

Cleverly turned out to be a lazy teacher who each day required his students to recite from a Latin grammar book and from catechism lessons. John found the Latin school to be boring; his schoolmaster was dull, and the atmosphere was cheerless.

John started skipping school. He found many ways to avoid going to school. Recalling his unhappy days at the Latin School, John Adams wrote in his memoirs that "I spent my time as idle children do in making and sailing boats and ships upon the pond and brooks, making and flying kites, in driving hoops, playing marbles, playing quoits [a game like horseshoes], wrestling, swimming, skating, and above all in shooting."

When his father learned that John had been a truant, he scolded his son for his misdeed, and pointed out that knowledge of Latin was a necessary requirement for anyone who wanted to study at Harvard College. John replied that he didn't want to go to college. He'd rather be a farmer. His father retorted, "A farmer? Well, I will show you what it is to be a farmer."

Early the next morning, the father took his son into the marsh to retrieve thatch. All day, under the hot sun, they worked in knee-deep mud, stooping, cutting, bundling and lifting bundles of thatching. At the end of the day's work, the elder Adams asked his bone-tired son how he liked farming. "I like it very well, sir," replied the tired and muddy son. "But I don't like it so well," stormed the elder Adams. "You will go to school. You will comply with my desires."

John Adams did not return to Latin School and Mr. Cleverly's teachings. Instead, the father arranged for him to receive private tutoring from Joseph Marsh, who was known for preparing his students to pass the entrance examinations at Harvard. Marsh loved teaching and encouraged his students to try their best. John Adams began to study in earnest, and soon found that he enjoyed attending school. In addition to studying the required Latin, he emerged himself in history, especially the history of England. He decided to become a serious scholar, reading books and writing essays, qualities that would stay with him for the rest of his life.

In the spring of 1751, after a year under Marsh's tutelage, John, then 16, was pronounced ready for Harvard. Marsh was supposed to be present and introduce John to the Harvard examiners, but he was sick, so John rode his horse to Cambridge alone.

After John was interviewed by the college's president and tutors, he was asked to take the entrance examination, which included a passage in Latin that he was to translate into English. John did not recognize some words and was afraid that he would fail the test. He was greatly relieved that he was allowed to use a dictionary. He then passed the test. He was almost light-headed with excitement as he galloped home to tell his parents that he was accepted by Harvard.

John Adams entered Harvard in the fall of 1751. There, the day began with morning prayers at 6:00, and ended with bedtime at 9:00. Freshmen studied logic, rhetoric (speaking and writing), physics, Greek, and Latin. On Saturdays, all the college students were required to attend the theology classes given by Harvard's president, Edward Holyoke.

Adams threw himself into all of his studies, especially math and natural and moral philosophy. In his junior year, he joined a play reading club, where members read plays and poems aloud. They also made speeches about school subjects and current events. John quickly developed a flair for public speaking. He liked dramatic subjects that allowed him to use vigorous gestures and expressions. Those communication skills would enhance his future career.

When he graduated from Harvard in the spring of 1755 with a bachelor of arts degree, his family expected him to take up theological studies. John had no intention of becoming a minister; instead he planned to become a teacher.

At his graduation, Adams made one of the commencement addresses. It made a strong impression on Thaddeus MacCarty, a minister in the town of Worcester who came to Cambridge to hire a Latin teacher for the grammar school. Three weeks after graduation, John Adams, not quite 20 years old, made the 60 mile trip to Worcester on horseback. John stayed with Mr. Mac-Carty while he taught Latin to the children in MacCarty's grammar school for a small salary. The people in Worcester were quite friendly, often inviting the new teacher to afternoon teas. Soon he knew everyone in town.

While he enjoyed teaching, John Adams had a burning desire to become a lawyer. He wanted to move ahead. In larger towns such as Boston, lawyers were becoming professional politicians. John demonstrated his talent for the legal arena during college debates, and especially when he delivered his commencement address. His topic was "Liberty cannot exist without law." His argument that laws were needed to keep liberty from being mere chaos shows that he may have planted the seed for cultivating a legal career.

After about a year of teaching grammar school students, John Adams asked James Putnam, one of Worcester's leading lawyers, to take him into his office to learn law. For two years he served his apprenticeship with Putnam, copying deeds and wills, studying law, preparing briefs, and discussing court cases. During the day he continued teaching the children at the grammar school.

In August 1758, two years after he began, John Adams completed his law studies under Putnam. He moved back in with his parents and began practicing law in Braintree writing wills and deeds and taking an interest in town affairs. On October 25, 1764, he married Abigail Smith, a brilliant and capable woman, who, in her own right, became one of the famous characters of American history.

Adams' legal practice took him to Boston, where, in 1770, he helped defend the British soldiers accused of murder in the Boston Massacre. It was an incident of justice versus unlawful authority. The court ruled that the soldiers shot and killed civilians because the soldiers were defending themselves against a threatening mob.

John Adams soon involved himself in patriotic maneuvers against the British. He became a delegate to the First Continental Congress in 1774. During the next three years in Philadelphia, he pushed Congress to separate the colonies from Britain. He helped write the resolutions that declared America independent, and defended the Declaration of Independence during debate in Congress.

During 1789 to 1797, Adams served under George Washington as the first vice president of the United States. He became president on March 4, 1797. Adams left the presidency in 1801. He died at his Quincy home on July 4, 1826.

Bibliography

Ferling, John. *John Adams: A Life.* Knoxville: The University of Tennessee Press, 1992.

McCullough. David. *John Adams.* New York: Simon & Schuster, 2001.

Peabody, James Bishop, ed. *John Adams: A Biography in His Own Words.* Volumes I & II. New York: Newsweek, 1973.

Shaw, Peter. *The Character of John Adams.* Chapel Hill: University of North Carolina Press, 1976.

Smith, Page. *John Adams*, Volumes I & II. Garden City, NY: Doubleday, 1962.

Thomas Jefferson

Third President
1801–1809

If Thomas Jefferson was a boy today, people might be calling the tall, lanky, freckle-faced, skinny kid from Shadwell, Virginia, an egghead, or a real brainy guy, which he was. Thomas Jefferson, destined to be the author of the Declaration of Independence, was born on April 13, 1743, the third child of Peter and Jane Jefferson. Thomas had two older sisters, four younger sisters and a younger brother.

Thomas' father, Peter Jefferson, a Virginia frontiersman, was a self-made man who taught himself to be a surveyor, which enabled him to purchase thousands of acres of land in the Virginia wilderness. He was also prominent in local affairs, holding such posts as justice of the peace, sheriff, judge, commander of the local militia, and representing his county in the Virginia House of Burgesses (the Virginia colony's government council under the supervision of the English governor).

Thomas' mother, Jane Jefferson, was the daughter of Isham Randolph, Adjutant General of Virginia. The Randolph family was among the early settlers of Virginia. When a cousin of Jane Jefferson died, she and her husband moved from Shadwell to Tuckahoe to care for the cousin's orphaned children. They stayed at Tuckahoe for seven years, returning to Shadwell in 1752, when Thomas Jefferson was nine years old. Thomas Jefferson once stated that his earliest memory was sitting astride on a horse's neck, steadied by a slave, on the 65-mile journey from Shadwell to Tuckahoe. More than likely he heard the story second-hand, because he was then only two years old.

Thomas got his first schooling when the family lived at Tuckhaoe. When they returned to Shadwell, Thomas was placed in a school operated by the Reverend William Douglas, who taught his students Greek, Latin, and French.

Thomas and his teacher did not get along. Douglas found his student inattentive and given to daydreaming. Thomas disliked his teacher and thought him boring.

While his father insisted that Thomas, his eldest son, attend boarding schools and become well educated, he also encouraged Thomas to become self-reliant. Thomas learned well. Whenever he came home to Shadwell from boarding schools, he would ride his horse in the forest and roam the country-side to study the trees, flowers and vegetation. Jefferson would become one of the best horsemen in Virginia. He first hunted alone when he was ten. Taking the new gun his father had given him, Thomas rode into the forest seeking prey. He found nothing. On the way home, young Thomas Jefferson, the hunter, came across a wild turkey in a pen. Tying the bird to a tree, he shot it, and proudly brought his trophy home.

Thomas was only 14 when his father died in August 1757 at the age of 50. He was greatly affected by the loss of his father, who had been the family's pillar of strength, and the parent to whom he was deeply attached. In his will, Peter Jefferson provided Thomas with the largest portion of his property (2,500 acres and 20 slaves), when he reached the age of 21. Meanwhile, the Shadwell property would be managed by several guardians named by his father.

Thomas became distressed over the loss of his father. Years later, in a letter to a grandson, Thomas Jefferson wrote. "I recollect that at 14 years of age, the whole care and direction of myself was thrown on myself entirely, without a relation or friend qualified to advice or guide me."

While his father had appointed competent guardians and overseers of the property, Thomas felt ill at ease under the watch and ward of his widowed mother. Thomas' relationship with his mother was cool. He seldom spoke of her. So little is known about Jane Jefferson that it is difficult to know if her son's coolness toward her was justified. The only time Thomas Jefferson wrote anything about his mother was on March 31, 1776. He noted in his diary, "My mother died about eight o'clock this morning, in the 57th year of her age."

Soon after his father's death, in order to further his education and to gain relief from the pressures of his uncomfortable domestic situation, Thomas became a boarder under the care of the Reverend James Maury at his home near Charlottesville, not far from Shadwell. Maury's school was recognized as one of the best in the Virginia province.

At school much of Jefferson's time was spent reading Greek and Latin, and he soon distinguished himself by his scholarship and industry. Although Maury focused on classical education and the arts, he particularly stressed the importance of competence in the use of the English language. Maury had collected what was considered an impressive library for that period, consisting of more than 400 volumes. Jefferson was encouraged to use the library often, and to familiarize himself with the current literature as well as the classics.

Maury gave his students more than book learning. He wanted them to enjoy the world around them. He would take his students for walks through the Blue Ridge Mountains in search of fossils, studying geology and other sciences. He also gave his students time to engage in other pursuits, such as riding horses and hunting. While studying under Maury, Thomas Jefferson learned how to dance and play the violin. He became an excellent violin player.

After two years of studying with Maury, 17-year-old Thomas Jefferson was restless and eager to make important changes in his life. He did not want to remain at Shadwell to live with his distant mother and his six sisters and a dull brother. He wanted to widen his circle of acquaintances, see more of the world, and to further his education. Thomas sought the advice of two of the guardians that his father had selected to guide his son. One of the guardians was a cousin, Colonel Peter Randolph; the other was John Harvie, who managed his business matters. Both guardians approved of Thomas' plan to further his education.

Jefferson did not have much choice in his selection of an institution of higher education. He could attend any of the New England colleges, but Thomas Jefferson was determined that he would stay in Virginia—he would always be a Virginian.

Taking his violin, a few books and some clothing, Jefferson set out from Shadwell on a five-day ride to Williamsburg, where he enrolled in the College of William and Mary on March 25, 1760. To Jefferson, who had never seen a town of more than 20 houses, Williamsburg was a wild and exciting place—he playfully referred to it on several occasions as Devilsburg. At the time of his arrival, the Virginia capitol had a population of 1,800 residents.

William and Mary College was divided into four schools: a grammar school for the instruction of boys to the age of 15; a school of philosophy; a postgraduate divinity school, and an Indian school. Thomas Jefferson attended the school of philosophy. He was instructed in natural philosophy (physics, metaphysics, and mathematics) and moral philosophy (rhetoric, logic, and ethics). A keen and diligent student, he displayed an avid curiosity in all fields, spending many hours on his studies. One of his college friends once wrote that Thomas "could tear himself away from his dearest friends, to fly to his studies."

For almost half of the time Jefferson spent at the college, the only professor whose classes he attended regularly was William Small, who taught mathematics and philosophy. A lively Scottish bachelor, Small was only nine years older than Jefferson and the only non-clerical member of the faculty. He had, Jefferson would write, "an enlarged and liberal mind," and the unconventional idea that a teacher should not break the spirit of the student.

William Small was greatly impressed with the questions Jefferson asked in class and his conversations out of class. He admired Jefferson's thirst for knowledge so much that he took Thomas under his wing. He introduced him to his close and influential friends in Williamsburg. Through Small, Jefferson met George Wythe, a distinguished lawyer, and Virginia's governor, Francis Fauquier. The governor, who was an economist and student of physics and natural sciences, impressed young Jefferson. Jefferson and his new friends often dined together at the governor's palace. At times he was invited to bring his violin and take part in Fauquier's chamber music concerts.

Thomas Jefferson completed his studies at William and Mary in the spring of 1762. On the advice of William Small, Jefferson decided to study law, and remain in Williamsburg to read, study and associate with his learned friends.

There were no law schools in the American colonies until after the American Revolution. To become a lawyer, one went to work for a lawyer and read his law books, ran his errands, helped prepare his briefs, and studied his actions in court. George Wythe offered Jefferson the opportunity to study law in his office. After five years of study under Wythe, Jefferson was admitted to the bar in 1767. In the next few years, he conducted a successful law practice in Williamsburg with clients from all across Virginia. His financial standing increased with various real estate deals that added to the holdings he had already inherited.

Jefferson was elected to the Virginia House of Burgesses in 1769.

Jefferson celebrated New Year's Day 1772 by marrying Martha Wayles Skelton, a widow.

In March 1775, Thomas Jefferson was elected a delegate to the Second Continental Congress, which appointed him chairman of a committee to draw up the Declaration of Independence. Jefferson presented the document to Congress on June 28, 1776. It was amended and adopted July 4, 1776.

On June 1, 1779, he was elected by the Virginia legislature to succeed his friend Patrick Henry as governor. On March 4, 1801, Thomas Jefferson took the oath of office as the third president of the United States. Probably the most outstanding event of Jefferson's presidency was the purchase of the Louisiana Territory in 1803 from France. For 15 million dollars, Jefferson doubled the size of the nation and kept European countries out of the central part of the continent.

Jefferson's last years were devoted to the creation of the University of Virginia, founded in 1818 in Charlottesville. He died on July 4, 1826, the 50th anniversary of the Declaration of Independence.

Bibliography

Bober, Natalie S. *Thomas Jefferson: Man on a Mountain.* New York: Atheneum, 1988.

Bowers, Claude G. *The Young Jefferson, 1743–1789.* Boston: Houghton Mifflin, 1945.

Cunningham, Noble E., Jr. *In Pursuit of Reason: The Life of Thomas Jefferson.* New York: Ballantine, 1988.

Randall, Willard Sterne. *Thomas Jefferson: A Life.* New York: Henry Holt, 1993.

James Madison

Fourth President
1809–1817

James Madison was a small, shy, and bookish boy. He was also frail, suffering from real or imagined health problems which would plague him for life. If he was a boy today, some teenagers might refer to him as a nerd.

Yet, for all his early health problems and smallness (he never weighed more than 100 pounds, his full-grown height was five feet, four inches, his voice was weak), James Madison had qualities that commanded attention. He was perhaps the hardest working and most widely respected man of his day.

Madison was born March 16, 1751, in his maternal grandparents' home at Port Conway in King George County, Virginia. His parents were James Madison, Sr., and Eleanor Rose (Nellie) Conway Madison. Both of his parents were members of aristocratic Virginia families. Young James was the eldest of 12 children (five died young). His mother was the daughter of a prominent planter and tobacco merchant. She remained close to her famous son throughout her life.

James Madison, Sr., was a wealthy landowner. He inherited an estate in Orange County in the Piedmont area of Virginia. On this land he built a large brick mansion he called Montpelier. He kept adding property to his estate, and became the largest landowner and leading citizen of Orange County. He served also as the county's sheriff and justice of the peace, and vestryman of the Anglican church.

James, Jr., spent his childhood at Montpelier. He was called Jemmy, to distinguish him from James Senior. His playmates were his younger brothers and sisters, and the children of his father's slaves. The childhood friendships he formed with the slave children later led him to become an outspoken foe of slavery. Yet he accepted slavery as a necessary evil in the management of the family plantation. His slave-owning father was known for his humane treatment of his slaves and for regarding them as human beings rather than chattel.

Jemmy's education in religion and in reading, writing, and arithmetic began at home under the guidance of his grandmother, Frances Taylor Madison. Jemmy's grandfather, Ambrose Madison, had amassed a fine library, which included copies of a popular English literary magazine, *The Spectator*. It featured a single theme in each issue and commented satirically on the men and events of the time. Grandmother Madison encouraged Jemmy to read the magazine. So James Madison, Jr., learned early about the entanglements of men in politics and governments.

In 1762, when Jemmy was 11, his father enrolled him in a boarding school near Dunkirk, Virginia, operated by Donald Robertson, a Scottish schoolmaster. Here, young Madison began to study Latin, Greek, and French. He also studied algebra, geometry, geography, and literature.

Robertson was a gifted teacher who encouraged his students to excel in their studies. He raised all kinds of questions, and made his pupils use logic and reason whenever they spoke. Years later, James Madison would praise Robertson as "a man of extensive learning, and a distinguished teacher."

James unhappily left Robertson's tutelage in September 1767, when his father withdrew him from the school to be taught at home by the Reverend Thomas Martin, the new rector of the Madison's parish church. Martin, who had become a resident at Montpelier, also taught James' brothers Francis and Ambrose, and his sister Nelly.

After two years of tutoring by Martin, James Madison was ready to enter college. Influenced by Martin's recommendation, the elder Madison decided that his son would attend the College of New Jersey (now Princeton University). It was a Presbyterian college, but James Madison, Sr., a sincere Anglican, apparently saw nothing extraordinary in selecting the College of New Jersey for his eldest son.

The college was then under the presidency of John Witherspoon, a Scotsman who strongly opposed British attempts to control the colonies' churches, and who early on supported the colonies' move toward independence from British control. He called King George III a scoundrel and spurred his students into political involvement. Witherspoon's thunderous voice commanded absolute attention from his listeners whenever he lectured to the student body. He insisted that the students use clear English. Writers and orators should keep their mouths shut until they had something to say and stop when they said it; trimmings were a waste of time, he told them.

In the summer of 1769 when he was 18 years old, James Madison, Jr., set out on horseback for Princeton, New Jersey. He was accompanied by his tutor, the Reverend Thomas Martin, and Martin's brother, Alexander, and Sawney, one of the Madison family's most trusted blacks. It took about two weeks to complete the 300 mile journey.

Since he had covered some college-level courses under Mr. Martin, the college administrators allowed him to begin his studies as a sophomore. Madison completed the four-year course in two years, but with considerable effort. His sleep, he wrote, "was reduced for some weeks to less than five hours in the twenty-four."

Sophomores were required to study the classic languages of Greek and Latin. They also began to study the sciences—logic, rhetoric, mathematics, and geography. During the next year they continued studying mathematics and science, and began to study moral philosophy, metaphysics, and history. Seniors also studied the Bible, the arts and sciences, as well as the Latin and Greek classics.

Young Madison soon learned that there was more to campus life than studies. He mingled with students from the northern and middle colonies, who freed him from any Virginia bias he may have had. He took an active part in the American Whig Society, a student protest group that stood for resistance to British rule. This would be the beginning of a political philosophy that would eventually lead him toward a life of public service.

James Madison graduated from the College of New Jersey on September 25, 1771, with a bachelor of arts degree. Since his health had deteriorated during his self-imposed heavy load of studies, James was too ill to travel. His father allowed him to stay at the college for another six months to study Hebrew and theology with the Reverend John Witherspoon. James had thoughts about entering the ministry.

In April 1772 the elder Madison decided that his son had spent enough time on college studies and ordered him to come home to Montpelier. He was needed to help run the plantation and to teach his younger siblings. James Madison was low in spirits when he returned home. His depression worsened when he learned that a close college friend had died. He became obsessed with the idea that he would also die young.

His father sent him to Warm Springs, a health resort whose mineral waters were supposed to cure all types of ailments, but they failed to help the moody Madison. Get out of the house. Get some exercise; ride a horse, suggested his doctor. Young James Madison took his doctor's advice, and this seemed to help.

As the colonies became more estranged from England, James Madison, Sr., decided in December 1774 to organize the Orange County committee on public safety with his son James, Jr., as his principal aide. Both father and son were ardent supporters of the revolutionary cause. At about this time James, Jr., bought 200 acres of his father's land for himself. He needed to own property in his own right if he wanted to vote or hold office.

On October 2, 1775, James Madison, Jr., was commissioned a full colonel in the Orange County Militia. He was then 24 years old. In 1776, he was a member of the Virginia constitutional committee, a body that drafted Virginia's first constitution and a bill of rights which later became a model for the Bill of Rights amended to the United States Constitution. In 1779, Madison was elected to represent Virginia at the Continental Congress. He was the youngest member of that body.

Madison is known as "The Father of the Constitution." It was his Virginia Plan, put forward at the Constitutional Convention of 1787, which provided the basic framework and guiding principles of the U.S. Constitution. Madison was the only participant to take day-by-day notes of the proceedings and the debates at the Convention, and therefore furnished the only comprehensive history of the event.

Though honored as the "Father of the Constitution" Madison was too modest to accept such a title. The Constitution was not, he would write, the offspring of a single brain, but "the work of many heads and many hands." To promote ratification of the Constitution, Madison collaborated with Alexander Hamilton and John Jay in the publication of *The Federalist Papers*. He wrote 29 of the 85 that were published.

James Madison was 41 when he married 26-year-old Dolley Payne Todd on September 15, 1794. Dolley was a popular figure in the Washington social circuit. During the War of 1812, she remained at the White House as British troops advanced on the capital. She helped save many national treasures from being destroyed.

Madison was elected to the first House of Representatives as a Federalist and served through President George Washington's administration (1789–1797). When John Adams was elected president, Madison retired to his home in Virginia. In 1801, when Thomas Jefferson was elected president, Madison entered the cabinet as Secretary of State. Eight years later, James Madison became the fourth president of the United States, serving from 1809 to 1817.

James Madison died at his Montpelier home on June 28, 1836. Dolley Madison died on July 12, 1849.

Bibliography

Fritz, Jean. *The Great Little Madison*. New York: G. P. Putnam's Sons, 1989.

Ketcham, Ralph. *James Madison: A Biography*. Charlottesville: University Press of Virginia, 1990.

Miller, William Lee. *The Business of May Next: James Madison and the Founding*. Charlottesville: University Press of Virginia, 1992.

Moore, Virginia. *The Madisons: A Biography*. New York: McGraw-Hill, 1979.

Rutland, Robert A. *James Madison: The Founding Father*. New York: Macmillan, 1987.

★ 5 ★

James Monroe

Fifth President
1817–1825

James Monroe was a tall, strong boy with broad shoulders and a large frame. He had a disarming, warm personality. He was athletic, becoming a good horseman and hunter. James Monroe was also daring and unwavering in accomplishing goals that eventually led him to the presidency of the Unites States.

The oldest of five children, James Monroe was born in Westmoreland County, Virginia, on April 28, 1758. His father, Spence Monroe, was a farmer who worked his 200 acres of land by a small stream that was known as Monroe's Creek. He was also a carpenter and circuit judge. His mother, Elizabeth Jones Monroe, was the sister of Judge Joseph Jones, twice a delegate from Virginia to the Continental Congress.

Spence Monroe wanted James to be better educated than he had been. So he enrolled his son as a day student at Campbelltown Academy, a school operated by the Reverend Archibald Campbell, rector of the Washington Parish, in which the Monroe family lived.

The academy, which admitted only 25 students, was considered the best school in Virginia. James, who was 11 when he enrolled in the school, progressed through the Latin and math courses at a rate faster than his classmates. Among his classmates were John Marshall, who would later become the fourth Chief Justice of the Supreme Court of the United States.

James left Campbelltown Academy in early 1774 after the death of his father. In accordance to the custom of the time, James, as the eldest son, then 14 years old, inherited all the family property. He also became responsible for the operation of the farm and the welfare of his mother, brothers and sisters. Fortunately, he was helped by his uncle, Judge Joseph Jones, the executor of his father's will. Judge Jones, concerned about future of the family of his sister Elizabeth, guided his nephew through the troubled times.

Judge Jones encouraged James Monroe to consider a legal and political career and suggested that he continue his studies at the College of William and Mary. Since the college was located in Williamsburg, the capital of the Virginia Colony, it would give him an opportunity to observe and learn from political activities that took place in the city during the legislative sessions.

In June 1774, at the age of 14, James enrolled in the College of William and Mary. Since he was already well prepared in classics, Latin and mathematics, he was placed in the philosophical school of the college. The philosophical school offered studies in natural philosophy, mathematics, astronomy, logic, and rhetoric. The school also offered studies in sophisticated literature.

Monroe's college life was interrupted by the Revolutionary War. The House of Burgesses, the Virginia colony's ruling body, had refused to obey British governor Dunmore's order to dissolve. He retaliated in April 1775 by seizing a store of gunpowder belonging to the town of Williamsburg.

The heated political events had an unsettling effect on the college students. They became directly involved in the everyday turbulence surrounding the capital. Many of them, including James Monroe, purchased muskets and began drilling to form a militia unit on the campus. On June 24, 1775, James joined a group of 24 men in a surprise attack on the Governor's Palace, from which they looted 200 muskets, 300 swords, and some pistols. The weapons were turned over to the Williamsburg militia.

Monroe continued his studies at William and Mary until January 1776, when he abandoned his college education and enlisted as a cadet in the Third Virginia Regiment. Not long after he joined, James Monroe was made a lieutenant. He was then 18 years old.

During the spring and summer, the Third Virginia Regiment trained in the Williamsburg area. In August, the 700 men and officers of the Third Regiment were ordered to join General George Washington's army on Long Island, New York. After a fatiguing march in the summer heat, the Virginians arrived at General Washington's headquarters in Manhattan on September 12. Soon Monroe would fight in the battles in Harlem and White Plains.

During Christmas of 1776, he was among those crossing the Delaware River with Washington to take part in the Battle of Trenton. As enemy troops were preparing to mount cannons to fire point blank at the Americans, Lieutenant Monroe led his company in a countercharge, driving the enemy back and capturing their cannons. Monroe was severely wounded during the action. He was struck by an enemy musket ball, which tore though his chest and shoulder, severing an artery. He would have bled to death if a doctor had not been nearby to promptly give him medical assistance.

James Monroe was promoted to the rank of captain for his bravery under enemy fire. Later, for his bravery during battles at Brandywine and Germantown, he was promoted to the rank of major. In June 1778, during the Battle of Monmouth, New Jersey, he scouted for General Washington.

During 1777-1778, Monroe was assigned to the staff of Lord Sterling (American born William Alexander), one of General Washington's brigade commanders. He had hoped that this assignment and his bravery in combat would enable him to get a commission in the Continental Army. When Washington failed to approve his request, Monroe resigned his militia commission and returned to Virginia in December 1778.

Shortly after his return to Virginia, James Monroe was introduced to Thomas Jefferson, governor of Virginia. Jefferson was impressed with Monroe and advised him to prepare for a career in politics and law. Following Jefferson's advice, Monroe re-entered the College of William and Mary in early 1780. Later, when the state capital was transferred from Williamsburg to Richmond, Jefferson offered Monroe a job in his administration and a chance to study law under his tutorship.

James Monroe's political career began in the spring of 1782 when he was elected a member of the Virginia House of Delegates from King George County in place of his uncle, Judge Joseph Jones, who had been named a delegate to the Continental Congress. He served as a member of the Continental Congress during 1783–1786, and as a United States senator from 1790 to 1794. Monroe was twice governor of Virginia.

His ambition and energy, together with the backing of President Madison, made him the Republican choice for the presidency in 1816. With little Federalist opposition, he easily won re-election in 1820. In an address before the U.S. Congress on December 2, 1823, President Monroe issued a warning to European powers that any attempt to interfere with their old colonies in the western hemisphere would not to be tolerated by the United States. He also warned foreign countries not to attempt colonization in the western hemisphere. This declaration became known as the Monroe Doctrine.

James Monroe married Elizabeth Kortright of New York on February 16, 1786. They were married until Elizabeth's death in 1830. James Monroe lived his last years with his daughter Maria in New York City. He died July 4, 1831.

Bibliography

Ammon, Harry. *James Monroe: The Quest for National Identity.* Charlottesville: University Press of Virginia, 1990.

Brown, Gerry, ed. *The Autobiography of James Monroe.* Syracuse, N.Y.: Syracuse University Press, 1959.

Hanser, Richard. *The Glorious Hour of Lt. Monroe.* New York: Atheneum, 1976.

★ 6 ★

John Quincy Adams

Sixth President
1825–1829

John Quincy Adams was a brilliant, industrious boy who was reared for public service by fiercely dedicated parents. They expected their eldest son to achieve greatness. He was born on July 11, 1767, in the family's farmhouse in Braintree (now Quincy), Massachusetts. He was the second of four children born to John and Abigail Adams.

In the year of his birth, the British parliament passed the unpopular Townshend Acts, which suspended the Massachusetts Assembly and levied duties on various products imported into the American colonies. The colonialists retaliated by organizing boycotts of certain British products and purchasing similar goods manufactured in the colonies. Their protests were often violent.

After John Adams became a lawyer, he moved his family to Boston. Tension between Bostonians and British troops erupted into violence when, on March 5, 1770, five people were killed in what became known as the Boston Massacre. John Quincy Adams was then three years old. Ironically, his father defended the British soldiers in court, which ruled that the killings of civilians happened because the soldiers were defending themselves against a threatening mob.

On December 16, 1773, when John Quincy was six years old, revolutionaries dressed as Indians boarded British ships in Boston harbor and dumped their cargo of tea into the water.

In 1774, John Adams took his family back to Braintree, where John Quincy witnessed patriots preparing to defend themselves against ever threatening British troops. One day a group of militiamen stopped by the Adams home and asked if the family could spare any metal to make bullets. John Quincy's patriotic mother, Abigail, joined with other neighbors to melt pewter utensils into bullets for the local militia. As the militiamen rested, John Quincy brought them water from the well, while his older sister Abigail, nicknamed Nabby, served slices of salt meat.

That same year, John Adams was called on to further the revolutionary cause in Philadelphia, where he served as a delegate to the First Continental Congress and helped write the Declaration of Independence. In so doing, he became a marked man—an enemy of the British government.

While John Adams was away in Philadelphia, Abigail took charge of John Quincy's education. She taught him at home, assisted by John Thaxter, who was her cousin and her husband's law clerk. As John Quincy learned the fundamentals at home, his parents insisted that he broaden his education by learning the Latin and French languages. He was also required to read history and to write letters. Writing to his father, who was in Philadelphia in October 1774, John Quincy reassured John Adams that he was trying very hard to "grow a better boy" so "you will have no occasion to be ashamed of me when you return."

On June 17, 1775, as part of the encirclement of Boston, American militia soldiers began attacking British troops at the Charlestown section of Boston. Their original objective was Bunker Hill, but since they were met with a heavy British counterattack at Breed's Hill, most of the fighting took place there.

When Abigail Adams heard the thunder of cannons signaling the arrival of deadly warfare, she led her eight-year-old son John Quincy to nearby Penn's Hill, from which they could safely watch the battle. The American rebels fought bravely, but were forced to retreat when they ran low on ammunition and gunpowder. While the British forces won the battle, they suffered heavy casualties. John Quincy would long remember those historic moments.

In March 1846, when John Quincy Adams was 79, he wrote a letter to Joseph Sturge, an English philanthropist, recalling his experiences of the Battle Bunker Hill battle.

The year 1775 was the eighth year of my age—Among the first fruits of the War, was the expulsion of my father's family from their peaceful abode in Boston, to take refuge in his and my native town of Braintree—Boston became a walled and beleaguered town—garrisoned by British Grenadiers.... For the space of 12 months my mother with her infant children dwelt, liable every hour of the day and of the night to be butchered in cold blood, or taken and carried into Boston as hostages, by any foraging or marauding detachment of men.... My father was separated from his family, on his way to the ... continental Congress, and there my mother, with her children lived in unintermitted danger of being consumed with them all in a conflagration kindled by a torch in the same hands which on the 17th of June lighted the fires of Charlestown—I saw with my own eyes those fires, and heard Britannia's thunders in the Battle of Bunker's hill and witnessed the tears of my mother and mingled them with my own, as the fall of [Joseph] Warren a dear friend of my father, and a beloved Physician to me. He had been our family physician and surgeon, and had saved my fore finger from amputation under a very bad fracture.

Dr. Joseph Warren was president of the illegal Massachusetts Provincial Congress. He had turned down a command position in order to fight with the rank and file. He was killed fighting alongside his enlisted comrades. When John Quincy Adams attended Harvard College, he refused to participate in the ceremonies opening a new bridge over the Charles River because they took place over the exact spot where Dr. Warren was believed to have died.

Since his early childhood John Quincy was an avid reader. During the revolutionary days he read the patriotic newspapers and pamphlets that reflected his father's anti–British sentiments. Young John Quincy eagerly embraced and advocated his father's political beliefs. He would hold an anti–British attitude throughout his adult life.

In the winter of 1777, after serving four years in the Continental Congress—and helping to write the Declaration of Independence—John Adams returned home to his family in Braintree. But the reunion was of short duration. As he prepared to reestablish his law practice, John Adams was summoned by Congress to travel to Paris, where he would replace Siles Deane, a member of the American mission that was seeking French help to fight the British.

Adams eagerly accepted the diplomatic assignment. John Quincy, who was preparing to enter Governor Dummer Academy in Byfield, Massachusetts, begged his father to take him along. Up to then, the education of their eldest son had been primarily left to his mother, but she, with the support of tutor John Thaxter, convinced John Adams that a trip to Europe would greatly enhance their eldest son's education.

In mid–February, 1778, the 24-gun frigate *Boston*, with John Adams and his 11-year-old son John Quincy aboard, sailed out of Marblehead Harbor for a hazardous six week voyage across the Atlantic Ocean to France. John Quincy immediately took an interest in shipboard activities. The ship's captain, Samuel Tucker, was favorably impressed with John Quincy, and took the time to teach him about the compass, navigation, and how to work the sails. John Quincy used every moment to advance his knowledge during the Atlantic journey. Several passengers taught him French.

A couple days into the voyage, the *Boston* spotted three British warships. Outnumbered, the *Boston* wisely ran and escaped the superior enemy. Respite was short, however, since a few days later the ship ran into a tremendous storm in the Gulf Stream. During the storm lightning struck three men on deck, killing one, while the wind carried away the *Boston*'s main topmast.

Four weeks out of Marblehead, the *Boston* came upon a vessel that turned out to be the British 14-gun privateer *Martha*. She fired on the *Boston*, but her captain struck his colors when he realized that he was up against a superior American warship. Her crew were taken prisoners aboard the *Boston*. Captain Tucker then set a prize crew aboard the captured enemy ship and ordered it to sail to Boston, Massachusetts.

On March 24, 1778, after more than five weeks at sea, the frigate *Boston* arrived in Bordeaux, France. Soon after the Adamses arrived in Bordeaux, John Adams was surprised to learn that the delegation he was to join had already accomplished its goal. France had agreed to help the Americans win their freedom from the British. He then hurried to Paris, where he conferred with Benjamin Franklin and Arthur Lee, the other two members of the diplomatic commission.

While John Adams was being introduced to the ways of French and European diplomacy, John Quincy was placed in Monsieur Le Couer's boarding school at Passy, a small town on the outskirt of Paris. Among his classmates were two grandsons of Benjamin Franklin and several American children. At the Le Couer academy, John Quincy Adams learned French and Latin, as well as music, dancing, drawing, and fencing. John Quincy liked attending the new school, but his father, who found it to be too expensive, was relieved when Congress terminated his diplomatic mission. Father and son left Paris in March 1779 for the seaport of Nantes, where they hoped to catch a ship sailing to Massachusetts. During their stay at the French seashore, the Adamses used their free time to study the French language and culture.

Several times they were the guests of American-born merchant Joshua Johnson, who had fled London to take up residence in France for the duration of British hostilities with the colonies. Among Johnson's family members were his daughter Louisa, whom John Adams would marry 18 years later.

As the weather grew warmer during the long wait in Nantes, French sailors taught John Quincy how to swim. He found swimming invigorating and strengthening, and over the years developed into an excellent swimmer. When he became president, he frequently swam nude in the Potomac River.

On June 17, 1779, the Adamses and a French diplomatic delegation sailed from Nantes aboard the French frigate *La Sensible* for Boston. During the Atlantic crossing, John Quincy Adams spent much of his time teaching English to members of the French delegation. *La Sensible* sailed into Boston harbor on August 2, 1799.

John Adams had hardly gotten his land legs back when Congress ordered him to return to Europe on another diplomatic mission. Spain had entered the war against England, and his new diplomatic assignment was to negotiate treaties of peace and commerce with Great Britain. As he prepared to return to Europe, John Adams decided that he would take his younger son, nine-year-old Charles, with him. John Quincy was to stay home and prepare himself to enter college. But his wife Abigail persuaded him to take both boys, insisting that a continued stay in Europe would enhance John Quincy's education and knowledge of world affairs.

On November 13, 1779, the frigate *La Sensible* made its return trip to France carrying three Adamses-John and his sons John Quincy and Charles, and John Thaxter, who was to tutor the two boys and serve as secretary to John Adams. Francis Dana, a young Boston attorney, went along to serve as secretary to the peace commission.

On January 19, 1780, Abigail Adams wrote a letter to John Quincy, reminding her oldest son that wisdom is the result of experience, and to make good use of the knowledge he would gain from his second trip to Europe: "It will be expected of you my son that as you are favour'd with superior advantages under the instructive Eye of a tender parent, that your improvements should bear some proportion to your advantages. Nothing is wanting with you, but attention, dilligence and steady application, Nature has not been deficient."

She was also concerned about his stubborness and temper: "I cannot fulfill the whole of my duty towards you, if I close this Letter, without reminding you of a failing which calls for a strict attention and watchfull [*sic*] care to correct. You must do it for yourself. You must curb that impetuosity of temper, for which I have frequently chid you, but which properly directed may be productive of great good."

On December 8, 1779, the Adams party made landfall at El Ferrol on the northwestern tip of Spain. Their ship had to seek the nearest safe port after it sprang a leak during stormy weather.

The Adamses had no choice but to travel overland through the rugged mountains along Spain's northern coast. After a sometimes dangerous and tiresome journey, they reached Paris on February 9, 1780. They took up residence at nearby Passy, where the boys were enrolled in a private school. In July, John Adams expanded his diplomatic mission by moving to Amsterdam, where he would persuade the Dutch to provide America with diplomatic recognition and commercial trade agreements.

While in Amsterdam, Adams enrolled John Quincy at the nearby Leyden University, recognized as one of the finest institutions of higher learning in Europe. Since he could speak no Dutch, John Quincy became an independent student, being allowed to take private lessons and attend lectures. By January 1781, he had become fluent enough in the Dutch language to be accepted as a regular student. Soon thereafter, he and Charles parted company. Homesick, Charles was sent back to Massachusetts.

In the spring of 1781, Congress appointed Francis Dana as a minister to Russia. His mission was to persuade Empress Catherine II the Great to sign a treaty that would recognize the American republic. Since John Quincy Adams was now fluent in French, the language of diplomats, he was asked to go along with Dana to Petersburg, then the capital of Russia. Though only 14, John Quincy, with his father's approval, accepted the new challenge.

On July 7, 1781, Dana and John Quincy Adams left Amsterdam for their long journey to St. Petersburg, where they arrived August 27, after having passed through Germany and Poland. Dana's mission was unsuccessful. The Russian empress wanted no quarrel with England. John Quincy Adams remained in St. Petersburg 15 months until his father sent for him. During his stay in St. Petersburg, he assisted Dana and continued his studies.

Young Adams left the Russian capital in late October 1782. After a long journey that took him through Finland, Sweden and Denmark, he arrived in the Dutch capital of The Hague on April 21, 1783. He remained in Europe until his father had completed his many diplomatic assignments, including the signing of the peace treaty with Great Britain. During this time he met Thomas Jefferson, who was then in Paris. They would become lifelong friends.

John Quincy returned to America in July 1785, landing in New York City, then the national capital. He went on to Haverhill, Massachusetts, where he lived with John and Elizabeth Shaw. John Shaw was the pastor of the town's Congregational parish. He had agreed to spend six months preparing John Quincy for college entry. His wife, Elizabeth Smith Shaw, was the younger sister to his mother, Abigail Adams.

Pastor Shaw set a tough schedule, and John Quincy took his studies seriously, seldom leaving the parsonage. Quite often he would work late at night, long after the household had retired. On March 15, 1786, John Quincy Adams was admitted to Harvard College as a junior, and was granted free tuition as a token of appreciation for his father's service to the nation. His father had graduated from Harvard in 1755.

John Quincy was a good college student, but like others, he had faults, among them being a late sleeper and skipping lectures in favor fishing trips. He joined Phi Beta Kappa and honed his political oratory at the fraternity's meetings.

John Quincy Adams graduated from Harvard on July 16, 1787. He ranked second out of a class of 51. He delivered one of the valedictory addresses at the commencement exercises. The speech, in which he called for citizens' support for national honor and integrity, was well received by the audience.

Now 20 years old, law seemed to be in Adams's future. With some reluctance, after graduation he rode to the small seaport of Newburyport to arrange to read law in the offices of Theophilus Parsons, a successful attorney and experienced instructor. Parsons charged his students $100 each for their apprenticeship.

John Quincy Adams completed his legal training in 1790 and began practicing law in Boston. His father helped him in various ways, offering advice and making available his large law library. The young attorney was unhappy, he attracted few clients, but he stuck to the job, because he believed his parents expected it of him.

When not practicing law, John Quincy Adams wrote newspaper articles in support of President Washington's administration. In 1794, President Washington, appreciative of the young Adams's support, and aware of his knowledge of the Dutch and French languages, appointed him minister to the Netherlands.

John Quincy Adams devoted his adult life to public service. President James Madison appointed him minister to Russia, and in 1814, he sent Adams to Ghent, Belgium, to help conclude peace with England following the War of 1812. During 1817–1825, he served as Secretary of State to President James Monroe.

The National-Republican Party selected him as its presidential nominee in 1824. The election failed to return a majority, and Adams was chosen president by the House of Representatives. After being beaten for reelection in 1828, he successfully ran for the House of Representatives in 1830. Adams suffered a stroke while on the floor of the House. He died two days later on February 23, 1848.

Bibliography

Clarke, Fred G. *John Quincy Adams.* New York: Collier, 1966.

Hecht, Marie B. *John Quincy Adams: A Personal History of an Independent Man.* Newtown, Conn.: American Political Biography Press, 1995.

Nagel, Paul C. *John Quincy Adams: A Public Life, a Private Life.* New York: Alfred A. Knopf, 1998.

Parsons, Lynn Hudson. *John Quincy Adams.* Madison, Wis.: Madison House, 1998.

Andrew Jackson

Seventh President
1829–1837

Andrew Jackson was the first poor boy to become president. Born into a hard and stormy life, the feisty Andy Jackson was always ready for a scrap. At age 13, he joined the militia to fight British soldiers during the American Revolution.

He was raised by impoverished Scots-Irish immigrant parents in the rough Tennessee frontier. They owned a small tract of land on Twelve Mile Creek at the Waxhaw settlements near the North Carolina boundary.

The Jacksons had immigrated from northern Ireland. Their first two sons, Hugh and Robert, were born in Ireland. On March 15, 1767, Elizabeth Jackson gave birth to her third son, whom she named after her husband Andrew, who had died a few days earlier. He had injured himself lifting a heavy log. The hard pioneer work killed him. Andrew Jackson's birthplace has been disputed. Some historians believe he was born at the home of Elizabeth Jackson's sister Peggy, Mrs. George McCarmie, across the border in North Carolina. Others say he was born a few miles farther south, in South Carolina, at the home of James and Christiana Crawford. In 1824 Andrew Jackson wrote: "I was born in South Carolina, as I have been told, at the plantation whereon James Crawford lived, about one mile from the Carolina Road and the Waxhaw Creek."

One thing is certain, Andrew Jackson was raised by a strong and caring mother. After her husband's death, Elizabeth and her sons went to live with her sister Jane and her husband George Crawford. They lived in a comfortable home at Twelve Mile Creek. Since her sister was ailing, Elizabeth found herself in charge of the Crawford household. Elizabeth Jackson and her sons lived with the Crawfords for about 12 years.

A deeply religious woman, Elizabeth Jackson did her best to provide her sons with direction and purpose. As a strong figure herself, she showed the boys how to live a fruitful life by helping those in need, but also how to protect themselves against the wanton ways of others. Many years later, as a grown man, Andrew Jackson would write this about his mother: "There was never a woman like her. She was gentle as a dove and as brave as a lioness."

Elizabeth Jackson had dreams of her youngest son becoming a minister and a community leader. She sent Andrew and his brothers to a school run by William Humphries. Here they learned how to read, write and do arithmetic. Later she sent Andrew to a school directed by the Presbyterian minister James White Stephenson, hoping that the religious curriculum would encourage him to seek the ministry. Andy was a quick learner, and could read at an early age. But he showed no interest in the ministry.

Since he had learned to read—a rarity in the 1770s rural America—at age nine, he took on the job of reading newspapers aloud to illiterate citizens, and thus learned public speaking skills. The newspapers received in the Waxhaw settlement came from Charleston and Philadelphia. One of his proudest moments as a public reader was, in August 1776, when he read from a Philadelphia paper that told of Congress adopting the Declaration of Independence.

Sandy, red-haired Andy Jackson was a spindly, long-legged boy. His beaky nose and jutting jaw warned of his fierce determination. Sensitive to ridicule, he fought anyone who dared tease him, but was equally quick to defend smaller boys from bullies, according to Marquis James, one of his more thorough biographers. He liked to shoot, fish, ride horses and wrestle. One of his classmates, recalling his wrestling matches with Andy, said, "I could throw him several times, but he could never *stay throwed*. He was dead game and never would give up."

He was easily offended, and at times showed signs of being a bully. Once a gang of boys challenged him to fire a gun that had been loaded to the muzzle. It was a prank. They wanted to watch him get tossed about from the discharge. Andy grabbed the gun and fired it. The sharp discharge threw him to the ground. Jumping up in a maddening frenzy, he yelled at the frolicking boys: "By God, if any one of you laughs, I'll kill him!" No one laughed or made a sound.

During his childhood and into his teens, Andrew Jackson suffered from habitual slobbering. He eventually overcame his disability.

Andrew Jackson was only 13 years old when the American Revolution swept the Waxhaw region. In May 1780, some 300 British cavalrymen, led by Lieutenant Colonel Banastre Tarleton, slashed out a savage victory over Waxhaw militiamen. More than 100 militiamen were killed, another 150 were wounded.

The wounded militiamen were taken to a meeting house that had been converted into a hospital. Townspeople, including Elizabeth Jackson and her sons Andrew and Robert, treated the wounded on the straw-covered floor.

Andrew's older brother Hugh, age 16, had already gone off to war, joining militia forces fighting the British at Stono Ferry. Hugh died there, not from an enemy bullet, but from exposure to the extreme heat that enveloped the summer battleground.

At their mother's encouragement, Robert and Andrew attended the drills and general musters of the local militia, where they learned the rudiments of military service. All summer there were scrimmages among the settlers. It was brother against brother, neighbor against neighbor. The settlers from the Scottish Highlands were Tories and fought for the British; the poor Irish were Whigs and revolutionists supporting the American colonies.

Seeking revenge for the Tarleton massacre, American soldiers, on August 1, 1780, attacked a British outpost at Hanging Rock. Reports of that event suggests that Andy and his brother Robert had joined the patriot troops as messengers. It was a half victory for the Americans. In their eagerness to celebrate a victory, they became inebriated from the rum they had captured from the British. When the enemy retaliated, the patriots panicked and rode off in wild confusion. It was a pathetic day for American forces.

On April 9, 1781, a force of British dragoons entered the Waxhaw area to support the Tories. They stormed a church where Andrew and his brother were. About 30 men were captured and the church was set afire. The boys managed to escape to the home of Thomas Crawford. A Tory neighbor informed the British of their whereabouts. Soon enemy troops surrounded the house and took the boys prisoners.

The British soldiers wrecked the house, destroying furniture, smashing dishes, and shredding clothing. While this was going on, the officer in charge ordered Andy to clean his muddy boots. The feisty Andrew Jackson refused to obey the officer's order. Instead he challenged the British officer to treat him like a prisoner of war. This infuriated the dragoon officer who drew his saber, aiming it at Andy's head. The boy ducked and threw up his left arm to ward off the blow, but he received a deep cut to the bone and a gash on his head. The officer then turned on Robert, who also refused to clean the boots. The angry British dragoon then raised his saber and inflicted a serious wound on Robert's head.

The dragoons then marched the Jackson boys, along with 20 other captives, 40 miles to a prison stockade in Camden, South Carolina. The boys, separated in prison, received no medical attention, little food, only a small amount of bread. Living under miserable conditions, the Jackson boys, along with many other prisoners, contracted smallpox in the stockade.

Learning of the capture of her sons, Elizabeth Jackson and some of her neighbors went to Camden to seek the release of the imprisoned boys. She gained an interview with the British commander and persuaded him to exchange her sons and five Waxhaw neighbors for 13 British soldiers that the Americans had captured. For Robert the help came too late. He died two days after his release. Andrew was delirious, but with the aid of his mother's nursing skills he recovered his strength in a few weeks.

With her son out of danger, Elizabeth Jackson and two other women from Waxhaw, traveled 160 miles to Charleston to nurse prisoners of war held in a British prison ship. Among the prisoners were relatives of the three volunteer nurses. The trip of mercy ended tragically. While nursing the prisoners, Elizabeth Jackson contracted cholera and died in November 1781. She was buried in an unmarked grave.

Andrew, age 14, was now an orphan. He still had family—uncles, aunts and cousins—but he found it difficult to live harmoniously with them. He was sullen, depressed and angry. His explosive temper made him unwelcome at many households. What may have saved him was an offer from a distant relative, Joseph White, a saddler, to come and live with him and work in his shop. Since he loved horses and was a good rider, Andrew eagerly accepted the offer. After six months of apprenticeship in the saddler's shop, he taught school for a short while.

When he was 17 Andy received a small inheritance. He picked up his few belongings and got on his horse and rode to Charleston. The restless Andrew Jackson wanted to see the world beyond the Waxhaw settlements. Somehow he made enough money to live a merry life, but in so doing he gambled away his earnings and had little left except a fine horse.

Coming to his senses, Andrew Jackson decided that he wanted to study to become a lawyer. In December 1784, at age 17, he rode to Salisbury, North Carolina, where he began studying law under the tutelage of Spruce McCay, an eminent lawyer and later a judge.

After two years of studying law under McCay, Andrew Jackson completed another six months of legal training in the office of Colonel John Stokes, a veteran revolutionary soldier. On September 26, 1787, the itinerant (circuit) court at Wadesborough, North Carolina, issued Andrew Jackson permission to practice law. Andy Jackson, a poor orphan and revolutionary boy soldier, was on his way to become the seventh president of the United States of America.

Andrew Jackson married Virginia-born Rachel Donelson Robards on January 17, 1794, after she had untangled a complicated divorce.

Rachel was a handsome woman with a sparkling personality. Her education was limited. She spent much time reading the Bible and performing religious work. She suffered a heart attack and died on December 22, 1828, at the Jacksons' home in Hermitage, Tennessee.

On February 15, 1891, Jackson was appointed attorney general of Tennessee's Mero District. He was elected Tennessee's first member of the U.S. House of Representatives in 1796, and in 1797 was elected to the U.S. Senate. After a few years of living quietly at his Hermitage home in Tennessee, he became a major general in the Army. In 1815 his troops defeated superior British troops in the Battle for New Orleans. In 1824 he lost to John Quincy Adams in a bid for the presidency despite winning the plurality of popular votes. On March 4, 1829, he became the seventh president of the United States, having easily defeated John Quincy Adams. He was reelected in 1832.

Since Andrew Jackson was considered a man of the people, his first inauguration in 1829 turned out to be a great celebration not previously seen at the White House. Thousands of uninvited supporters of Jackson crowded into the White House to partake in a reception in the East Room for invited dignitaries. Instead the room was jammed with a rowdy crowd of 20,000 people who ruined rugs and furniture and broke chinaware, causing thousands dollars worth of damage. The also consumed all the cake, ice cream and orange punch that was to be served to the invited guests.

Andrew Jackson died on June 8, 1845, at his home in Hermitage.

Bibliography

Buell, August C. *History of Andrew Jackson*. Volumes I & II. New York: Charles Scribner's Sons, 1904.

James, Marquis. *The Life of Andrew Jackson*. Indianapolis: Bobbs-Merrill, 1938.

Remini, Robert V. *Andrew Jackson*. New York: Perennial Library, Harper & Row, 1969.

_____. *Andrew Jackson and His Indian Wars*. New York: Viking Penguin, 2001.

_____. *Andrew Jackson, Volume One, The Course of American Empire, 1767–1821*. Baltimore: The Johns Hopkins University Press, 1998.

Martin Van Buren

Eighth President
1837–1841

Martin Van Buren was the first president to be born an American citizen, rather than a British subject. His predecessors all were born prior to the Declaration of Independence and thus entered the world as British subjects.

Van Buren was born on December 5, 1782, in the village of Kinderhook, near Albany, New York. His parents were Abraham and Maria Van Buren, both of Dutch descent, whose families had lived in New York for several generations. His mother, formerly Maria Van Alen, was a widow with three children-a girl and two boys-when she married Abraham. From his mother's second marriage, Martin would have two older sisters and two younger brothers.

Martin Van Buren, nicknamed Mat, was a small but sturdy boy with sandy curls that receded with age. As a grown man, he stood a bit under five feet, six inches tall. When he became president, he was distinguished by a crown of unruly white hair and prominent sidewhiskers. Since Dutch was spoken in their home, Martin Van Buren grew up speaking Dutch better than English. Long into adulthood, he would speak English with a Dutch accent.

Abraham Van Buren was a farmer who owned six slaves that he had inherited from his father. He was also a tavern keeper, the tavern being part of the family home, which was located on a post road between New York City and Albany. The tavern was frequently visited by politicians and lawyers on their way to and from the state capital of Albany. The tavern also served as a polling place during elections.

Among the politicians who made stops at the Van Buren tavern were Aaron Burr and Alexander Hamilton. Thus, at an early age, Martin Van Buren became acquainted with the ways of politicians, as he heard their discussions of issues and events. He learned well. He became a clever politician.

While the tavern was his main business, Abraham Van Buren also worked a small truck farm growing cabbage that he sold to neighbors and at the village market in Kinderhook. Martin helped with the farming and delivered the home-grown vegetables to customers.

For a number of years, Abraham Van Buren served as a clerk to the village community. In this capacity he met all types of people, from the lowest citizens to the most powerful officials and ambitious lawyers and politicians. Since the clerk position required him to get along with people, Abraham mostly listened and took no sides in political discussions. This trait he passed on to his son Martin, who, throughout his life, would try to please both sides in political and private discussions.

Martin learned the basics at a dreary, poorly lit, one-room school house in Kinderhook. He was a good student and quickly learned to read and write English and some Latin. He was a great talker and was never at a loss for words, a skill he had developed from serving and conversing with the customers in his father's tavern.

Young Mat stayed in school until he was 14 years old. Through his father's friendship with influential townsmen, he landed a job as a law clerk with Francis Silvester, a respected lawyer in Kinderhook. As a clerk, Martin swept floors, ran errands, copied documents, and studied law. He also read political papers and pamphlets he found in his employer's office.

Martin Van Buren quickly established himself as a clear thinker and clever debater. At times Silvester allowed him to present and summarize minor cases in court. Since he was short, Martin had to stand on a bench in order to be seen by the jury he addressed.

While he worked for Silvester, Martin became interested in politics. His boss was a member of the Federalist Party, which believed in a strong central government and supported policies that favored wealthy businessmen. These views did not sit well with Martin, whose political position followed his father's support for the Democratic-Republican Party, which endorsed the anti–Federalist policies of Thomas Jefferson.

Martin worked for Silvester for five years until 1801. While he politely avoided discussing political issues with his employer, Martin Van Buren adopted the manners and tastes of the wealthy Silvesters. To improve his appearance, Martin learned to dress fashionably. He socialized with influential people. He became popular; good manners helped him gain new friends.

Martin became more interested in politics, so at the age of 18, he began working to help Thomas Jefferson win the presidential election of 1800. Young Martin admired the ideas of Jefferson, who believed that in a democratic society, the power should be in the hands of its citizens. As a reward for his campaign for Jefferson, the Democratic-Republican Party in Kinderhook, led by John Peter Van Ness, elected him a delegate to their congressional caucus in Troy in 1801. That same year, Van Buren campaigned for Van Ness, who won a seat in the U.S. House of Representatives.

Meanwhile, after leaving the law office of Francis Silvester, the Van Ness family encouraged Martin Van Buren to move to New York, where he could broaden his legal skills by working in the law office of William Peter Van Ness, brother of John Peter. Following intensive study under William Peter Van Ness, Martin Van Buren became a lawyer himself in November 1803. He then returned to Kinderhook and joined the law practice of his half brother, James Van Alen.

On February 21, 1807, Van Buren married Hanna Hoes, his childhood sweetheart. She was a distant cousin related to Van Buren through his mother. Hanna bore him four sons.

In 1808, the newlyweds moved to Hudson, the county seat. That same year he was appointed to his first public office, surrogate of Columbia County, succeeding his half brother in that post. (In New York, a surrogate is a legal officer who helps probate wills and settlements of estates.)

In 1812, at the age of 30, Van Buren decided to embark on a political career. After helping other politicians win, he decided to run for the New York state senate. He won the senate race, and was reelected in 1816. During his New York state senate service, he sponsored a bill to abolish imprisonment for debt—one of the first legislators to do so in the United States. In the early nineteenth century, people who were unable to pay their bills were often put into prison.

Van Buren was elected to the United States Senate in 1821. During the presidential campaign of 1828, Van Buren supported Andrew Jackson. When Jackson became president, he made Van Buren his secretary of state. Van Buren was elected vice president in 1832, and, with Jackson's blessing, the Democrats nominated him for the presidency in 1836. Van Buren easily won the election that year over the main Whig candidate, William Henry Harrison.

Van Buren's political career reached its zenith with the presidency and quickly began its decline. The nation got caught up in a depression that began in 1837, and as president, Van Buren was blamed. In the election of 1840, he was badly beaten by William Henry Harrison. After spending several years in Europe, Van Buren retired in 1855 to Lindenwald, his home in Kinderhook, where he died on July 24, 1862.

Bibliography

Alexander, Holmes. *The American Talleyrand: The Career and Contemporaries of Martin Van Buren, Eighth President*. New York: Russell & Russell, 1935.

Lynch, Dennis Tilden. *An Epoch and a Man: Martin Van Buren and His Times*. New York: Horace Liveright, 1929.

Niven, John. *Martin Van Buren: The Romantic Age of American Politics*. New York: Oxford University Press, 1983.

Van Buren, Martin. *The Autobiography of Martin Van Buren*. New York: Chelsea House, 1983. (This edition is an edited reprint of the 1920 U.S. Government Printing Office edition.)

★ 9 ★

William Henry Harrison

Ninth President
1841

William Henry Harrison was born into a wealthy and prominent Virginia family. His father, Benjamin Harrison V, was a signer of the Declaration of Independence, and a governor of Virginia for three consecutive one-year terms, from 1781 to 1784.

His mother, Elizabeth, was the daughter of Colonel William Bassett, who owned the Eltham Plantation in New Kent County, Virginia. She married William Henry's father when she was 18. She bore him seven children, William Henry being the youngest. A distant relative of Martha Washington, she was noted for her beauty and kindness.

William Henry was born on the Berkeley Plantation in Charles City County, Virginia, on February 8, 1773. The plantation, comprising about 100 acres on the banks of the James River, was first settled in 1619 by adventurous British families. The plantation was named after Richard Berkeley, leading financier of the settlement.

As a child, William Henry Harrison lived in a three-story brick manor house on the Berkeley Plantation. The house was built in 1726 by his grandfather, Benjamin Harrison IV, who had served in the Virginia House of Burgesses from 1736 until his death in 1745. The original three-story mansion remains today. Its beautifully landscaped hilltop site overlooks the historic

James River. Adjacent to the manor house were two smaller buildings, one which was used by private tutors instructing William Henry and his siblings in basic reading and writing.

The idyllic life at the Berkeley Plantation ended for William Henry when the American Revolution took a bad turn for the patriots in Virginia. They were unable to cope effectively with the superior British forces led by General Charles Cornwallis, who raided the Hampton Roads area, including the banks of the James River all the way to Richmond.

The Harrisons escaped with their lives, but the mansion was plundered in January 1781 by troops under the command of the traitor Brigadier General Benedict Arnold. The home was stripped of its furnishings, paintings and decorations were burned, livestock were slaughtered, and slaves and horses were carried off. After having left the Berkeley property to the fate of the invaders, the Harrison family found temporary haven in the Richmond area.

William Henry Harrison began his formal education at the age of 14 when he entered Hampden-Sydney College at Farmville, Prince Edward County. There he studied rhetoric, geography, history, mathematics, Greek and Latin. He joined the college's literary society, and showed a strong interest in military history. But he didn't stay long at Hampden-Sydney. His father pulled him out of the college when a strong Methodist revival swept over the college. The Harrisons were Episcopalians.

Since the elder Harrison wanted his youngest son to be a doctor, sometime in 1790 William Henry began medical studies under Doctor Andrew Leiper in Richmond. Later he went to Philadelphia to study medicine under the tutelage of the renowned physician Benjamin Rush.

While studying in Philadelphia, William Henry learned that his father had died at the Berkeley plantation on April 24, 1791. William Henry was then 17 years old. In his will, Benjamin Harrison V appointed his old friend Robert Morris as William Henry's guardian. Robert Morris, a successful Philadelphia merchant, known as the financier of the Revolution, was instrumental in obtaining funds to buy munitions and other supplies for General Washington's army. While his father had left William Henry a small tract of land at the Berkeley Plantation, there was no money for him to continue his medical training.

William Henry Harrison, having lost interest in medical studies and having no desire to become a Virginia planter, sought out the advice of a family friend, Henry Lee, a famous cavalry officer of the Revolutionary War. Lee had just begun his first term as governor of Virginia. Governor Lee suggested that the youngster seek an officer commission in the Army. The six foot tall, skinny William Henry, who had long wanted to follow in the family tradition of serving in the military, quickly agreed to the proposal.

Soon Governor Lee presented William Henry with a commission as an ensign in the First Regiment of the Infantry. The commission was signed by President George Washington on August 16, 1791. William Henry kept his guardian, Robert Morris, in the dark about obtaining an army commission. When Morris learned what his 18-year-old ward had done he became quite upset, but agreed that military service might serve him well in the future.

Harrison's first army assignment was as a recruiting officer in Philadelphia, where he signed up a company of 80 men. Leaving Philadelphia in September 1791, the young ensign marched the recruits over the Allegheny Mountains to Fort Pitt (Pittsburgh), where they built flatboats and sailed down the Ohio River to Fort Washington (Cincinnati) in the Northwest Territory.

The fort's commander, General Mad Anthony Wayne, made Harrison his aide after a year's service there. The fort was established to protect settlers against Indians. In 1794 he fought under Wayne when he defeated a coalition of Indian tribes at the Battle of Fallen Timbers, which opened most of the Ohio area to settlements.

In the spring of 1795, while Harrison was in the town of Lexington, Kentucky, on military business, he met Anna Tuthill Symmes. The two fell in love and were married on November 25, 1795.

After resigning from the Army in 1798, Harrison became secretary of the Northwest Territory. He was its first delegate to Congress, and helped obtain legislation dividing the Territory into the Northwest and Indiana Territories. In 1801 he became governor of the Indiana Territory, serving 12 years.

As governor, Harrison was also in charge of Indian affairs. He negotiated treaties with Indian tribes and bought large tracts of land from them for the government to be used as settlements. But the Indians became hostile when they realized that they had lost millions of acres of valuable hunting grounds. The Shawnee chief, Tecumseh, along with his brother Tenskwatawa, known as the Prophet, began uniting the tribes to fight the settlers.

Fearing the growing strength of the Indians, Harrison decided to strike quickly. In November 1811, he marched an army of 1,100 men along the Wabash River toward the Prophet's encampment, located where the Tippecanoe River empties into the Wabash. The soldiers camped for the night on the Tippecanoe River.

The Indians made a surprise attack against Harrison's troops just before dawn on November 7, 1811. Harrison rallied his troops and in more than two hours of fighting beat back the Indians. Harrison lost more than 180 killed and wounded in the battle. The Battle of Tippecanoe was no great victory, but it led to the breakup of the Indian alliances. Harrison was both praised and criticized for his action. The battle earned him the nickname "Old Tippecanoe."

In the War of 1812 Harrison won more military laurels when he was given the command of the army in the Northwest with the rank of brigadier general. He recaptured Detroit from the British, and at the Battle of the Thames, north of Lake Erie, on October 5, 1813, defeated a combined English and Indian force.

Following the war, Harrison embarked on a political career. He served in the House of Representatives (1816–1819) from Ohio, the Ohio state senate (1819–1821), and the U.S. Senate (1815–1828).

In 1828, he was appointed American minister to Columbia, but was recalled when he offended his host by lecturing Simón Bolivar, the South American revolutionary leader, on the dangers of dictatorship. Thereafter his political fortunes went sour. In 1834, with few friends and little income, Harrison found himself accepting a position as clerk of common pleas in Hamilton County, Ohio.

His political star rose again when he emerged as the Whig Party's presidential candidate in the election of 1836, but he lost to Martin Van Buren. Harrison and Van Buren faced each other again in the 1840 presidential election. Harrison won easily, carrying 19 states, while Van Buren carried only seven.

It was cold, windy day in Washington, D.C., when 68-year-old William Henry Harrison was inaugurated president in March 1841. He insisted on delivering a lengthy inaugural address without wearing a hat, gloves, or overcoat. Sometime later he got caught in a rainstorm while out strolling and returned to the White House drenched. The cold developed into pneumonia and he died on April 4, 1841. William Henry Harrison was the first president to die in the White House.

Bibliography

Cleaves, Freeman. *Old Tippecanoe: William Henry Harrison and His Time.* Newtown, Conn.: The American Political Biography Press, 1990.

Dowdey, Clifford. *The Great Plantation: A Profile of Berkeley Hundred and Plantation Virginia from Jamestown to Appomattox.* Charles City, Va.: Berkeley Plantation, 1980.

Montgomery, H. *The Life of Major-General William H. Harrison, Ninth President of the United States.* Cleveland, Ohio: Tooker & Catchell, 1853.

★ 10 ★

John Tyler

Tenth President
1841–1845

For a man who had a major influence on the American presidency, there is little information about the childhood of John Tyler, America's tenth president. A probable reason for the lack of childhood data is that many of the Tylers' family papers were destroyed during the Civil War. Most likely his boyhood was not much different from that of other young scions of wealthy Virginia plantation owners.

John Tyler was born March 29, 1790, at his father's 1,200-acre estate, called Greenway Plantation, in Charles City County. He was the sixth of eight children; he had five sisters and two brothers. His father, John Tyler, Sr., was a tobacco planter who owned 40 slaves. He served as governor of Virginia from 1809 to 1811, when he was appointed a U.S. Circuit Court judge for Virginia. Little is known about his mother, Mary Armistead Tyler. Her father, Robert Armistead, was a prominent planter. She died when John was seven years old.

As a boy, John Tyler was generally mild mannered, bright and headstrong, a trait he inherited from his father. As a youth he was very slight in build; his thin face was dominated by high cheekbones and a prominent Roman nose he would later joke about. Throughout his life, John Tyler was prone to suffer from a variety of illnesses. Always serious-minded, he was inclined to moodiness.

An anecdote about his early schooling tells about 11-year-old John Tyler rebelling against his cruel Scottish schoolmaster, William McMurdo, whose authority had never been questioned by the parents or guardians of his pupils. At times he used birch switches to whip his students. Under John's leadership, the boys physically overpowered their teacher, threw him down and proceeded to tie his hands and feet. Then they locked in him in a closet. The teacher lay in this uncomfortable position for several hours before he was found and freed.

When Judge Tyler learned the reason for their rebellious action, he had no sympathy for the severe teacher. The judge was a powerful and determined man, yet he could be very compassionate when dealing with his children. Often he would sit on the front lawn of the Greenway Plantation playing his violin for the children, or he would read poetry and tell them stories about the Revolution. Young John inherited his father's love of music and he learned to play the violin. He considered himself a good "fiddle" player.

In 1802, at the age of 12, John Tyler entered the preparatory school of the nearby College of William and Mary. In 1804, he began studies at the college proper, graduating in 1807.

The college curriculum in those days was mainly classical languages and English literature, but William and Mary undergraduates also studied history and political economy. The text used by John Tyler in the economics course was Adam Smith's book *The Wealth of Nations*, a classic study of economics. John Tyler was much impressed by the writings of Adam Smith. Later, when he became a politician, his speeches on the tariff and free trade were drawn almost verbatim from this influential work.

Among John Tyler's college friends were Winfield Scott, who studied at William and Mary for a short time before undertaking the study of law in Petersburg, Virginia. Scott would become a famous general, and in 1852, was the Whig Party's unsuccessful presidential candidate.

When Tyler graduated from the College of William and Mary, the subject for his commencement speech was female education. Most faculty members thought it was an interesting, well delivered address, but the college president, Bishop James Madison, considered it overloaded with high-flown expressions.

After graduating from the College of William and Mary, John Tyler returned to Charles City and began to study law under his father's direction. When his father became governor of Virginia in 1808, he studied in the Richmond office of Edmund Randolph, former United States attorney general in

President George Washington's administration. Tyler was admitted to the bar in 1809. He was then 19 years old.

In October 1809, young John Tyler met President Thomas Jefferson when his father invited his old friend to dinner at the governor's mansion in Richmond. Jefferson had then completed his second term as president of the United States.

During the War of 1812, John Tyler, who supported the conflict, served briefly as captain of a small militia company raised to defend Richmond. The company was called the Charles City Rifles. It saw no action, and was disbanded when the British threat to Richmond ended in 1813.

With the support of Edmund Randolph, Tyler entered the political arena, when, in 1811, he was elected a member of the Virginia House of Delegates. His entry into politics eventually led him to the governorship of Virginia, followed by service as a United States representative and senator.

In 1840, he was chosen by the Whig Party to run as William Henry Harrison's vice president. The Whigs were successful. Harrison and Tyler were elected, and on March 4, 1841, Harrison was inaugurated as president. Immediately after the inauguration ceremony, Vice President Tyler returned to his home in Williamsburg. On April 5, 1841, Fletcher Webster, chief clerk of the Department of State and son of Daniel Webster, secretary of state, rode up to Tyler's home and delivered a message informing him that President William Henry Harrison had died.

Tyler rode to Washington the next day.

As the first vice president to accede to the presidency on the death of a president, Tyler began his term amid great controversy regarding his status. No president had died in office before, and no one in Washington knew what to do. Was Tyler president for the rest of Harrison's term? Or was he an "acting president"? The Constitution was not clear on his status. Tyler himself was convinced he was already president in full. But when he reached Washington, he found himself embroiled in a mounting controversy.

The cabinet had already decided that Tyler should bear the title of "Vice President, Acting President." Furthermore, he was told that all administrative matters would have to be approved by them. John Tyler quickly dispelled any doubts as to his own status: "I am very glad to have in my Cabinet such able statesmen as you," he told them. "But I can never consent to being dictated to as to what I shall or shall not do ... I am the President.... When you think otherwise, your resignation will be accepted."

Caught off guard by his bold stance, the cabinet members backed down. He was then sworn into office as president of the United States. Later, their decision was confirmed by the Congress. The policy established by John Tyler in 1841, that the vice president becomes the president upon the death of a president remains in force to this day.

When he entered the White House, Tyler was married to Letitia Christian. A frail woman, she suffered a stroke and died on September 10, 1842. Tyler met his second wife, 24-year-old Julia Gardiner, after a tragic accident aboard a naval ship that killed her father. They were married on June 26, 1844.

At the end of his presidency in 1845, Tyler retired to Sherwood Forest, his 1,200-acre plantation, located about 18 miles west of Williamsburg. As the Civil War began in 1861, John Tyler called for a peace conference of the states. When his suggestion failed, he called for Virginia to secede from the Union.

After Virginia left the Union, he was elected to the Provisional Congress of the Confederacy. He died on January 18, 1862, while preparing to take his seat in the Confederate House of Representatives, meeting in Richmond.

Bibliography

Chitwood, Oliver Perry. *John Tyler: Champion of the Old South.* Newtown, Conn.: American Political Biography Press, 1990.

Seager, Robert, II. *And Tyler, Too: A Biography of John & Julia Gardiner Tyler.* New York: McGraw-Hill, 1963.

James K. Polk

James Knox Polk was born on November 2, 1795, on the family farm in Mecklenburg County, North Carolina. He was the first of ten children born to Samuel and Jane Knox. He had five brothers and four sisters.

His father, Samuel Polk, caused an uproar when his infant son was taken to be baptized by a Presbyterian minister, who required both parents to profess their faith, according to Presbyterian custom. For Mrs. Polk, a devout worshiper, this was no problem. Samuel Polk thought otherwise. He didn't think that part of the baptism ritual was necessary. An argument between the minister and the father followed, ending with Samuel Polk stalking out of the church with his wife and unbaptized son. Yet James Knox Polk was raised as a Presbyterian. In his later years he joined the Methodist church. He was baptized on his deathbed.

James Polk was of Scots-Irish ancestry. Through his mother's ancestral line, James was a great-grandnephew of John Knox, founder of Scottish Presbyterianism. James lived the first ten years of his life in Mecklenburg County in a large house built by his father. The house was actually two log cabins joined with a common roof that also covered a connecting passageway. James and his siblings were taught to read, write, and do arithmetic by their parents. At times they were taught by private tutors. His stern mother believed in raising her children according to strict Presbyterian doctrine.

The land that Samuel Polk farmed was a gift from his father, Ezekiel Polk, who had served as a cavalry captain in the Mecklenburg militia during the Revolutionary War. The elder Polk was an ambitious man. In 1803, in his search for more fertile farm land, he moved his family to the Duck River valley southwest of Nashville, Tennessee. Three years later, in 1806, Samuel Polk moved his family to Tennessee, settling on a large tract that his wealthy father had put aside for him in the Duck River area.

While he farmed his new property, Samuel Polk also worked as a surveyor, often taking his son James along on surveying trips. Since James was a frail boy, prone to stomach pains, he stayed close to the surveying camp, cooking and tending to the horses. After one surveying trip in 1812, when James was 17 years old, his sufferings from stomach pains became so severe that he was taken to Danville, Kentucky, to undergo a very risky operation for removal of gallstones. The operation was performed by Doctor Ephraim McDowell, who was renowned for his pioneering work in abdominal surgery.

Since there was no anesthetic available at that time, James was required to drink enough liquor to dull his pain. He was strapped to a wooden table, and was further restrained by the doctor's assistants. Happily, the risky operation was successful.

After the operation, Samuel Knox accepted the reality that his son James would never be strong enough to perform the hard labor of a farmer or surveyor. Instead, he arranged to have his son work as a clerk for a merchant to learn the business. However, James did not like the job, and quit after a few weeks.

Eager to get an education, James Polk convinced his father to send him to school. In July 1813 James enrolled in a Presbyterian school run by the Reverend Robert Henderson outside Columbia, Tennessee. For about a year, young Polk studied Greek and Latin. After a year he transferred to a more demanding institution, the Murfreesboro Academy. There, in addition to the classic languages, he studied mathematics, science, and philosophy.

In 1816, when he was 21 years old, James entered the University of North Carolina at Chapel Hill as a sophomore. He received classic education, with emphasis on Greek, Latin, and philosophy. He excelled in mathematics. He enjoyed public speaking and debates, and was chosen president of the Dialectic Society.

James Polk graduated from the University of North Carolina with honors in 1818. He was chosen to deliver the Latin welcoming address at the com-

mencement ceremonies. The honors came with a price. In his drive to succeed, he was close to collapse as his health was deteriorating.

When his father arrived at the university in July to take him home, James
was too ill to travel back to his new home in Columbia, Tennessee. While his
son studied at the University of North Carolina, Samuel Polk built the family a two-story brick home in Columbia. (Today the home is museum, con-
taining many items and furnishings from the career of James Knox Polk.)

By October 1818, James was strong enough to travel to his lavish new
home in Columbia. There he laid out plans for his future. He wanted to be a
politician, and one of the best ways of entering politics is to become a lawyer.
So, with the aid of his father, in 1819 he began studying law in the Nashville
office of Felix Grundy, a skilled criminal lawyer. Grundy would later serve as
attorney general in President Martin Van Buren's administration.

When Grundy was elected to the state legislature in Murfreesboro, he
arranged for Polk to become clerk of the senate, a bureaucratic post responsible for directing the flow of legislative paperwork. The job paid $6 a day while
the senate was in session. After completing his legal studies with Grundy,
James Polk passed the Tennessee bar examination in 1820 and opened his own
legal office in Columbia.

When he was 27 years old, Polk decided that he was going to pursue a
political career. In 1823, he was elected to the Tennessee state legislature, and
in 1824, as a member of the Democratic Party, he was elected to the House
of Representatives. While serving in Congress, Polk formed a friendship with
Andrew Jackson, who was then a U.S. senator.

Polk was reelected to the House of Representatives six times, and in 1835
became the speaker of the house. In 1839, he left the House of Representatives, ran for governor of Tennessee and won. His political star waned when
he twice lost bids for reelection as governor, in 1841 and 1843.

But another chance came when the 1844 Democratic National Conven-
tion in Baltimore became deadlocked between incumbent President Martin
Van Buren and Lewis Cass of Michigan. Aging former President Andrew
Jackson had urged Polk to seek the presidency. When the convention dead-
locked, Jackson's friend began touting Polk as the party's presidential choice.
On the ninth ballot Polk became the unanimous choice of the convention.
James Polk then went on to win a close election over Henry Clay, the Whig
nominee for president. He assumed the presidency on March 4, 1845.

During his presidency, Polk succeeded in expanding the area of the United

States. Texas was admitted as a state, the boundary of the Oregon Territory was extended, California was acquired from Mexico, as was New Mexico, and the Rio Grande was recognized as a border between Mexico and the United States.

Throughout his political life, James Polk received much assistance from his wife, Sarah Childress Polk, whom he had married on January 1, 1824.

James Knox Polk set out to become a one-term president; he did not seek reelection. Leaving Washington after the inaugural of his successor, Zachary Taylor, Polk embarked on an extensive southern tour; he fell ill, probably from cholera that had broken out in New Orleans. He became progressively weaker and died on June 15, 1849.

Bibliography

Greenblatt, Miriam. *James K. Polk, 11th President of the United States.* Ada, Okla.: Garrett Educational Corporation, 1988.

McBride Morrell, Martha. *The Life and Times of President James K. Polk.* New York: E.P. Dutton, 1949.

McCormac, Eugene Irving. *James K. Polk—A Political Biography,* Volumes I & II. Newtown, Conn.: American Political Biography Press, 1995.

Zachary Taylor

Twelfth President
1849–1850

Zachary Taylor was a president who in his younger days had shown little interest in politics; he had never cast a vote in any election when he became president. His formal education was limited. His writing suffered from bad grammar and poor spelling. His handwriting was terrible. But as he grew older, Taylor developed a greater regard for education. He sent his three daughters to be educated in eastern boarding schools. His son attended Harvard and graduated from Yale. As post commander in the Army, he made certain that there were adequate schools for the children of soldiers stationed there.

Zachary Taylor was born into a family of wealthy Virginia planters on November 24, 1784. His parents were Richard and Sarah Taylor. Richard Taylor had fought in the Revolutionary War, enlisting in 1775 as a lieutenant in the First Virginia Regiment commanded by Patrick Henry. He participated in several important battles, including White Plains and Brandywine, finishing the war as a lieutenant general. During the war he married Sarah Dabney Strother from Culpeper, Virginia. One historical account tells that she permanently disfigured her hands when molten lead spilled on her when she was making bullets.

Zachary Taylor's birth took place at Montebello, the home of Richard's cousin, Valentine Johnson, who lived in Orange County, Virginia. Zachary was the third of eight children to be raised by the Taylors. He had four brothers and three sisters.

Richard and Sarah Taylor were then in process of moving from Hare Forest, their home in Orange County, to their new residence near what is now Louisville, Kentucky. At that time Kentucky was still part of Virginia. Richard felt that the Virginia farm was not producing enough income to support his growing family.

While the Taylors were well-to-to, their new home in Kentucky was a log cabin, but with the help of slave labor, Richard Taylor was soon able to build a two-story house next to the cabin. The house, which was named Springfield, became the centerpiece of his new prosperous plantation. Altogether, he came to own more than 1,000 acres of land in Kentucky.

Not much is known about Zachary Taylor's education. He received only the most basic of educations. He initially learned to read and write from his mother. For a short period he was taught by Elisha Ayer, an itinerant New England schoolmaster. Later he studied briefly under Kean O'Hara, a classical scholar.

Zachary Taylor most likely picked up some practical education from helping his father run his plantation. He was a stocky, strong boy who liked the outdoors. He hunted and fished in the frontier region. Once, to test his endurance, he swam across the Ohio River to the Indiana side and back to the Kentucky side. Zachary worked on his father's plantation until he was 23 years old.

In the spring of 1808, President Thomas Jefferson, in response to growing problems with England, increased the size of the Army. Zachary saw this as an opportunity to follow the military tradition of his father and grandfather. With the aid of his congressman, Zachary Taylor was one of 26 Kentuckians recommended to serve in the Army as second lieutenants. Taylor's commission, dated May 3, 1808, appointed him first lieutenant in the 7th Infantry Regiment. His pay was $30 per month and two rations per day. Taylor accepted his appointment on June 6, 1808.

Since the Army had not yet organized the newly created 7th Infantry Regiment, Zachary Taylor had to wait months before being assigned to active duty. In the fall he was ordered to report to Washington, Kentucky, to help with recruiting for the new regiment.

In the spring of 1809, Taylor led two companies of soldiers to New Orleans, where they joined with other troops to defend the town and the vast Louisiana territory recently purchased from France by President Jefferson.

New Orleans was an unhealthy town. The low-lying swampy area was a breeding ground for mosquitoes. Among the 2,000 troops there, 686 died of fewer and dysentery. While in New Orleans, Taylor came down with dysentery. When he recovered slightly, the Army sent him home to Louisville to recuperate.

During his convalescent period, Taylor met and married Margaret Mackall Smith. His father gave them a wedding present of 324 acres of farmland at the mouth of Beargrass Creek. Taylor later sold the property, and used his earnings to buy more property, eventually becoming a rich man with land holdings in Kentucky, Louisiana, and Mississippi.

After recuperating from his illness, Taylor returned to his regiment, only to learn that there was no assignment for him. He remained in Louisville until July 1811, when he took command of Fort Knox, a frontier post near Vincennes in the Indiana Territory. The fort was in disarray. The officers were feuding among themselves, the troops were untrained, and the post was in shambles. Captain Zachary Taylor, then 27 years old, quickly restored military discipline to the troops, and thereby received high praise from General William Henry Harrison, who was governor of the territory.

This was a splendid beginning of a great military career. He became known as the best Indian fighter in the Army. He participated in the Black Hawk War in the Illinois Territory in 1832, and later fought in Florida during the Seminole Indian wars. In the Mexican war in 1846, Taylor's troops won major victories at Monterrey and Buena Vista. For his victories in the Mexican War, Taylor was promoted to the rank of major general. Zachary Taylor became a national hero for his victories in the war with Mexico. His popularity appealed to the Whig Party, which, in June 1848, nominated him for president. In the election, he defeated the Democratic candidate, Lewis Cass.

Taylor served only 16 months as president. On July 4, 1850, Taylor participated in ceremonies at the Washington Monument. After enduring the blistering heat during the ceremonies, Taylor became ill with cholera. He died five days later, on July 9, 1850.

Bibliography

Bauer, K. Jack. *Zachary Taylor: Soldier, Planter, Statesman of the Old Southwest.* Baton Rouge: Louisiana State University Press, 1985.

Dyer, Brainerd. *Zachary Taylor.* Baton Rouge: Louisiana State University Press, 1946.

Hoyt, Edwin P. *Zachary Taylor.* Chicago: Reilly & Lee, 1966.

★ 13 ★

Millard Fillmore

Thirteenth President
1850–1853

Life began roughly for Millard Fillmore.

He was born on January 7, 1800, in a log cabin located in the Locke Township, Cayuga County, New York. The second of nine children, Millard had five brothers and four sisters. His parents, Nathaniel and Phoebe Millard Fillmore, were struggling to eke out a living by farming a tract of poor land, consisting mostly of clay and rocks. Nathaniel had foolishly bought the property, sight unseen, from unscrupulous land speculators. Before settling in New York, they had lived in Bennington, Vermont.

Bad luck haunted Nathaniel Fillmore. In 1802, he lost his land through a defective land title. He then moved his family to Sempronius, now Niles, near Lake Skaneateles, one of the Finger Lakes. There he took perpetual lease on a 130-acre farm, thus becoming a tenant farmer.

Millard's education was limited. While his father probably was literate, he had little time for self-education, spending most of the days toiling in the fields. From his mother, who was the daughter of a doctor, Millard learned how to read and write.

Millard Fillmore would recall in later years that among the family's early treasures were "a Bible, a hymn book, and an almanac," which his mother used to teach him how to read, write, and do arithmetic.

From an early age, Millard was required to help his father work the farm. Living at the edge of the wilderness, he also wanted to explore the area, and fish and swim in nearby Lake Skaneateles. Whenever he indulged in such pleasures, his hard-working father berated him for wasting time. Millard was a strong boy who did his farm chores well. He plowed the fields, cultivated the crops, and cleared land for more farming. By the time he was 15 years old, he was a skilled frontier farmer.

Any formal education in the early life of Millard Fillmore was virtually non-existent. Yet he was eager to learn. When he was nine years old, he received his first formal schooling in the village of New Hope. There an abandoned log house had been furnished with benches and a blackboard to write on. The students were instructed in reading, writing, and arithmetic. Time for schooling was limited. Since Millard's main job was to work on his father's farm, he could only attend school during the winter.

During the War of 1812, Millard Fillmore wanted to join the Army, but his father denied him permission to enlist. In those days, it was not unusual for young boys to join the military services.

Nathaniel Fillmore was an unhappy father. Disgusted with his own failures as a farmer, he was determined that his five sons would never have to till the soil for a living. Since he had no money to send Millard to school, in 1815 Nathaniel Fillmore arranged for him to work a three-month trial period for Benjamin Hungerford, who operated a wool-carding and clothing mill in Sparta (now West Sparta). If the trial period was successful, Millard would be apprenticed as a cloth dresser.

Millard was not happy about the move from his home in Sempronius to Sparta. Hungerford turned out to be a difficult employer. Millard had visions of learning a trade, but instead found himself chopping wood. After an angry exchange of words about his wood chopping duties, Hungerford relented and let him perform some shop work, but Fillmore left after fulfilling his three months' obligation.

Later in 1815, Millard Fillmore began a second apprenticeship period with Alvan Kellogg and Zaccheus Cheney at their carding and cloth dressing shop in New Hope. While he was learning the carding trade, Millard also served as a bookkeeper for Mr. Cheney. Whenever there was a slowdown of work at the mill, Millard would help his father with farm work.

During the time he worked in the clothing mills, Millard became painfully aware of his lack of education. While he could read, he had little understanding of the meaning of the words. At 17, after he had joined a newly established lending library in Sempronius, he purchased a dictionary, determined to improve his knowledge of the English language.

He became an avid reader, and, at the age of 18, had gained enough knowledge to land a teaching job at a school in Scott, near Skaneateles Lake. He was paid ten dollars a month.

In 1819, he enrolled in a newly established academy at New Hope. It was an exciting time for Millard. He was getting better education, and he had a girlfriend, 21-year-old Abigail Powers, a teacher at the academy. She was studious and ambitious, and helped Millard with his studies. They fell in love, but did not marry until 1826.

Another important thing happened to Millard in 1819. His father left his rented farm and moved his family 12 miles away to Montville, where he became a tenant farmer of County Judge Walter Wood. Nathaniel Fillmore, eager to have his son learn a profession, asked Judge Wood to allow him to clerk in his law office for two months. The judge agreed, but in order to let Millard study the legal profession full time, he would have to free himself of his indenture to the owners of the cloth dressing shop in New Hope.

Realizing that Millard Fillmore had little money, the judge offered to lend him the $30 he needed to buy his freedom. Millard taught school to repay his debt. Millard's legal clerkship with Judge Wood did not run smoothly. The judge owned a great number of tenant farms, and young Fillmore was required to help his employer administer his holdings. At times this meant evicting some of the farmers from the land they tilled. Fillmore disliked his job, and in 1821, after an argument over Millard's handling of a minor legal case, he abruptly left the employment of Judge Wood and returned home to his parents, then living in East Aurora.

Millard Fillmore continued his legal studies while teaching school. In 1823 he gained admission to the New York bar. He opened a law practice in East Aurora, and then in Buffalo, New York, which in 1830 he made his permanent home.

Fillmore began his political career in 1824 when he supported President John Quincy Adams for president. During 1829–1831, he served as a New York state assemblyman; he served in the House of Representatives during 1833–1835 and 1837–1843. In 1832 Fillmore helped found the Whig party in western New York.

During the 1840s, Fillmore worked with the conservative wing of the

Whig Party in New York. In 1848 the Whigs chose an outsider, General Zachary Taylor, as their presidential candidate. They named Fillmore as the vice presidential candidate. The Whigs won the election, and almost immediately the nation became embroiled in the slavery issue—whether slavery should be extended to the new territories or be abolished altogether.

President Taylor took a firm stand against appeasing the South, while Fillmore took no stand on the issue when it was debated in Congress.

Taylor died unexpectedly, and on July 9, 1850, Millard Fillmore became president. In September 1850, Fillmore signed into law a series of measures that made up the Compromise of 1850. Among these measures were the admission of California as a free state; organization of other areas taken from Mexico into the territories of New Mexico and Utah and abolishment of the slave trade in Washington, D.C. Unfortunately, these measures did not end the turmoil over slavery. The problem would revisit the nation within a few years.

While Millard Fillmore had little success as a president, he established the first permanent library in the White House. Fillmore and his wife Abigail were ardent readers and book collectors, having more than four thousand volumes in their home in Buffalo, New York.

During the Whig presidential convention of 1852, Fillmore was defeated by General Winfield Scott. The divided Whigs were then defeated in the general election by Democrat Franklin Pierce. Millard Fillmore returned to Buffalo but remained active in politics. He supported the Union during the Civil War, but felt that the conflict was needless. He was often critical of President Abraham Lincoln's handling of the war. After retiring from politics, Millard Fillmore became active in civic life of Buffalo. He died there at age 74 on March 8, 1874.

Bibliography

Deam, James M. *Millard Fillmore*. Berkeley Heights, N.J.: Enslow, 2003.

Rayback, Robert J. *Millard Fillmore: Biography of a President*. Buffalo, N.Y.: Henry Stewart, 1959. (Published for the Buffalo Historical Society.)

Scarry, Robert J. *Millard Fillmore*. Jefferson, N.C.: McFarland, 2001.

★ 14 ★

Franklin Pierce

14th President
1853–1857

When Franklin Pierce was 12 years old he attended the Hancock Academy in New Hampshire. One Sunday, a homesick Franklin decided that he'd had enough of schooling and walked the long way to his home in Hillsborough. He was warmly welcomed by his parents, General Benjamin and Anna Pierce.

The elder Pierce had led the local militia to victories in the American Revolution, and as a result, he enjoyed a status in the area of Hillsborough that gave him influence in local politics.

After feeding his son, the father hitched his horse up to the carriage and without any explanation drove his son back toward Hancock. Halfway to the school, the father told his son to get out of the carriage and walk the rest of the way to school. His father's words on leaving Franklin were: "Now, remember not to come home again until you are invited."

Though not born to great wealth on November 23, 1804, Franklin Pierce had more advantages than most local people in rural New Hampshire. Like most parents who were raised in troubled times, Benjamin and Anna Pierce wanted their eight children to have a better education than their own.

Before the Hancock Academy, Franklin Pierce learned to read and write at a little brick schoolhouse in Hillsborough. Franklin's studies at Hancock

Academy had not been sufficiently advanced so he was sent to Francestown Academy to prepare him for college. He also studied for a short period at the Phillips Exeter Academy. In September 1820, Franklin Pierce enrolled in Bowdoin College in Brunswick, Maine. His son's college education, including room and board, would cost General Pierce about $200 a year.

During his sophomore year he met an incoming freshman named Nathaniel Hawthorne, the future author. They formed a lasting friendship. When Pierce ran for president, Hawthorne wrote his campaign biography. Another college pal was the poet Henry Wadsworth Longfellow, who was a year behind Pierce.

At first, young Franklin enjoyed the social life at Bowdoin so much that his schoolwork took second priority. Soon after the third year began, the school announced the standing of the students, and Pierce found himself the lowest in his class. This was too much for his pride so he began to apply himself. For three months he would rise at four o'clock in the morning in order to get a head start on his studies. After the regular classes, he would study until midnight. By graduation day in 1824, Franklin Pierce ranked fifth in his class.

In addition to classical languages and math, Franklin also studied history, chemistry, mineralogy, and philosophy. In his junior year, Pierce joined a school chum during spring break to teach briefly at a rural elementary school in Hebron, Maine. Having been born the son of a Revolutionary war veteran, Franklin Pierce was aware of his heritage at an early age. The patriotic youngster joined the Bowdoin Cadets, the college's march and drill club, which elected him captain.

After graduating from Bowdoin in the fall of 1824, Pierce returned to the homestead in Hillsborough to take over the post office duties of his father. At the same time he studied law under the tutelage of John Burnham, a prominent local lawyer.

Deciding that the local environment was not the best place to study law, Pierce moved to Portsmouth, the bustling seaport of New Hampshire. There he read law in the office of Attorney Levi Woodbury. When Franklin studied at Francestown Academy, he boarded with Woodbury's mother, so student and teacher renewed their old relationship.

In the Spring of 1826, Franklin Pierce went to Northampton, Massachusetts, to take an intensive law course under the direction of Judge Samuel Howe. After his lengthy legal studies, Franklin was admitted to the New Hampshire bar in 1827.

That year Benjamin Pierce won election to the state's governorship, and he vowed to pull his son up the political ladder with him. With father and son both being Democratic Party members and supporters of the new administration of President Andrew Jackson, Franklin Pierce was easily elected to the New Hampshire legislature in 1829. In 1833, Franklin Pierce, without formal opposition, was elected to represent New Hampshire in the U.S. House of Representatives. In 1836, he was elected to the U.S. Senate, then being 32 years old, the youngest member of the Senate.

Pierce resigned from the Senate in 1842 to practice law in Concord, New Hampshire. When the Mexican War broke out he enlisted in the Army as a private. Soon commissioned as a brigadier general, he served under General Winfield Scott in the campaign against Mexico City. Pierce resigned from the Army after the war.

Staying active in politics, Franklin Pierce found himself a presidential candidate when the Democrats held their nomination in Baltimore in June 1852. With the four major candidates unable to get the two-thirds majority vote, Pierce was nominated on the 49th ballot. He went on to defeat the Whig Party's nominee, General Scott, to become the 14th president of the United States.

For Franklin Pierce his inauguration as the president of the United States on Friday, March 4, 1853, was not a happy event. Three months before the inauguration day, Pierce, his wife Jane, and 12-year-old son Benjamin boarded a train in Boston for Concord, New Hampshire, to make final preparation for departure for Washington, D.C.

About a mile from the railroad station in Boston, an axle broke and the car in which the Pierce family was traveling slipped off the track, toppled off the embankment and rolled into the field below. President-elect Pierce and his wife were uninjured, but their son was caught in the wreckage and horribly killed before their eyes. Having lost two other children through illness, the Pierces were stunned and shocked by the loss of their last child. The Pierces never fully recovered from this disaster. Mrs. Pierce refused to attend the inauguration.

When Chief Justice Roger B. Taney administered the oath, Pierce raised his right hand and broke precedent by affirming, rather than swearing to the oath of the presidency. Pierce, believing that the death of his son was punishment for his sins, refrained from using the Bible during the oath taking ceremony. Overcoming his emotional problems, President Pierce then astonished the spectators by reciting his lengthy inaugural address of more than 3,000 words without reference to text or notes.

As a pro-slavery president, Pierce was unable to govern satisfactorily. He alienated the North by his tough enforcement of the Fugitive Slave Act, and he failed to restore civil order when abolitionists and pro-slavery immigrants fought each other in the Kansas Territory. The events in Kansas became a prelude to the Civil War.

In 1856, Pierce's own Democratic Party refused to support him. Instead they nominated James Buchanan, who won the election. Pierce left the White House a discredited figure. He spent his last years in virtual seclusion, and died in Concord, New Hampshire, on October 8, 1869.

Bibliography

Bell, Carl Irving. *They Remember Franklin Pierce.* Springfield, Vt.: April Hill, 1980.

Boas, Norman F. *Jane M. Pierce (1806–1863): The Pierce-Aiken Papers.* Stonington, Conn.: Seaport Autographs, 1983.

Nichols, Roy Franklin. *Franklin Pierce: Young Hickory of the Granite Hills.* Newtown, Conn.: American Political Biography Press, 1993.

★ 15 ★

James Buchanan

Fifteenth President
1857–1861

While James Buchanan was an excellent scholar, he was kicked out of the Dickinson College in Carlisle, Pennsylvania, for disorderly conduct. He smoked cigars, and engaged in beer drinking contests. He was saved from expulsion when the college accepted his passionate plea and promise to behave. The fact that the college faculty had great respect for his father, James Buchanan, Sr., a hard-working farmer and merchant, influenced their decision to reinstate him.

James Buchanan, Sr., was an Irish immigrant who owned a 300-acre farm and operated a general store near Mercersburg, Pennsylvania. The younger James Buchanan was born on April 23, 1791, in log cabin at Stony Batter near Cove Gap, a frontier settlement outside Mercersburg. (The cabin is now located on the campus of the Mercersburg Academy.) James Buchanan, Sr., was married to Elizabeth Speer, who bore him 11 children. Eight lived to maturity. James, Jr., was their second child and first son.

On the 100 acres of Stony Batter land, the elder Buchanan farmed, kept an orchard, and operated a general store. By 1794 he had prospered enough to buy a 300-acre farm near Mercersburg. In 1776, Buchanan bought a large tract in Mercersburg and on it built a large house to serve both as his home and place of business.

James, Jr., was a tall, strong boy, but he had a peculiar eye disorder. One eye was nearsighted, the other farsighted. Also, the left eyeball was located higher up in the socket than the right. To compensate for his eye problem, he would cock his head down and look to one side to focus his vision. This move gave some people the impression that he was shy. James Buchanan grew up with four sisters and three brothers. Their mother, Elizabeth Speer Buchanan, from Lancaster, Pennsylvania, had little schooling, but she loved to read and recite poems to her children. She encouraged them to learn and often tested their powers of reason by engaging them in arguments.

Since James was the eldest son, his father expected him to be his indispensable assistant. While he did his best, the boy seldom received praise from his father. When he was eight years old, he began working in his father's store, where he served customers, learned the value of money and kept records. He did a good job serving as his father's bookkeeper. Throughout his adult life, Buchanan would excel in neatness and accuracy when working with figures and record keeping.

Thanks to his father's business success and his mother's interest in education, James received a good education. His first schooling was at the Old Stone Academy in Mercersburg, where he studied reading, writing, and arithmetic, as well as Latin and Greek. A quick learner, James's studies at Old Stone Academy qualified him to enter Dickinson College at the age of 16, in 1807. His courses included Latin, Greek, mathematics, geography, logic, history, literature, and philosophy.

At first, James attended to his studies at Dickinson, but when his fun-loving classmates ridiculed him for taking his studies seriously, he yielded to temptation and joined in the revelry. He took part in boisterous drinking bouts, and smoked cigars, all contrary to regulations of the college.

At the end of his first year, while at home in Mercersburg, James received a letter from the college president, Dr. Robert Davidson, stating that he had been expelled due to his disorderly conduct. His disappointed father berated him for his misconduct, arrogant attitude, and disrespect for his teachers. Realizing that he couldn't discuss his problem with his irate father, James sought out the help of Dr. John King, the family minister, who was also president of the board of trustees of Dickinson.

After giving James a lecture, then having him promise to conduct himself properly and concentrate on his studies, Doctor King persuaded the college to reinstate the errant Buchanan.

When he returned to college, James was a more serious student. He received good grades and stayed out of trouble. Still, he remained aloof and arrogant, feeling that he was superior to the other students. This attitude would cost him honors.

The college had two literary societies, Belle-Lettres and the Union Philosophical Society. The societies picked their candidate for top student honors. The victor was assured valedictorian status at commencement exercises.

The Union Philosophical Society picked Buchanan as their top student, but the faculty rejected their nomination on the grounds that it would be bad for the college's morale to honor a troublesome and disrespectful student. The faculty's decision caused an uproar on the campus. Buchanan complained loudly over their ruling, as did his literary society. However, all had calmed down by commencement day, September 19, 1809, when Buchanan was allowed to deliver the valedictory address. James Buchanan left Dickinson a wiser but bitter student.

James's father, who wanted his son to become a lawyer, made arrangements for James to study law by clerking in the office of James Hopkins in Lancaster, Pennsylvania. James began his legal studies in December 1809, and in November of 1812 he was admitted to the bar. In February 1813 he became a practicing attorney in Lancaster. Later he was appointed prosecutor for Lebanon County, Pennsylvania.

As a member of the Federalist Party, James Buchanan disapproved of President James Madison's handling of the War of 1812, but his opposition changed when British forces burned Washington, D.C. At a public rally in Lancaster in 1814, Buchanan gave a rousing patriotic speech, and then joined the Lancaster County Dragoons. The company was a privately formed paramilitary group responding to the burning of Washington by taking up arms. The volunteers marched to Baltimore, Maryland, where they offered their services to the major in charge of the Third U.S. Cavalry, but the Army had no use for untrained volunteers.

However, the major suggested that they obtain horses for the Army, either by stealing or from volunteers donating their horses. When the British threat dissipated, Buchanan's group returned to Lancaster.

Shortly after returning to Lancaster, Buchanan made his first entry into the political arena. He was elected to the Pennsylvania state legislature, serving two terms, 1815–1816, as a Federalist. Years later he would join the Democratic Party.

During the summer of 1819, Buchanan became engaged to Ann Caroline Coleman, daughter of a wealthy iron trader in Lancaster. Her family disapproved and gossip spread that Buchanan was a fortune hunter. A series of unhappy events led Ann to break off the engagement, and a week later she died, a possible suicide. The experience shocked Buchanan. He never became seriously involved with any other woman for the rest of his life.

After this tragic episode, Buchanan channeled all his energies into an extraordinary political career that stretched over five decades, as congressman, minister to Russia, U.S. senator from Pennsylvania, secretary of state, minister to Great Britain, and president. In 1856, James Buchanan was nominated for president by the Democratic Party, with John Breckinridge of Kentucky as his running mate. The campaign platform was based on the finality of the Compromise of 1850 and the non-intervention of Congress concerning slavery in the territories.

Buchanan defeated opponent John Fremont in the electoral college, though he failed to receive a majority of the popular vote. Buchanan's presidency was a stormy one, and his lifelong pattern of avoiding taking sides, hampered his governing. He would make no definite decision on the slavery issue, and Congress ignored his leadership. The election of Abraham Lincoln as president in 1860 added fuel to the fire, and the attack on Fort Sumter on April 12, 1861, started the Civil War. After his presidency, James Buchanan retired to his Lancaster estate, called Wheatland, and died there on June 1, 1868.

Bibliography

Brill, Marlene Targ. *James Buchanan: Fifteenth President of the United States*. Chicago: Childrens Press, 1988.

Horton, R.G. *The Life and Public Service of James Buchanan*. New York: Derby & Jackson, 1856.

Klein, Philip Shriver. *President James Buchanan: A Biography*. University Park: The Pennsylvania State University Press, 1962.

Young, Jeff C. *James Buchanan*. Berkeley Heights, N.J.: Enslow, 2003.

★ 16 ★

Abraham Lincoln

Sixteenth President
1861–1865

"I was born Feb. 12, 1806, in Hardin County, Kentucky. My parents were both born in Virginia, of undistinguished families—second families, I should say. My mother, who died in my tenth year, was of a family of the name of Hanks.... My father, at the death of his father, was but six years of age; and he grew up literally without education. He moved from Kentucky to what is now Spencer County, Indiana, in my eighth year.... There I grew up."

This is how Abraham Lincoln described his ancestry in a biographical sketch he wrote just before he was nominated for president by the Republican Party in May 1860. "Somehow," he added, "I could read, write, and cipher ... but that was all." Contrary to Lincoln's self-deprecation, he was an energetic youngster who worked hard to educate himself and to help his parents escape poverty.

His parents, Thomas Lincoln and Nancy Hanks, were married in 1806 and built their first home, a small cabin, in Elizabethtown, Kentucky. Their first child, Sarah, was born there in February 1807. In 1808 the Lincolns moved and resettled on their 348 acre Sinking Spring Hill farm, located about three miles south of Hodgenville, in Hardin County (now Larue County), Kentucky. Their home was a one-room log cabin with dirt a floor. It was here that Abraham Lincoln was born on February 12, 1809. He was named after his paternal grandfather, who was killed by an Indian while he was clearing a field. Another son, named Thomas after his father, was born in 1811, but he died two years later. While Thomas Lincoln worked his farm, he supplemented his meager farm income by doing odd jobs such as cabinet making and carpentry. He always owned a horse, and at times he worked as a timber cutter and prison guard.

In 1813 Thomas Lincoln lost his Sinking Spring Hill farm because of a defective land title. He then moved his family ten miles north to a farm located near Knob Creek, Kentucky. The Knob Creek farm was fertile and easy to till, and the region was more thickly populated. Since the Cumberland Trail from Louisville to Nashville passed close by, the Lincoln family was often in contact with travelers. And Abraham and his sister Sarah had playmates. Abraham often fished in the Knob Creek, which ran close to his home. Once, when heavy rain raised the water level, Abraham fell into the swollen creek while trying to cross it to hunt for partridges. Luckily, his playmate, Austin Gollaher, pulled him to safety. Neither boy could swim.

While his mother had given both her husband and her son basic instructions in reading and writing, Abraham would get his first taste of schooling when he walked his sister Sarah to school in Knob Creek. He went with his sister more to keep her company than to learn anything at the school.

Since there were no public schools in the early frontier days, parents in the settlements would collect money to hire a teacher who held classes in a one-room schoolhouse. Children of all grade levels would sit in the same room and together they would recite the lessons given by the teacher. These schools were often referred to as "blab schools."

The Knob Creek school, located about two miles away from the Lincoln home, was such a blab school. Its first teacher was Zachariah Riney. He was followed by Caleb Hazel, who taught spelling, reading, writing, and arithmetic (in those days called cipher) to Sarah Lincoln. While Abraham, then about five years old, wasn't a regular student, he did pick up a bit of knowledge while waiting for his sister to finish class. Since Caleb Hazel was a neighbor of the Lincolns, it is quite possible that he tutored young Abraham when the school was not open.

Abraham was eager to learn, so he studied his sister's textbook, *Dilworth's Speller*. The textbook contained spelling and grammar lessons, prose and verse for reading, tables of numbers with their proper spelling, and a listing of the states and territories. It also contained writings of moral and religious nature, as well as instructions about behavior. Along with studying the *Dilworth Speller*,

Nancy Lincoln required her children to read the Bible. They were also required to attend Sunday church services. While Abraham Lincoln was very close to his mother, he did not get along with his father. At times the elder Lincoln would trash his son for no apparent reason. When his father died in 1851, Abraham Lincoln did not attend his funeral.

Thomas Lincoln lost his Knob Creek farm when non–Kentucky residents brought suit against him and other occupants of the rich valley, claiming prior title. Having neither the money nor the inclination to fight for his claim in court, he sought out property in Indiana. Here the government had surveyed the land and offered buyers guaranteed titles to their new property.

In the late fall of 1816, the Lincolns left Knob Creek for their new home in the wilderness area of what is now Spencer County, near Little Pigeon Creek. Thomas Lincoln hastily build a crude shelter to ward off the oncoming winter. There they lived while he cleared the land and built a log cabin. Abraham Lincoln, who was then seven years, learned how to swing an axe and helped his father clear the land for farming. Thomas Lincoln kept the family going through the winter by hunting and killing wild animals, such as deer and bears, for food. The skins and furs they got from the animals kept the family warm.

In February 1817, just before his eighth birthday, Abraham tried his luck in hunting. He spotted a flock of wild turkeys near the cabin. Using his father's rifle, he killed one of the birds. But killing animals was not for him. Recalling the incident years later, Lincoln said that he had "never since pulled a trigger for any larger game."

After about a year of clearing, Thomas Lincoln and his son Abraham had enough land to plant corn, wheat and oats. They also raised some sheep and hogs, and acquired a few cows. By October 1817, things were going so well for Thomas Lincoln that he began making small repayments on the $320 government loan he had made to purchase the farm.

Then tragedy struck. In the late summer of 1818, a dreaded disease called milk sickness killed many people in the Little Pigeon Creek community. The illness was caused by the milk from cows that roamed the forest and ate the poisonous white snakeroot plant. The inflicted person usually died within seven days of being struck down by the illness. Abraham's mother, Nancy Hanks Lincoln, fell sick with the milk disease and died on October 5, 1818.

Thomas remained a widower for about a year. In December 1819, he went to Elizabethtown, Kentucky, where he proposed to a widow named Sarah

Bush Johnson, the mother of three children who ranged in age from five to nine years. She accepted the marriage proposal, and after he paid her debts, they quickly packed up her belongings and moved her to her new home in Indiana.

With his expanded family, Thomas Lincoln, with the help of Abraham, made his cabin larger and put down wood flooring to accommodate the four newcomers. He also installed a sleeping loft for the children, cut a hole for a window, and built a solid door.

Sarah Bush Lincoln was a warm and outgoing woman who quickly brought order to the Lincoln household. She blended the two families harmoniously, and treated her own and Lincoln's children with absolute impartiality.

Abraham Lincoln grew fond of his stepmother who, while illiterate herself, encouraged him to study, read, and seek ways to improve his life. Some historians believe that Lincoln was referring to his stepmother when years later he wrote to his law partner, William H. Herndon, that "all I am or hope to be, I owe to my angel mother."

Abraham Lincoln's schooling was sketchy. Common free schools were not available in the Indiana area where he lived. Settler families had to depend on itinerant teachers to instruct their children. The first school Abraham attended in the Little Pigeon Creek community was operated by Andrew Crawford, a justice of the peace and neighbor of the Lincoln family. The school, a so-called "blab school" where students of all ages recite their lessons together, was located about a mile and half from the Lincoln home.

Teachers at these primitive schools merely taught their students reading, writing and arithmetic. It was a rarity when an itinerant teacher would instruct in other subjects. Crawford was an exception, requiring his students to read and study the Bible, and giving them instructions in etiquette.

After one term, Crawford gave up teaching, and Abraham did not attend school for two years, until James Swaney opened one about four miles away from the Lincoln home. The distance made it difficult for Abraham to attend school on a regular basis, since he was required to help his father with farm chores. Later, for about six months, he attended a school taught by Azel W. Dorsey, and that ended Abraham Lincoln's formal education. He was then 15 years old.

Abraham Lincoln possessed a quick and inquiring mind that led him to educate himself. He would read everything he could lay his hands on. When he came across a passage that struck him, he would write it down on a piece of paper, or in his scrapbook, and memorize it. While the Bible was the Lincoln family's main reading matter, Abraham would borrow books from the more literate neighbors.

Among his favorite reading were Parson M. L. Weems's fanciful biography of George Washington, *The Pilgrim's Progress* by John Bunyan, the poems of Robert Burns, and the plays of William Shakespeare. He would often quote favorite passages from these writers.

Abraham was a good storyteller, often using the rough barnyard language and coarse humor of the backwoods to amuse his listeners. Sometimes his storytelling sessions interfered with his chores, much to the annoyance of his stern father. After attending church, Abraham would gather his brothers and sisters, get on a stump or log, and mimic the preacher's sermon.

At 15 Abraham Lincoln was almost six feet tall (as an adult he was six feet, four inches tall). He had long, gangling arms and legs and a sunken chest. He often seemed lost in his dreams, but he was a powerfully strong young man. He was a good wrestler; no one could put him down.

When Abraham was 17 years old he got a job with James Taylor, who operated a packing house and ferry where the Anderson River flows into the Ohio River. His duty was to run a small ferry across the Anderson River. While he had the physique of a grown man, Abraham was not paid a man's wages. He received only 37 cents a day for his ferrying job.

In the spring of 1828, James Gentry, who owned a store in Rockport, was sending a flatboat with a cargo of meat, corn, and flour down the rivers for sale in New Orleans. Gentry's son Allen was in charge of the boat, and Abraham was hired as a helper. He was to receive eight dollars a month, plus his passage back by steamboat.

In New Orleans, the first big city he had ever seen, Abraham Lincoln observed a population of great mixture—French, Spanish, Mexican, Creole, and, for the first time, see slaves sold at a slave market. There is apparently no record of the impression the slavery auction had on young Lincoln. Upon returning home, Abraham dutifully handed over his earnings to his father. This he did regularly until he reached maturity.

Thomas Lincoln had become dissatisfied with farming in Indiana. He sold his farm in Little Pigeon Creek for $125, and in 1830, moved to Macon County, Illinois. He lived in Illinois for the rest of his life.

Abraham, now of age, was on his own. He made a second flatboat trip to

New Orleans, and in 1831 set out for New Salem, in Sangamon County near Springfield, Illinois. His first job in New Salem was working as a clerk in a general store for $15 a month plus sleeping quarters in the back. In 1832 he volunteered for service in the Army during the Black Hawk War, and was elected captain of a company of volunteers. He saw no action during his military service.

Lincoln became a popular figure in New Salem. He delighted people with his wit, intelligence, and integrity. He helped the less literate citizens with their reading and writing, and took part in community affairs. When the general store he operated failed, he was appointed postmaster for New Salem. He used that job as springboard for entering politics, and in 1834 was elected to the Illinois state legislature. When the legislature was not in session, Lincoln studied law and received his license to practice in 1837.

On November 4, 1842, Lincoln married Mary Todd of Lexington, Kentucky.

In November 1846, Lincoln was elected to the U.S. House of Representatives. In 1856, he joined the Republican Party, and was elected president in 1860. President Abraham Lincoln was shot by an assassin on April 14, 1865, while attending a play at Ford's Theater in Washington, D.C. He died the next day.

Bibliography

Angle, Paul M., ed. *The Lincoln Reader.* Brunswick, N.J.: Rutgers University Press, 1947.

Arnold, Isaac N. *The Life of Abraham Lincoln.* Lincoln: University of Nebraska Press, 1994.

Browne, Francis Fisher. *The Everyday Life of Abraham Lincoln.* Lincoln: University of Nebraska Press, 1995. (Reproduction of original 1866 edition.)

Donald, David Herbert. *We Are Lincoln's Men: Abraham Lincoln and His Friends.* New York: Simon & Schuster, 2003.

Herndon, William H., and Jesse W. Weik. *Abraham Lincoln: The True Story of a Great Life.* New York: D. Appleton, 1924. (For an updated version with a new introduction, refer to *Herndon's Life of Lincoln*; New York: Da Capo Press, 1983.)

Kunhardt, Philip B., Jr. Philip B. Kunhardt, III, and Peter W. Kunhardt. *Lincoln: An Illustrated Biography.* New York: Portland House (Random House), 1992.

Thomas, Benjamin P. *Abraham Lincoln: A Biography.* New York: Alfred A. Knopf, 1952.

Warren, Louis A. *Lincoln's Youth: Indiana Years, Seven to Twenty-one, 1816–1830.* Indianapolis: Indiana Historical Society, 1991.

★ 17 ★

Andrew Johnson

Seventeenth President
1865–1869

Andrew Johnson, who was born into poverty, became the only president of the United States who never had a day of formal schooling. His meager education began at the age of 14 when his mother forced him into virtual servitude by having him become an apprentice to a stern tailor in Raleigh, North Carolina.

The future president was born on December 29, 1808, the second son of Jacob and Mary "Polly" McDonough Johnson. Andrew was born in a small cabin located next to Casso's Inn in Raleigh, where his father worked as a porter and handyman. Jacob also tended horses, served as a church sexton, and rang the town's bell. His mother was a seamstress at the inn.

Andrew Johnson's father died when Andrew was three years old. He died as the result of performing an act of heroism in saving another's life. In December 1811, Jacob Johnson was hired to accompany a group of Raleigh's leading businessmen on a fishing party at Walnut Creek. His job was to clean the fish. Thomas Henderson, editor of the *Raleigh Star*, was paddling a canoe, when the canoe overturned, dumping him and his two passengers into the frigid water. One passenger, who could not swim, panicked and desperately clung to Henderson, causing them both to sink to the bottom of the creek.

Jacob Johnson dove into the icy water, and with immense effort managed to pull both men safely ashore. The rescue effort ruined his health. He caught a chill, which developed into pneumonia, and he died shortly thereafter. Since he was poor, Jacob Johnson was buried in an unmarked grave in a potter's field.

Editor Henderson paid tribute to Jacob Johnson in an obituary published in the January 12, 1812, issue of the *Raleigh Star*, noting that "he was esteemed for his honesty, sobriety, industry, and his humane, friendly disposition." Continuing, Henderson wrote, "Among all whom he was known and esteemed, none lament him, except perhaps his own relatives, more than the publisher of this newspaper, for he owes his life on a particular occasion to the kindness and humanity of Johnson."

Mary Johnson, poor and uneducated, struggled to care for Andrew and his eight-year-old brother, William. In 1814 she married a man named Turner Dougherty. Her lot did not improve, since the man she married was also poor and illiterate.

Mary wanted her sons to be educated, but since there were no free schools in Raleigh, she opted for the boys to learn a trade. She apprenticed them to local businessmen. Under the apprenticeship system of the 1800s, a boy learned a trade by being an indentured servant to his employer until he became of age or was released earlier by his employer.

When William turned 14, his mother contracted with Editor Henderson to have him become an apprentice printer at the *Raleigh Star*. A year later Henderson died and the contract ended. In November 1818, Mary Johnson Dougherty, determined that her boys should learn a trade, went to James J. Selby, a local tailor, and made her mark on a document that apprenticed them to work in his shop until they reached the age of 21.

Selby had a large and busy tailor shop. His customers included the most influential citizens of the city. Journeymen tailors and the apprentices worked in the back of the shop from early morning to late at night. The apprentices sat cross-legged on a tailor's bench, cutting, stitching, patching, and pressing, with no letups except for meals. Theirs was a long, hard road toward learning a trade.

To keep his workers from becoming bored, Selby hired someone to read to them while they worked. The readers usually read aloud from newspapers, journals, and pamphlets. One reader, Dr. William G. Hill, volunteered his services. He devoted his leisure time to reading aloud from his favorite books, which included *The American Speaker*, a collection of great speeches by American and British statesmen. The book also contained essays on a variety of subjects, including how to become a good speaker. Andrew Johnson looked forward to the reading sessions. He tried to remember passages from the book read by Dr. Hill.

Businessmen who employed apprentices had an obligation to ensure that their workers could read simple instructions. James Litchford, Selby's foreman, was responsible for teaching the alphabet to the apprentices. Andrew Johnson was an eager student, and his enthusiasm for learning impressed Dr. Hill so much that he gave Andrew one of his books.

Unlike other apprentices, Andrew Johnson did not live at the tailor shop. He was allowed to stay at home under a special arrangement that his mother had made with Mr. Selby. This arrangement allowed Andrew time to roam the neighborhood with his buddies. One night, in June 1824, Andrew and some of his companions threw pieces of wood against the window at the house of a woman who had two daughters. While they thought to impress the girls, their mother was not amused and threatened to prosecute the boys.

Andrew and his brother William took the threat seriously. The law dealt harshly with apprentices who got into trouble. They could be arrested and jailed. Rather than risk going to jail, Andrew and William Johnson decided to run away. So on the night of June 15, 1824, the two Johnson brothers threw some of their belongings in a bag and left Raleigh to escape punishment.

As soon as he learned of the disappearance of the Johnson brothers, the angry tailor Selby placed an advertisement in a local newspaper offering a ten dollar reward for their capture. He was particularly interested in apprehending Andrew. "I will pay the above Reward to any person who will deliver said apprentices to me in Raleigh, or I will give the above Reward for Andrew Johnson alone," Selby declared in his ad.

The runaways didn't stop running until they arrived in Carthage, a town about 50 miles away. There they rented a small shack in which they set up a tailor shop. Andrew had learned his trade well, and managed to make a meager living as a journeyman tailor. Feeling unsafe in North Carolina, however, the boys later fled across the state line to the town of Laurens, South Carolina.

The Johnson brothers plied their trade in Laurens for two years, but then Andrew decided to return to Raleigh and clear his name and debt with Mr. Selby. The tailor had since moved his business out of Raleigh, and when Andrew contacted him, Selby refused to have anything to do with his former apprentice.

Unable to clear his name, the dejected Andrew Johnson decided to leave North Carolina for good. So, in August 1826, Andrew set out for new adventures in Tennessee, where William had already settled. Andrew's travels to Tennessee ended at Columbia, where he found a job with another tailor. His stay in Columbia was brief. When he learned that things were not going well for his mother, he returned to Raleigh, and convinced her and his stepfather to live with him in Tennessee. They traveled across North Carolina in a two-wheeled cart drawn by a pony, and arrived in Greenville in eastern Tennessee in September 1826.

Andrew found temporary work with tailors in Greenville and nearby Rutledge until March 1827, when he opened his own shop in Greenville. On the door of his shop, he nailed a simple sign, "A. Johnson, Tailor."

When Andrew Johnson arrived in Greenville, he became acquainted with Eliza McCardle who, according to legend, told her girlfriends that "there goes my beau," when she first saw him arrive in town. She was the daughter of a shoemaker and lived with her widowed mother.

Andrew courted the charming brown-haired girl, and on May 17, 1827, 18-year-old Andrew Johnson and 17-year-old Eliza McCardle were married. The newlyweds set up housekeeping in the back room of his tailor shop.

Having been more educated than her husband, Eliza began teaching Andrew how to read and write, how to do arithmetic, and how to talk. As he learned to express himself, Andrew gained friends, who would often assemble at his shop to discuss and debate current political issues. Once a week, Johnson participated in the student debates at Greenville College and, when they were discontinued, he went to Tusculum College to further hone his debating skill.

In 1829, with the backing of his eager friends and disgruntled citizens, Andrew Johnson won his first political victory-alderman to the Greenville town council. He served as the town's mayor from 1830 to 1833. In 1832, at age 23, Andrew Johnson, had never attended school, was appointed a trustee of the nearby Rhea Academy.

Johnson's political career took him to the U.S. House of Representatives and the U.S. Senate. During 1853–1857, he was governor of Tennessee. In the presidential campaign of 1864, Johnson was chosen as the running mate for Abraham Lincoln. In 1865 upon the assassination of Lincoln, he became president of the United States.

Although Johnson attempted a continuation of Lincoln's plan for reconstruction, he was unsuccessful in carrying out this program. Johnson was often at odds with the Congress. When he allegedly violated one of the restricted laws imposed on the president, the Tenure of Office Act, by dismissing Secretary of War Edwin M. Stanton, the House voted to impeach him. He was tried by the Senate in the spring of 1868 and acquitted by one vote.

After his presidency ended, Andrew Johnson returned to Tennessee. He was defeated when he tried to get elected as U.S. senator and representative in Congress, but was elected to the Senate in 1875. He died on July 31, 1875.

Bibliography

Benedict, Michael Les. *The Impeachment and Trial of Andrew Johnson*. New York: W.W. Norton, 1973.

Crane, William D. *Andrew Johnson: Tailor from Tennessee*. New York: Dodd, Mead, 1968.

Reece, B. Carroll. *The Courageous Commoner: A Biography of Andrew Johnson*. Charleston, W.Va.: Education Foundation, 1962.

Stryker, Lloyd Paul. *Andrew Johnson: A Study in Courage*. New York: Macmillan, 1929.

Thomas, Lately. *The First President Johnson: The Three Lives of the Seventeenth President of the United States of America*. New York: William Morrow, 1968.

Trefousse, Hans L. *Andrew Johnson: A Biography*. New York: W.W. Norton, 1989.

Winston, Robert W. *Andrew Johnson: Plebeian and Patriot*. New York: Henry Holt, 1928.

Ulysses S. Grant

Eighteenth President
1869–1877

As a child, Ulysses S. Grant was cruelly teased about his name. Wags in his hometown of Georgetown, Ohio, called him "Useless." Grant seems not to have been offended by the crude remark. In his memoirs, Grant recalled that "my life in Georgetown was uneventful."

He was born on April 27, 1822, the first of six children born to Jesse Root Grant and Hanna Simpson Grant of Point Pleasant, Clermont County, Ohio. In 1823 the family moved to Georgetown, where life for Ulysses was anything at uneventful.

Jesse Grant operated a tannery where animals were slaughtered and their hides processed into leather. Ulysses detested the tannery. He liked all animals, and couldn't stand the cruelty of the tannery business. While Jesse Grant accepted his son's reluctance to work in the tannery, he didn't exempt Ulysses from doing other work. There was plenty to do, especially when he opened a small livery business near the tannery.

From the time Ulysses was seven years old, his father put him to work handling horses for the livery and the farm. While he was too small to lift heavy loads by himself, he worked the horses to haul wood used in the house and shops. By the time he was 11, he was plowing the fields and driving horse-drawn wagons for his father's business.

From early childhood, Ulysses Grant demonstrated a remarkable talent for handling horses. As a toddler, he often played around the horses of tannery customers. When he was five years old, he learned how to stand on the back of a trotting horse, holding the reins to keep his balance. Ulysses's horsemanship soon became well known in the community. He had a special knack for breaking and training young horses. When a circus came to town, the ringmaster would offer a prize to anyone who could ride a spirited trick horse. Ulysses took up the challenge and usually won.

Grant's love of horses stayed with him for life. It also caused him a haunting embarrassment, which he poignantly described in his memoirs. Ulysses was eight years old when he had earned enough money to buy a horse from a farmer named Robert Ralston. Jesse Grant, needing another horse for his trade, offered the farmer $20 for the animal. The farmer declined the offer, saying the colt was worth $25.

Ulysses begged his father to pay the full price for the horse. His father yielded, and when Ulysses arrived at Ralston's house, he said: "Papa says I may offer you twenty dollars for the colt, but if you won't take that, I am to offer twenty-two and a half, and if you won't take that, I am to give you twenty-five." Farmer Ralston got his twenty-five dollars and the last laugh. Ulysses Grant got his horse, but as he wrote in his memoirs, "This transaction caused me great heart-burning." He was the butt of jokes among the boys in the village for a long time.

Schooling for Ulysses began when he was five or six years old. He was enrolled in a one-room school which was supported by the town's parents, who paid an annual subscription fee to keep it in business. The teacher used textbooks that were basic readers and grammars. The students ranged from those of Ulysses's age to youths pushing 21.

In 1836, when he was 14, Ulysses spent the winter in Maysville, Kentucky, where he studied at an academy run by two male teachers. Unfortunately, their curriculum did not teach Ulysses anything that he didn't already know. He overcame his boredom by enrolling in the local debating society, where he expressed himself well on issues of the day.

In the winter of 1838, Ulysses was enrolled in the Presbyterian Academy in Ripley, Ohio, ten miles from Georgetown. Again, Ulysses found the schooling boring. "I was not studious in habit, and probably did not make progress enough to compensate for the outlay for board and tuition," Grant wrote in his memoirs.

Jesse Grant was determined that his firstborn should get the best education possible. He asked Ohio Senator Thomas Morris to appoint Ulysses to the prestigious and free United States Military Academy at West Point, New York. Normally he would have asked his congressman, Thomas L. Hamer, for the appointment, but they were not on speaking terms after a political argument. Morris turned the letter over to Hamer, who cheerfully appointed Ulysses to the Military Academy, thus ending the breach between him and Jesse Grant.

During his 1838 Christmas vacation from the Presbyterian Academy in Ripley, Ulysses's father told him the good news of getting an appointment to the U.S. Military Academy.

"But I won't go," Ulysses blurted out.

"I think you will," replied the father.

Years later, acknowledging his father's firm stand on education, Ulysses wrote in his memoirs that "I thought so, too, if he did."

Ulysses Grant arrived at West Point in May 1839 at age 17. He passed the entrance examination, but he didn't like to study. "I rarely ever read over a lesson a second time during my entire cadetship," he recalled in his memoirs. He was good at math; French was his worst subject.

Grant had a love for literature and frequently visited the academy's library, where he found novels that he could read in his quarters. "I read all of the works of Bulwer's then published, Cooper's, Marryat's, Scott's, Washington Irving's works, Lever's, and many others," he wrote in his memoirs. In addition to reading fiction, Grant sought relief from the military routine by taking drawing courses offered by Robert Walter Weir, a well-known painter. Grant drew well, and several of his artworks have survived.

Grant did not like attending the military academy. He had no intention of making the Army a career. He planned to resign from the Army as soon as he had completed the obligatory service time. Ulysses Grant finished 21st among the 39 cadet who made up the graduating class of 1843. He was 16th in engineering, 25th in artillery tactics, and 17th in geology. Only in horsemanship did he excel. No cadet could rival Grant in the handling of horses. This was clearly demonstrated on graduation day, when, during a riding exhibition, he and his horse set a West Point jumping record that stood for 25 years.

Assignments after West Point were based on class standing. Grant requested the cavalry, but there was no vacancy. On September 30, 1843, 21-

year-old Second Lieutenant Ulysses S. Grant reported for duty at Jefferson Barracks, St. Louis. His first Army assignment was as quartermaster—supply officer—to the regiment stationed at Jefferson Barracks.

During the Mexican War, as a second lieutenant, Grant fought under the command of General Zachary Taylor. At the end of the war, he was transferred to Pascagoula, Mississippi. Army life was not for Grant. He had married Julia Boggs Dent and found that the rigors of military service were not conducive to a happy family life. On April 11, 1854, Grant resigned from the Army.

Shortly after the Civil War began in 1861, Grant once again became a soldier. After several minor assignments, he was appointed brigadier general by President Abraham Lincoln. Four years later, on April 9, 1865, the victorious General Grant would accept the surrender of Confederate Army General Robert E. Lee at Appomattox, Va.

In May 1868, the Republican Party nominated Grant for president. He won the November election over Democratic Party candidate Horatio Seymour. Grant was sworn in as president on March 4, 1869, and was reelected to a second term in 1872.

After retiring from the presidency, Grant became partner in a financial firm which went bankrupt. About that time he learned that he had cancer of the throat. He began writing his memoirs to pay off his debts and provide for his family. The book was published by a company owned by his friend Mark Twain. Grant died on July 23, 1885, just two months after the book was published.

Bibliography

Grant, Ulysses S. *Memoirs and Selected Letters*. New York: The Library of America, 1990.

McFeely, William S. *Grant: A Biography*. New York: W.W. Norton, 1982.

Perret, Geoffrey. *Ulysses S. Grant: Soldier and President*. New York: Random House, 1997.

Simpson, Brooks D. *Ulysses S. Grant: Triumph Over Adversity, 1822–1865*. Boston: Houghton Mifflin, 2000.

Smith, Jean Edward. *Grant*. New York: Simon & Schuster, 2001.

Rutherford B. Hayes

Nineteenth President
1877–1881

Rutherford Birchard Hayes was born October 4, 1822, in the town of Delaware, Ohio, in the shadow of tragedy. His father, Rutherford Hayes, Jr., had died of typhus fever ten weeks before he was born. His mother, Sophia Hayes, then mourning the recent loss of a daughter, had two other children, son Lorenzo and daughter Fanny. Two years later, Lorenzo drowned in an ice skating accident.

Rutherford Birchard Hayes was the second child of Rutherford and Sophia Hayes to bear that name. Their first child, who died at birth in 1814, had also been given that name.

The Hayes family moved from Vermont to Delaware, Ohio, in 1817. The family lived in the first two-story red brick house built in the town. The house was surrounded by profitable farmland.

Rutherford's father was a successful merchant who operated a lucrative distillery. He also invested in land purchases. When he died, he left a large estate, which gave his widow and children financial security.

Rutherford was born a frail child whose survival was at first doubtful. The doctor who delivered him was paid $3.50 for his services by his mother's brother, Sardis Birchard, who would become his surrogate father. The newborn son, who had red hair like his father, was nicknamed Rud, which was also his father's moniker.

While she pampered her children, Sophia Hayes also taught them how to read, write, and spell. However, she was especially fearful of Rutherford's health, and kept him inside for a long time. After Lorenzo died, his sister Fanny was his only playmate.

Fanny, who was two years older than Rud, was a very bright and energetic girl. She taught him games to play and read him stories. As they grew older, she interested him in Shakespeare's plays and Sir Walter Scott's poetry. Fanny was also tomboyish. She played boys' games, and was a superb rifle shot. Rud had to play hard to keep up with her. Sardis Birchard, concerned over Sophia's overindulging of Rutherford, convinced his sister to let her son have more freedom. So, at the age of seven, Rud was allowed to go out and play with other children.

Rutherford Hayes got his first schooling at age 12 in 1834. His mother had gone to nurse his sick uncle Sardis, and had boarded Rud and Fanny with relatives Arcena and Thomas Wasson in Delaware. The Wassons enrolled the Hayes children in a public school run by Daniel Granger, a brutal schoolmaster who was notorious for his flogging.

At the age of 12, Rutherford Hayes began keeping a diary. In it he noted that schoolmaster Granger, when excited, "appeared to us as a demon of ferocity. He flogged great strapping fellows of twice his size, and talked savagely of throwing them through the walls of the schoolhouse. He threw a large jackknife, carefully aimed so as just to miss, at the head of a boy who was whispering near me."

Rutherford and Fanny feared for their lives, and begged Wasson to take them out of the school, but he refused, insisting that Granger was a good man. When their mother returned from her stay with Sardis, the children were placed in a small private grade school in Delaware that was operated by Joan Hills Murray. Later, casting aside his bad learning experience with Granger, Rutherford considered Mrs. Murray to be his first true teacher. He excelled in her school and became a champion speller.

When Rud completed his basic education with Mrs. Murray, she honored him as the school's outstanding student. The honor included an award—a book or a Jew's harp. To the dismay of his mother and sister, but to the amusement of Uncle Sardis, he chose the Jew's harp as his prize.

In the fall of 1836, 14-year-old Rutherford Hayes was enrolled in the Norwalk Academy, a Methodist boarding school run by the Reverend Jonathan E. Chaplin in Norwalk, Ohio. Uncle Sardis chose the school because it was located only 16 miles from his home in Lower Sandusky, Ohio, from where he could keep an eye on his young nephew.

Sardis Birchard played an important part in the life of Rutherford B. Hayes. A life long bachelor, Sardis was a self-made businessman and provided the funds for his nephew's education. As a successful merchandiser and land speculator, Sardis Birchard had a reputation for honesty and fairness. Indians frequently traded at his general store in Lower Sandusky.

Rutherford did well at Norwalk. Along with the routine classic studies, the Norwalk curriculum emphasized speaking and writing. Rud wrote his mother that he had written a composition on the subject of liberty, and that he delivered a good speech on William Pitt. So confident was Rud of his progress at Norwalk that he suggested to his mother that he would be ready for college in four months. Skeptical Sophia Hayes conferred with her brother and together they decided that Rud needed some college preparatory education. In the fall of 1837, he began attending classes at Isaac Webb's Preparatory School in Middletown, Conn.

A former Yale tutor, Isaac Webb accepted only 20 boys of good character into his school. The students arose at 6:30, had breakfast, and attended prayer services given by Congregational ministers. The school was in session from nine to twelve noon, one to four, and six to nine. Rud's expenses for tuition, room and board totaled $250 a year, which Uncle Sardis Birchard paid.

Rutherford enjoyed his studies at Webb's school. He made good grades and won prizes for his translations of Latin and Greek poems. He also studied ethics and theology. After a year of studying under Webb, the family had to decide at which college Rutherford should continue his studies. Isaac Webb thought that Rutherford, who was still 15, was too young to go college, and urged that he continue his studies at the Middletown school. Sardis Birchard also thought his nephew should stay another year at the Webb school, and then enter Yale University.

But Sophia Hayes had her own plan for Rutherford's education. He would return home to the Buckeye State, and in August 1838 she enrolled him in Kenyon College at Gambier, Ohio, not far from the family home. Rud had no trouble passing the entrance examination to Kenyon, which included Latin, Greek, mathematics, grammar, and elementary knowledge. He found the college quaint—neither his tutors nor the study requirements challenged him, and he disliked the Episcopalian college's strict regulations.

In the summer of 1839, Kenyon College underwent a religious revival in which the entire student body was converted except Rud and nine other hold-outs. He never faced dismissal; since he was otherwise an excellent student, his teachers overlooked his rebellious attitude. Rutherford became a leader at Kenyon College when, in his junior year, was elected president of the Philo-mathesian Society, which debated current political and social issues. In 1842, Rud attended a political meeting in Dayton, where he met his hero, the great compromiser, Henry Clay.

In addition to his required college studies, Rud read history and biogra-phy, fiction and poetry. In August of 1842, Rud graduated from Kenyon Col-lege with honors. He was named valedictorian, and in his oration he spoke of "college life," noting that the successful student "labors to become a useful member of the society in which he lives and thus prepares himself to deserve the only reputation which is valuable and lasting."

Rutherford planned to be a lawyer after he graduated from Kenyon Col-lege. At first he had no thought of attending a law school; instead he entered the law office of Thomas Sparrow in Columbus, Ohio, where he would work and study for the legal profession. Realizing that he needed more legal instruc-tion, and with the support of Uncle Sardis, Rutherford entered Harvard Law School, earning a bachelor of law degree in 1845. He joined the Ohio bar that year and opened a law practice with another lawyer in Lower Sandusky, where Uncle Sardis helped channel business to his new office.

In 1849 Hayes moved to Cincinnati, where he gained fame as a criminal lawyer and defender of fugitive slaves. In 1852 he married Lucy Ware Webb of Chillicothe, Ohio. He served with the 23rd Ohio Volunteer Infantry dur-ing the Civil War, rising from the rank of major to major general when the war ended. He was wounded four times during the war. Elected to Congress while on active service, he later won three terms as governor of Ohio. He became president in 1877 after winning a disputed election, which was settled by a special electoral commission appointed by Congress.

Rutherford B. Hayes died at his home in Fremont (formerly Lower San-dusky), Ohio, on January 17, 1893.

Bibliography

Barnard, Harry. *Rutherford B. Hayes and His America*. Newtown, Conn.: American Political Biography Press, 1992 (originally published in 1954 by the Bobbs Mer-rill Company, Indianapolis., Ind.).

Eckenrode, H. J. *Rutherford B. Hayes: Statesman of Reunion*. New York: Dodd, Mead, 1930.

Hoogenboom, Ari. *Rutherford B. Hayes: Warrior and President*. Lawrence: University Press of Kansas, 1995.

Trefousse, Hans L. *Rutherford B. Hayes*. New York: Times Books, Henry Holt, 2002.

★ 20 ★

James A. Garfield

Twentieth President
1881

When James Abram Garfield was born on November 19, 1831, in a log cabin built by his father in the village of Orange in Cuyahoga County, Ohio, his mother, Eliza Ballou Garfield, described her son, weighing ten pounds, as "the largest Babe I ever had."

The unusually big baby took his physical features from his father, Abram Garfield, a large and strong man who was known throughout Ohio as a champion wrestler. James never knew his father, who died when his son was 18 months old. James was named for his father and an older brother, James Ballou Garfield, who had died in infancy. He was the youngest of four children, two boys and two girls, to live to maturity.

James Garfield's father died after fighting a forest fire that threatened his crop. He caught a cold fighting the fire, and died soon thereafter from pneumonia. After her husband died, Eliza Garfield sold off more than half of her land, keeping the rest for farming, to help the family survive. Her oldest son, 11-year-old Thomas, helped his mother to farm the remaining land, while the daughters Mary and Hitty were taught how to card wool clipped from their sheep.

Eliza Garfield, a high-spirited and deeply religious woman, found her son James to be an exceptionally bright child. She decided that he should get an education. So when James was three years old, his sister Hitty would take him with her to the district school she attended at Chagrin Falls. There he learned to read.

The walk to the school at Chagrin Falls, three miles distant, a round trip of six miles, was long and tiresome for the young children. So Eliza Garfield decided that the village of Orange should have its own school. She donated some of her land and got her neighbors to build a log cabin school on it.

A bright student, James Garfield quickly mastered spelling, arithmetic, and grammar. While few books were available, James developed a passion for reading. He would read and reread books until he could reel off their content from memory. He liked history, especially stories about the American Revolution. And he let his imagination run wild when he read adventure stories, including tales of the seas.

In 1842, when James was 11, his mother remarried, but the marriage lasted only a year, then Eliza moved back to her home town. Her husband then divorced her. Meanwhile, James Garfield took various jobs to support himself and his mother. He chopped wood and performed farm and carpentry work.

In the summer of 1848, James, eager to strike out on his own, decided to leave home. So, against the wishes of his mother, he set out for Cleveland, where he planned to work as a sailor on board a lake schooner. When a drunken captain chased him off his ship, a disappointed Garfield found a job working for his cousin Amos Letcher aboard the canal boat *Evening Star*, which carried copper ore and coal from Cleveland to Pittsburgh. One of his duties was to lead horses that pulled barges along the Ohio and Pennsylvania Canal, a waterway used to transport goods and people.

It was a boring job made worse by the fact that James could not swim. He fell into the water 14 times, but was saved by hanging on to the lines, or by being plucked out of the water by someone. A hard worker, he was later promoted to bowman at 14 dollars a month. Garfield's seafaring days ended after six months when he fell sick with malaria and had to return home. It took him several months to recover.

While recuperating from his illness, Garfield did a lot of reading, as his mother encouraged him to forget about being a seaman and concentrate on getting an education. As his health improved, James agreed with his mother that even a sailor needs education, and in March 1849 he enrolled at the Geauga Seminary, a Baptist school in nearby Chester, Ohio, which was about ten miles away from his home. His course of study at Geauga included algebra, philosophy, grammar, mental arithmetic, botany, geography, elocution, Latin and Greek. He enjoyed participating in debates with other students. This helped him to become an excellent public speaker after he entered politics.

To pay for his schooling at Geauga, Garfield spent the summer working as a carpenter and farmhand. In his second year at the school, he took the state test for a teacher's certificate, which he passed, and at age 18, he was certified as a teacher. His first teaching job at a district school in Solon, Ohio, paid him $13 a month plus room and board.

By the fall of 1851, James Garfield was ready for college. He enrolled in the Western Reserve Eclectic Institute (now called Hiram College) in Hiram, Ohio. He chose the school because it was run by the Disciples of Christ, a church he had recently joined. Religion became an important part of his life. He worked hard at the Eclectic Institute, impressing both the faculty and fellow students with his scholastic abilities. He became a teacher as well as a student, and he preached during church services nearly every Sunday.

In the autumn of 1854, Garfield enrolled at Williams College in Williamstown, Massachusetts, as a junior. He graduated with the highest honors in the class of 1856. Before he left Williams College, he had agreed to return to the Eclectic Institute in Hiram as a teacher at a salary of $600 a year. He taught with skill, enthusiasm and effect, and grew in power as a preacher and lecturer. At the end of his first year, Garfield had become chairman of the board of instruction, and in 1857, at the age of 26, he was made president of the Eclectic Institute.

In 1958, Garfield married Lucretia "Crete" Rudolph, a classmate at the Geauga Seminary and his pupil at the Eclectic Institute, where they began dating.

In 1858 he also decided to widen his career field by studying law. While he entered his name as a law student at a law office in Cleveland, he actually studied in Hiram for two years. He was admitted to the Ohio bar in 1860.

Garfield entered politics in 1859, when a committee of Ohio Republicans asked him to run for the state senate. He accepted the offer and won the election. At the age of 28, he became the youngest member of the Ohio General Assembly. During the 1860 presidential campaign, James Garfield made many speeches supporting the Republican candidate Abraham Lincoln.

During the Civil War he served in the 42nd Regiment of the Ohio Volunteers. As the result of his battlefield achievements, he was promoted to major general in the Army. After the Battle of Chickamauga, in which he performed heroically, Garfield resigned his commission to take a seat in the House of Representatives on December 7, 1863.

In June 1880, the Republican Party picked Garfield as its presidential candidate. He narrowly won the election over the Democratic candidate, Major General Winfield Scott Hancock. After being sworn in as president on the Capitol steps on March 4, 1881, Garfield's first act was to kiss his 80-year-old mother. It was the first time that a president's mother had attended an inauguration.

On July 2, 1881, when a vacation-bound Garfield arrived at the Baltimore and Potomac railroad station in Washington, he was shot in the back by a disgruntled office seeker. Garfield was taken to the White House, where doctors operated and attempted to remove abscesses and bone fragments. Using bare fingers and unsterilized instruments, common practice in those days, the probing led to blood poisoning.

In September Garfield asked to be removed from the heat of Washington. He was taken to the seaside resort of Elberon, New Jersey, to recuperate, but he died there on September 19, 1881.

Bibliography

Booraem, Hendrik V. *The Road to Respectability: James A. Garfield and His World, 1844–1852*. Cranbury, N.J.: Associated University Presses, 1988.

Leech, Margaret, and Harry J. Brown. *The Garfield Orbit: The Life of President James A. Garfield*. New York: Harper & Row, 1978.

Peskin, Allan. *Garfield*. Kent, Ohio: The Kent State University Press, 1978.

Chester A. Arthur

Twenty-first President
1881–1885

Chester Alan Arthur was born on October 5, 1829, in a small log cabin in North Fairfield, Vermont, to parents who were always on the move. The cabin was the parsonage of his Irish-born father, William Arthur, a Baptist minister with strong beliefs, who did not hesitate to speak his mind to the congregations. His mother, Malvina Stone Arthur, was a native of Berkshire, Vermont. Like her husband, she was very religious, and strongly supported her husband's views.

Because of the Reverend Arthur's often barbed tongue and unpopular opinions—he also held strong abolitionist (anti-slavery) beliefs—he was forced to move from parish to parish. Young Chester moved five times during his first nine years, before the family finally settled in Union Village (now Greenwich), New York, in 1839.

When his second son was born, the proud William Arthur named him Chester for Dr. Chester Abell, the physician who delivered him, and Alan for his own father. Chester Alan Arthur was the fifth of eight children to live to maturity.

Although Chester Arthur received his basic education from his energetic father at home, he did not inherit the elder Arthur's explosive temperament. He was well-mannered and friendly, skillfully avoiding arguments.

In 1844, the elder Arthur moved his family to Schenectady, New York, where he became pastor of the First Baptist Church. Chester Arthur, 15 at that time, then enrolled at the Schenectady Lyceum, a college preparatory school. Tuition rates at the Lyceum were $3.50 per quarter for students in the common English branches; for those studying English, Latin and Greek, the tuition cost rose to $5 per quarter. All students were charged 50 cents per quarter for their stationery.

"Chet" Arthur, as he was known to the Lyceum students, was a good scholar, well liked by students and faculty. He was editor of the school paper, *The Lyceum Review,* which featured required sermons, poetry, and campus news. In the fall of 1844, Chester Arthur got his first taste of politics when he joined a group of students supporting Henry Clay, the Whig Party's presidential candidate.

In September 1845, upon completing his preparatory work at the Lyceum, Arthur enrolled as a sophomore at the Union College in Schenectady. The tuition at Union College cost him $28 during his three years at the school; room and board was about $125 a year. The college offered a variety of courses, including science courses and civil engineering, but Arthur chose to pursue the traditional classical curriculum. College records do not show what Arthur actually studied, but it is known that he studied French, for which he received a grade of 97. According to the Union College catalog, his studies may have included algebra, plane and solid geometry, rhetoric, history, political economy, and moral philosophy.

The school day at Union College began with breakfast, attended by prayers, at 6:30 a.m. Another mandatory prayer meeting was held at 5 p.m. Chet Arthur, the minister's son, was fined at various times for being absent from prayers. While he attended to his studies, Arthur also engaged in undergraduate high jinx and enjoyed playing school pranks. He liked to carve his name or initials at various places throughout the college. Once he cut his name, "C. A. Arthur," in a window sill of the college chapel.

The popular extra-curricular college activity in the 1840s was debating, and Union College had several societies whose activities, besides being rhetorical, were also social and political. Arthur joined the Delphian Institute, a literary society, and was elected its president. To help pay for his expenses, he taught at an elementary school in Schaghticoke, New York, during the winter months.

Although he appeared to take his studies lightly, Chester Arthur was an excellent student, receiving high marks in mathematics, Greek, and Latin. He graduated in July 1848 in the top third of his class. He was one of six graduates to be elected to the Phi Beta Kappa Society. After graduating from Union College, 18-year-old Chester Arthur returned to Schaghticoke to resume his grammar school teaching, at a pay of 15 dollars a month.

Teaching was not in Arthur's future plans. He wanted to become a lawyer, and in 1849 enrolled at a law school in Ballston Spa, New York. Unable to keep up with school expenses, he returned home to his father's home, then at Lansingburg, to continue his legal studies.

In 1851, Pastor William Arthur helped his son get a job as principal of a small academy in North Pownal, Vermont, where the father preached at a new church. In the mid–1800s, small academies with small budgets usually hired young college graduates like Arthur who had not yet established a career.

At the North Pownal academy, Chester Arthur combined the duties of preparing boys for college and preparing himself for his chosen profession. After two years of this experience, during which he saved a few hundred dollars from his $35 monthly salary, he set out for New York, where he served as a law clerk in the legal firm headed by Erastus C. Culver. Arthur was admitted to the New York bar in 1854, and became a member of the law firm of Culver and Parker. He formed his own law firm in 1856.

The Culver firm achieved famed in 1852 when it supported a plea by a group of free blacks to liberate seven slaves. Young Arthur spent much of his time as a clerk in the Culver firm handling details of the appeal. In another case that he handled himself, he obtained $500 damages from a transit company that had a black woman thrown off a New York City horse-drawn street car because of her color.

In 1856 Arthur accompanied his friend Dabney Herndon on a visit to relatives in New York. Arthur fell in love with Herndon's cousin Ellen Herndon. On October 25, 1859, Chester and Ellen were married.

Arthur had beome interested in politics, and in 1860 he helped organize the New York State Republican Party and supported the election of Abraham Lincoln as president. Arthur's political connections paid off when President Ulysses S. Grant in 1871 appointed him collector of customs for the port of New York. He lost that job in 1878, when President Rutherford B. Hayes ordered a reform of the government's merit system.

In 1880 the Republican Party nominated Chester Arthur to be vice president on the national ticket headed by James A. Garfield. In the election, the

Garfield-Arthur ticket beat the Democrats in the popular vote by less than one-tenth of one percent, but dominated the electoral college with 214 votes to 155. President Garfield was shot by an assassin on July 2, 1881, and died on September 19, 1881, and Chester Alan Arthur became the twenty-first president of the United States.

As president, Arthur gave the nation an honest administration. He backed and signed a bill to reform the civil service, which prohibited salary kickbacks as well as firing employees for political reasons. His administration was credited with modernizing the U.S. Navy.

When he lost the support of his party, Arthur chose not to run for reelection in 1884. After the presidency, he returned to his home in New York. On November 18, 1886, he died of a cerebral hemorrhage.

Bibliography

Howe, George Frederick. *Chester A. Arthur: A Quarter-Century of Machine Politics.* New York: Dodd, Mead, 1934.

Reeves, Thomas. *Gentleman Boss: The Life of Chester Alan Arthur.* New York: Alfred A. Knopf, 1975.

Young, Jeff C. *Chester A. Arthur.* Berkeley Heights, N.J.: Enslow, 2002.

Special thanks to the Schaffer Library, Union College, Schenectady, N.Y., for providing information about Chester A. Arthur's life while attending that college.

★ 22 ★ and ★ 24 ★

Grover Cleveland

Twenty-second President
1885–1889

Twenty-fourth President
1893–1897

Grover Cleveland was a tall, stout, strong, friendly, and fun-loving, yet responsible youngster. He was born in Caldwell, New Jersey, on March 18, 1837, the fifth of nine children born to the Reverend Richard Cleveland and his wife Ann Neal Cleveland. He had five sisters and three brothers.

His parents were poor, because Richard Cleveland, although a Yale graduate, dutifully complied with his parents' orders that he become a minister. At the time of Grover's birth, his father was earning $600 a year as pastor of the First Presbyterian Church at Caldwell. Fortunately, his mother received a small income from her father's estate to help pay family expenses.

Richard Cleveland named the new baby Stephen Grover Cleveland to honor Stephen Grover, who served as minister of the church from 1787 to 1837. The family seldom used the first name Stephen, and the boy stopped using it when he became a teenager.

In 1841, when Grover was four years old, the Reverend Cleveland moved his family to Fayetteville, New York, where he became pastor of the Presbyterian church. The Cleveland family lived in a 2½ story frame house—a manse provided free by the church—but even so, the family had a tough time making ends meet on Pastor Cleveland's meager salary.

Grover was raised in a strict, modest home. As the son of a minister he had to participate in evening worship services in the Cleveland house. Along with his brothers and sisters, he was required to memorize passages from the Bible. The Clevelands also taught their children the values of religious virtues and honesty. Throughout his life—as a child, young adult, and as an astute politician—Grover Cleveland was known to be a thoroughly honest person.

Every child in the Cleveland household was required to do chores, and as he grew older, Grover assumed more manly duties, such as cutting wood, carrying water, and working the garden, which provided the family with vegetables.

Grover's childhood had its lighter moments, when he was allowed to play with his buddies, or go on fishing expeditions to nearby lakes. He also liked to play pranks; once he attached a rope to a school bell, and rang it to awake the town in the dead of night. One Halloween night, Grover and his friends carried off the front gates of several homes in Fayetteville. (As president, Cleveland often reminisced about his childhood in Fayetteville. He especially liked to tell listeners about the pranks in which he and his buddies took part.)

In Fayetteville, Grover Cleveland's formal studies began at the district school, a little frame house where pupils of all ages studied under a single schoolmaster. When he was 11 years old, his parents enrolled him in the Fayetteville Academy (whose bell he rang one night).

Grover was a good student who received good marks. Historians cite an essay he wrote in September 1846 to show his value of time: "...If we expect to become great and good men and be respected and esteemed by our friends we must improve our time when we are young.... A great many of our men were poor and had small means of obtaining an education but by improving their time when they were young and in school they obtained their high standing."

The instructions Grover received at the Fayetteville Academy did not quite satisfy the educational-minded Reverend Cleveland. So he created home courses for Grover and his siblings to study religion, Latin and mathematics.

In 1850, when Grover was 13, his father's health began deteriorating. To relieve the strain of daily religious work, he accepted the post of district secretary of the Central New York Agency of the American Home Missionary, at $1,000 a year. He then moved his family to Clinton, New York.

At Clinton, the Cleveland children enjoyed educational advantages superior to those in Fayetteville. Grover attended the Clinton Liberal Institute, where he studied Latin and other subjects he hoped would prepare him for college. He enjoyed studying Latin, and used one of his father's Latin books in the classroom.

While Grover's father had a better paying job, it was not enough to support his large family. In 1852, to help his father, 15-year-old Grover quit school and looked for work in Fayetteville. John McVicar, deacon in his father's former church, offered Grover a job clerking in his general store for $50 a year plus board and lodging. Grover worked long hours at the McVicar store. He lived above the store in a barely furnished, unheated room, which he shared with another boy. He slept on a rope bed covered by a straw mattress.

Grover arose before six o'clock in the morning and prepared the store for opening at seven o'clock. During the day he made deliveries, ran other errands, moved boxes and barrels as needed, and waited on customers when the storekeeper was busy. He worked for McVicor for a year and returned to Clinton in March 1853. Upon arriving home, he learned that his father's health was failing. The father resigned his post with the American Home Missionary, and took a less demanding post as pastor of the Presbyterian Church at the village of Holland Patent, New York.

After having delivered three sermons to his new congregation, the Reverend Cleveland died suddenly on October 1, 1853.

As his father was laid to rest, Grover faced the disappointing reality that he would be unable to attend college—he had hoped to attend Hamilton College in Clinton. Now, along with his older brother William, he assumed the responsibility of providing for his virtually destitute mother and younger brothers and sisters.

William, a teacher at the New York Institution for the Blind, secured a place for Grover as an assistant teacher. The institution took in blind children from all over the state and educated them. In 1853, 116 students were being educated there. Grover taught reading, writing, arithmetic, and geography.

More prison than a school, the Institution, which was run by an overly strict superintendent, depressed Grover Cleveland so much that he resigned his job after a year of trying to educate his blind learners. He returned to Holland Patent, hoping to find a job with a future.

Having no success in finding a worthwhile job in Holland Patent and its neighboring towns and cities, Grover Cleveland decided to seek his fortune in the West. In May 1855, he borrowed $25 from a family friend for his western journey. He invited a friend to go along. Their first stop was a Buffalo, New York, where they visited Grover's uncle, Lewis F. Allen, who raised cattle in the suburb of Black Rock.

The visit to his uncle house changed Grover Cleveland's life. In addition to raising cattle, Allen recorded their lines of breeding in his *American Shorthorn Herd Book*. Allen persuaded Grover to stay and help him edit the book manuscript, for which he would pay his nephew $50 a month and free board and room. Grover accepted the offer.

Grover did his job well, and he enjoyed learning a new trade. Her also enjoyed visiting the 600-acre farm where his uncle raised cattle.

When his editorial job was finished, Grover discussed his future with his uncle. Allen offered him a career in the cattle business, but Grover said he was more interested in becoming a lawyer. Allen arranged for him to meet with a judge, but when the judge asked Grover some questions he thought to be impertinent, he stormed out of the judge's office.

His uncle counseled him to control his temper, then sent his nephew to visit Henry W. Rogers, head of the distinguished law firm of Rogers, Bowen and Rogers. The senior Rogers had little interest in training law clerks, but interviewed Grover as a courtesy to Allen.

When Grover arrived for the interview, Rogers seated him at a desk and handed him a copy of the large weighty bible of the legal profession, Blackstone's commentaries on law. (William Blackstone was an English jurist whose doctrines on English law became exceedingly influential on American jurisprudence.) Pointing to it, he declared, "There's where you begin."

Grover was not given any specific job at the law firm, and spent much of his time studying the Blackstone tome. He also watched how the lawyers and their clerks prepared legal documents. He was paid four dollars a week while at the Rogers law firm. Gradually he learned the law profession.

Grover Cleveland qualified to take the bar examination, and in May 1859, the New York State Supreme Court admitted him to the bar. Rogers, Bowen and Rogers immediately offered the new 22-year-old lawyer a job with the firm, at a salary of $600 a year.

As a young lawyer, Cleveland took an interest in politics. In 1862, at age 25, he was elected supervisor of the Second Ward. During 1863–1865, he was assistant district attorney for Erie County. In 1865 he ran unsuccessfully for district attorney. He then returned to private practice in Buffalo.

As a bachelor, Grover Cleveland lived a happy-go-lucky life, frequenting saloons and enjoying going on fishing and hunting trips with his cronies. Consequently, the chubby Cleveland grew fat, with a heavy bull neck and paunch which hung over his beltline.

In 1870, Cleveland was elected sheriff of Erie County. His subsequent political positions included being elected mayor of Buffalo in 1882, followed by serving as governor of New York during 1883–1885. In that office his opposition to graft and opportunism earned him a nationwide following.

The Democratic Party nominated him for president in 1884. He served two terms as president, the first from 1885 to 1889. After losing the presidential election of 1888, Cleveland was again re-nominated by the Democratic Party in 1884. He won that election and served his second presidency from 1893 to 1887.

Cleveland was the only president to be married in the White House. He married 21-year-old Frances Folsom on June 2, 1886. Her father had died when she was 11, and as administrator of her father's estate, Cleveland had taken a special interest in the child. Over the years, Cleveland's feeling for the girl blossomed into romance, and after her college graduation, he proposed to her. They did not announce their engagement until a few days before the wedding.

Grover Cleveland died on June 24, 1908. His last words were, "I have tried so hard to do right."

Bibliography

Brodsky, Alyn. *Grover Cleveland: A Study in Character*. New York: St. Martin's, 2000.

Hoyt, Edwin P. *Grover Cleveland*. Chicago: Reilly and Lee, 1962.

Jeffers, H. Paul. *An Honest President: The Life and Presidency of Grover Cleveland*. New York: William Morrow, HarperCollins, 2000.

Lynch, Denis Tilden. *Grover Cleveland: A Man Four-Square*. New York: Horace Liveright, 1932.

★ 23 ★

Benjamin Harrison

Twenty-third President
1889–1893

Benjamin Harrison, the twenty-third president of the United States, came from a political family whose public service dates back to the formative years of the nation. His great-grandfather, Benjamin Harrison V, signed the Declaration of Independence and later served as governor of Virginia. His grandfather, William Henry Harrison, was the ninth president of the United States. His father, John Scott Harrison, served two terms in the United States House of Representatives.

Benjamin Harrison was born on August 20, 1833, at North Bend, Ohio, in the home of his grandfather, William Henry Harrison. The "Big House," as the family called the 16-room, two-story home, was the main feature on the grandfather's 3,000 acre farm. Facing south, the majestic home stood about 300 yards back of the Ohio River. The grandfather's vast property extended westerly to a fertile delta area referred to as Point Farm.

At the time of Benjamin Harrison's birth, his grandfather was serving as the American ambassador to Colombia. The grandfather had assigned his son, John Scott, to manage the estate during his absence. He also deeded 600 acres of fertile farmland at the Point Farm area to his son, who built a two-story house on the property. The new house was under construction when Benjamin was born. It was called The Point.

Benjamin's mother was Elizabeth Irwin Harrison, the second wife of John Scott Harrison. She died in childbirth shortly after Benjamin's seventh birthday. Benjamin was the fifth of his father's 13 children.

Benjamin Harrison had a slender, wiry physique. His passion for outdoor life helped him grow into a stocky, muscular boy with short, stubby legs. As an adult he stood about five feet, six inches tall. While he was honest and a hard worker, he could be quite stubborn at times, insisting upon having his own way. These traits he carried with him to the presidency.

Benjamin grew up as a typical farm boy, doing such chores as hauling wood and water, and tending the livestock. For recreation he hunted, fished, and swam in the Ohio River. There were no schools nearby, so Benjamin's father built a one-room log cabin schoolhouse on his property. The cabin had a fireplace, several small windows, and seats that were benches without backs. He hired tutors to educate his children. Since the children were required to help with the farm chores, most of their schooling took place during the winter.

Benjamin was a good student who enjoyed studying and learning. As he progressed in his studies, he was encouraged to explore his grandfather's large library at North Bend. His tutors urged him to read books on American history and the lives of famous Americans. He also read books on Greek and Roman history.

In 1847, when Benjamin was 14, his father sent him to Cincinnati, where he enrolled in Cary's Academy, a preparatory school. The school was named after its founder, William Cary. After Benjamin Harrison entered the school, its name was changed to Farmers' College. The three years he spent at Farmers' College shaped his life in several important ways.

He studied under Dr. Robert Hamilton Bishop, a renowned teacher of history and political economy. Under Bishop's guidance, Benjamin developed a life long interest in history, politics, and sociology. In his classes, instead of textbooks, Bishop often used actual government documents, which the students were required to read, study, and discuss.

While at Farmers' College, Benjamin became a skillful debater and speaker after adhering to the helpful advice and criticism offered by Doctor Bishop. Benjamin was impressed with Doctor Bishop's formula for learning: "Education is getting possession of your mind, so you can use facts as the good mechanic uses his tools." Benjamin took this advice to heart. Throughout his career as lawyer, soldier, senator, and president, he insisted on having a thorough knowledge of the projects he was about to undertake.

Lack of money prevented John Scott Harrison from sending Benjamin to an eastern college, as he had planned. Instead, Benjamin would attend Miami University in Oxford, Ohio. In the fall of 1850, Benjamin enrolled as a junior. He skipped the freshmen class since he was given credit for his college preparatory studies at Farmers' College. In 1850, Miami University had 250 students who followed a strict regime. Their day began with mandatory chapel services at 7:30 a.m. Mornings were devoted to classes and student recitations. Afternoons were study periods, and all students were supposed to be in their rooms by 7:00 p.m.

Despite the university's strict regimen, Benjamin Harrison found time to join the Union Literary Society, a debating club with its own library, where he found books that helped him in his academic studies. His association with the literary society enabled him to develop his public speaking and debating skills. His colleagues, acknowledging his proficiency, elected him president of the Union Literary Society. He was also a member of the Phi Delta Theta fraternity, which was founded at Miami University in 1848.

Despite his studies and social activities, Benjamin also found time to court Carrie Scott, the girl he had a crush on since they were students together at Farmers' College. She was a student at the nearby Oxford Female Institute. By the time he graduated, they became secretly engaged. They married in 1853.

Benjamin Harrison graduated from Miami University on June 24, 1852. He ranked fourth in a class of 16. In his commencement speech, entitled "The Poor of England," he denounced nineteenth century England as a land of "poor laws and paupers."

During his attendance at Miami University, Harrison excelled in political economy and history. His family and some of his professors had hoped he would enter the ministry, but the 18-year-old graduate chose the legal profession. At the suggestion of his father, Benjamin Harrison applied for a clerkship position in the Cincinnati office of the legal firm of Storer and Gwynne. In early 1854, Harrison passed the Ohio bar examination.

Eager to set up his own legal practice, Harrison and his wife moved to Indianapolis. During his first year as an attorney, he managed to survive by getting small fees from doing routine real estate transactions. His luck changed when a cousin's friend got him a job at $2.50 a day announcing orders and directions of the federal court in Indianapolis. The job put him in touch with other attorneys who noticed his good work ethic and attention to details.

In March 1855, he formed a law partnership with William Wallace, son of former Indiana governor David Wallace. William's brother Lew wrote the famous novel *Ben-Hur: A Tale of Christ.* The partnership prospered, and by the time the partners separated six years later, Harrison's reputation as a successful lawyer had been firmly established.

During these years, Harrison decided get to into politics. He joined the Republican Party, and in 1857 he was elected city attorney of Indianapolis. He scored another victory in 1860 when he was elected reporter of the Indiana Supreme Court.

During the Civil War, Benjamin Harrison served with the Seventeenth Indiana Infantry, rising from second lieutenant to brigadier general. He fought admirably on the battlefield, and his forces made it possible for Union forces to advance to Atlanta in 1864.

Harrison was elected to the U.S. Senate in 1881 and served until 1887. In 1888 the Republicans nominated Harrison for president. Harrison gained the majority of electoral votes despite losing the popular vote to Grover Cleveland. He was defeated for reelection in 1892.

In October of 1892, just before the election, Harrison's wife, Carrie, died. In 1896, Harrison remarried. His new wife was Carrie's niece, Mary Scott Lord Dimmick.

In retirement, Benjamin Harrison resumed his law practice and wrote books about the United States government. He died on March 13, 1901, in Indianapolis.

Bibliography

Northrop, Henry Davenport. *The Life and Public Service of Benjamin Harrison, the Great American Statesman.* Philadelphia: Royal, 1892.

Siervers, Harry J. *Benjamin Harrison: Hoosier Warrior.* Newtown, Conn.: American Political Biography Press, 1996.

Stevens, Rita. *Benjamin Harrison: Twenty-third President of the United States.* Ada, Okla.: Garrett Educational Corporation, 1989.

Wallace, Lew. *Life of Gen. Ben Harrison.* Hartford, Conn.: S. S. Scranton, 1888.

★ 25 ★

William McKinley

Twenty-fifth President
1897–1901

William McKinley was a fun-loving boy whose playful antics almost caused him to drown in a creek near his home in Niles, Ohio. William and his buddy, Joseph G. Butler, Jr., went swimming together in the Mosquito Creek. Joseph could swim; William could not swim, so he waded out into the creek. Getting into deep water, he lost his footing and began sinking. Joseph tried to save him, but he, too, almost drowned as they thrashed about trying to get to safe ground.

The two boys were finally rescued by a young man named Jack Shealer. Later, when he learned to swim, William would confidently swim and fish in the creek that nearly caused his demise.

William was born on January 29, 1843, in Niles, Ohio, the seventh of nine children born to William and Nancy McKinley. He was named William McKinley, Jr. He dropped the junior part of his signature upon the death of his father in 1892.

The McKinleys lived in a two-story colonial style frame building that stood on a corner of the town's main street. One part of the first floor was a grocery store.

William's father operated an iron manufacturing firm in Niles. His mother, a devout Methodist, devoted herself to church work and to raising her children. She was a stern but loving mother who insisted that her children do their share of family chores. In her strong desire to educate to educate her children, she enrolled them in Sunday school before they attended regular school.

Five-year-old William McKinley entered a one room school as the war with Mexico drew to a close in 1848. The girls sat on one side of the room and the boys on the other. The teacher instructed them in the basics; reading, writing and arithmetic. Their teacher, Alva Sanford, for whom the children had some affection despite his hard demands, allowed them time for fun and games. The students, reflection the prevailing patriotism of the grown-ups, played soldiers, wearing paper hats, carrying wooden guns, and brandishing wooden swords.

In 1852, when William was nine years old, his family moved about ten miles away to the town of Poland in Mahoning County, where the McKinley children would have better educational opportunities. In 1854, after attending the local public school for a time, William enrolled in a private high school, the Poland Academy, which was operated by the Methodist church.

In moving from Niles to Poland for the sake of his children's education, William McKinley Senior was forced to spend time away from his family in order to manage his various iron furnaces. He would only live with his family during the weekends, riding horseback between Niles and Poland.

When William McKinley, Jr., attended the Poland Academy its faculty consisted of four teachers, including Miss E. M. Blakelee, who was a gifted instructor. As a friend of William's oldest sister Anna, who became a teacher in Canton, Ohio, Miss Blakelee greatly influenced his studies. Years later, McKinley gave Miss Blakelee credit for influencing his youthful development. Her intellectual ability and firm and resolute manner of teaching contributed significantly toward shaping the character of the future president of the United States.

At the Poland Academy, William became totally absorbed in his studies and was rarely seen without a book in his hand. He took a special interest in mathematics, Greek and Latin, and poetry. William was a serious student who excelled at public speaking and debating. He helped organize the Everett Literary and Debating Society, named in honor of Edward Everett, the famed Massachusetts educator and orator.

In 1860, when he was 17 years old, McKinley entered Allegheny College in Meadville, Pennsylvania, as a junior. He attended Allegheny for only one term, however, because he became ill and had to return home.

While he fully intended to return to college after he recuperated from his illness, this was not to be. By then the nation was in a serious financial depression, and William's father, strapped by money problems, was unable to further finance his son's college education.

William then decided to put to use the rudiments of education he had learned while attending public schools and the Poland Academy—he found a job as a teacher in Poland's Kerr district school about three miles from his home. In those days a degree in education was not a requirement to teach, especially in the lower grades.

Every day McKinley walked the six mile round trip to the school and back home. He earned twenty-five dollars a month during the school session. When the term was over in the spring of 1861, he found a job as clerk in the Poland post office.

When the Civil War began on April 12, 1861, William McKinley decided that it was his duty to join the army. He joined the 23rd Ohio Volunteer Infantry. His superior officer was Major Rutherford B. Hayes, the future president of the United States.

His regiment fought against Confederate forces in Virginia, Ohio, and West Virginia. Having been promoted to commissary sergeant, he often distributed food to the soldiers under difficult conditions. During the Battle of Antietam, McKinley bravely drove a mule team loaded with meat and coffee through heavy enemy fire to supply troops at the front. For his brave action he was promoted to second lieutenant and made an aide to General Hayes. He was mustered out of the army on July 26, 1865, with the rank of major.

Returning to Poland after his military service, McKinley decided he wanted to pursue a legal career. He began studying law in the office of Charles Glidden, a prominent attorney in Youngstown, Ohio. Greatly impressed by McKinley's diligent studies, Glidden urged him to attend a law school.

In the fall of 1866, McKinley entered the Albany Law School in Albany, New York. By the following spring, McKinley felt that he had learned enough to practice law. He returned to Poland; was admitted to the bar in 1867, and opened up a law office in Canton, where he became associated with the local Republican Party. In 1896, his popularity helped him get elected to his first public office, prosecuting attorney of Stark County.

While prosecuting attorney, he married Ida Saxton. Their marriage was tragic one, for both of their daughters died at early age, and Ida became a life-long invalid.

McKinley had a successful career as a politician. In 1876 he was elected to the House of Representatives, and during 1892–1896 served as governor of Ohio. In June 1896, the Republican Party nominated William McKinley as its presidential candidate. McKinley did little active campaigning, mostly meeting delegations of supporters at the front porch of his home in Canton, while surrogate speakers stumped the for McKinley nationwide. He won the election against Democrat William Jennings Bryan, and assumed the presidency on March 4, 1987.

In 1900 McKinley was elected for a second term. The following year, on September 6, 1901, at the Pan-American Exposition in Buffalo, New York, McKinley was assassinated by an anarchist. He died on September 14, 1901.

Bibliography

Armstrong, William H. *Major McKinley*. Kent, Ohio: The Kent State University Press, 2000.

Hoyt, Edwin P. *William McKinley*. Chicago: Reilly & Lee, 1967.

Leech, Margaret. *In the Days of McKinley*. New York: Harper & Brothers, 1959.

Morgan, H. Wayne. *William McKinley and His America*. Syracuse, N.Y.: Syracuse University Press, 1963.

Olcott, Charles S. *William McKinley*. (Two volumes.) Boston, Mass.: Houghton Mifflin, 1916.

Theodore Roosevelt

Twenty-sixth President
1901–1909

Theodore Roosevelt was born rich, but he was also born weak, thin, and asthmatic. With his father's encouragement, he built up his body with exercise to become an ardent bodybuilder, an outdoorsman, and a man of action who would be a dynamic national leader. Theodore Roosevelt, Jr., was born in a house on Twentieth Street in New York on October 27, 1858. His father was a wealthy glass merchant, and his mother, Martha Bulloch Roosevelt, was a southern belle raised in Georgia.

The second of four children, Theodore, Jr., who was nicknamed "Teedie," was often pampered because of his illness. He was propped up with pillows, and would sit up in bed so he could breathe easier. If this didn't help, his father would pick him up and walk with him, hour after hour. Some nights his father would bundle Teedie into a horse-drawn carriage and drive him through the city at top speed to force air into his lungs. Often his father took him to the country for a few days, hoping that fresh air would improve his breathing. Years later, Theodore, Jr., would write of his father: "One of my memories is of my father walking up and down the room with me in his arms at night when I was a very small person, and sitting up in bed gasping."

Treatment for asthma in the mid–nineteenth century was primitive. Black coffee and the smoking of strong cigars were often prescribed for victims.

Teedie's father usually had his son drink coffee when dealing with his asthma attacks. When asthma attacks left him weak, Teedie would rest in his father's library where he would study the illustrations in the books. He became quite interested in drawings of insects and animals. Soon the pictures would not satisfy his curiosity. He began collecting insects, bird feathers, rocks, flowers, leaves, bugs and garden snakes. Well on his way to become a naturalist, Teedie called his collection the Roosevelt Museum of Natural History.

One day when he was about seven, Teedie was sent to a market to buy strawberries for breakfast and there discovered a seal that had been killed in the New York harbor laid out for display. Fascinated by the seal, he spent several days studying and measuring it. When the seal was removed from display, the owner gave him the skull, which later became the centerpiece of the Roosevelt Museum of Natural History.

Theodore Jr.'s interest in natural history may have been inspired by his father, who helped to establish both the American Museum of Natural History and the Metropolitan Museum of Art. The senior Roosevelt generously gave both time and money for these causes.

Although business was important to the elder Roosevelt, he never discussed financial matters in front of the children. The youngsters lived a good life; there had always been servants and money to pay for their needs and wants. Life as they lived it was accepted as the norm.

In the summer of 1868, the Roosevelt family spent their summer vacation at Tarrytown in New York. While Teedie continued to have his asthmatic attacks, he also did a great deal of walking, riding and swimming. In 1869, Theodore Roosevelt, Sr., took his family to Europe. He kept the family busy visiting historical places, picture galleries and museums, cathedrals and ruins, walking through beautiful gardens, and exploring in German forests and the Swiss Alps.

One reason for the European trip was to visit his mother's two brothers, who had been living in England since the end of the Civil War. Having fought for the Confederate cause in the war, they sought refuge in England while waiting for a pardon they never received. Teedie was aware of the Civil War struggle and how it had split the Roosevelt family. While his mother's family actively supported the southern cause, his father's relatives gave their support to the Union.

As he grew older and was called Teddy, the son who adored his father seldom spoke of his father when the Civil War was discussed. He was embarrassed, or perhaps ashamed, that his father had not fought in the war. Theodore Roosevelt, Sr., had taken the easy way out during the war. He had paid a substitute—a common practice—to fight for him on the Union side. He explained that he feared he might find himself fighting against his wife's relatives.

The elder Roosevelt wanted to serve his country in some capacity. He found a way when Congress passed a bill encouraging soldiers to send part of their pay home. He was appointed a civilian allotment commissioner, and traveled on horseback to army camps urging soldiers to send part of their military pay back home to their families. After the war, he worked with the Soldiers' Employment Bureau where he helped injured veterans to find work.

The Roosevelts returned to New York after their year-long European vacation on May 25, 1870. The stay in Europe had not improved Teddy's health condition as his parents had hoped. He had received lots of physical exercise while sightseeing in Europe, yet Teddy still had asthma and was undersized and weak. Impatient with his persistent illness, the parents took him to a doctor for a thorough checkup. The physician reported that their son would need to get a thorough change of routine—he would need plenty of fresh air and more exercise.

It was at this point that Theodore Senior took his sickly son aside for a man-to-man talk. Always an active man, he dreaded the thought that his son might become an invalid. As Teddy's older sister Corinne recalled, his father said, "Theodore, you have the mind but not the body, and without help of the body the mind cannot go as far as it should. You must make your body. It is hard drudgery to make one's body but I know you will do it."

The young boy, eager to please his father, accepted the challenge. "I'll make my body," he vowed.

Teddy began exercising, first at a gymnasium operated by John Wood that was frequented by upper-class New Yorkers. As he progressed, his father had Wood set up private gym on the second-floor porch of their house. There Teddy worked out on weights, pulled himself up on horizontal bars, and pounded away on a punching bag.

The exercise program improved his health. He experienced fewer asthma attacks. As he grew stronger, Teddy Roosevelt took on more strenuous activities. He spent more time hiking, swimming, boxing, shooting, and mounting specimens of birds and small animals. Having set up his own taxidermy workshop, he appeared to be well on his way to becoming a naturalist.

When it was discovered that he had trouble reading signs and seeing letters, he acquired his first pair of glasses. "I had no idea how beautiful the world was," he wrote, "until I got those spectacles."

In October 1872 Theodore Roosevelt, Sr., took his family for another trip abroad. When they returned to New York in November 1873, he decided that it was time to make plans for Teddy to enter college. Then 15 years of age, Teddy Roosevelt had never attended a school. Since his father didn't think he was well enough to attend a school, he had tutors come to the house. Still, when it came time to prepare his son for college, the father hired another tutor.

Arthur Cutler, a recent Harvard graduate, and subsequently founder of the Cutler School of New York, was hired to prepare Teddy for the Harvard entrance examination. Until now, Teddy's education had been spotty. While he was an avid reader and knew a great deal about the world from his many travels abroad, his knowledge amounted to a nest of unrelated facts. Cutler developed a tough study program that had Teddy studying six to eight hours daily, five days a week, for two years. The studies were conducted at the Twentieth Street home in New York, and at the family's new summer home at Oyster Bay.

Simultaneously with studies, Teddy kept up with his physical training program, as well as his interest in natural science. The family assumed that he would pursue a career in science after he graduated from college. He passed the college examination, and, on September 27, 1876, he set off for Cambridge, Massachusetts, to begin his life at Harvard University.

Theodore, as he now wanted to be called, did well in his Harvard studies. He studied hard and was always full of boundless energy. At the time when 50 was passing at Harvard, he averaged 75 and ranked in the upper half of his class. He joined a variety of university activities, including the rifle club and the finance club, and was elected vice president of the Natural History Society. He also wrote for the *Harvard Advocate*.

Theodore Roosevelt's writing career was launched in the summer of 1877, when he published a short pamphlet called *The Summer Birds of the Adirondacks*. In this pamphlet he describes the appearance and songs of 97 species of the area. This was followed in 1979 by *Notes on Some of the Birds of Oyster Bay, Long Island*.

Roosevelt's father, suffering from cancer, died on February 9, 1878. Theodore was devastated by his father's death, and it would take him a long time to overcome his grief. Theodore Roosevelt, Sr., who had always provided well for his family while he was alive, also provided well for them in his death.

Theodore Roosevelt in sculling outfit at Harvard, circa 1877 (Theodore Roosevelt Collection, Harvard College Library).

Theodore, Jr., received an income of about $8,000 annually from his father's estate. (In today's terms, it was worth well over $100,000.)

Teddy graduated from Harvard, Phi Beta Kappa and magna cum laude, on June 30, 1880. He had lost interest in science and shifted his interest toward law, politics, and writing. Meanwhile, also in 1880, he married his college sweetheart, Alice Hathaway Lee. He went on to attend Columbia Law School.

During his last year at Harvard, Roosevelt began writing *The Naval War of 1812*. The book was published by G.P. Putnam's Sons in 1882, and immediately established the author as a notable historian. The book has endured as a classic in American naval history.

Theodore Roosevelt's political career began in 1881. When he was only 23 years old, he was elected to the New York State Legislature. From 1895 to 1897, he served as police commissioner of New York City.

President William McKinley offered him a post as assistant secretary of the Navy in 1897, but he resigned the post the next year to fight in the war against Spain. He organized a volunteer cavalry regiment, called Rough Riders because many of them were cowboys. Roosevelt was acclaimed a hero when he led a charge on Kettle Hill (wrongly called San Juan Hill) in Cuba.

After the Spanish-American War he was elected governor of New York in 1898. When President William McKinley began his second term on March 4, 1901, Theodore Roosevelt was sworn in as his vice president. On September 6, 1901, President McKinley, attending the Pan American Exposition in Buffalo, New York, was shot by an anarchist. He died September 14, and Theodore Roosevelt was sworn in as president. At age 42 he was the youngest man to become president. (John F. Kennedy was the youngest man ever elected president.)

In June 1904, Theodore Roosevelt won the Republican Party's presidential nomination, and on November 8, 1904, he was elected president in his own right. Having promised to serve just one full term, Roosevelt retired to his home at Sagamore Hill, Oyster Bay, New York, after the inauguration of his hand-picked successor, William Howard Taft, on March 3, 1909.

Roosevelt was married twice. Alice died from Bright's disease and childbirth complications in 1884. His second marriage was to Edith Kermit Carow. They were wed in London, England, on December 2, 1886.

President Theodore Roosevelt died on January 6, 1919, at his home in Oyster Bay, New York.

Bibliography

Brands, H.W. *T.R.: The Last Romantic.* New York: Basic Books, 1997.

Dalton, Kathleen. *Theodore Roosevelt: A Strenuous Life.* New York: Alfred Knopf, 2002.

Miller, Nathan. *Theodore Roosevelt: A Life.* New York: William Morrow, 1992.

Morris, Edmund. *The Rise of Theodore Roosevelt.* New York: Coward, McCann & Geoghegan, 1979.

Roosevelt, Theodore. *Theodore Roosevelt: An Autobiography.* New York: Da Capo Press, 1984. (Paperback reprint of the original edition published in 1913 by Charles Scribner's Sons.)

William H. Taft

William Howard Taft, born in the Mount Auburn section of Cincinnati, Ohio, on September 15, 1857, spent his boyhood trying to live up the high expectations of his domineering father, Alfonso Taft, a distinguished lawyer. He raised his nine children (one had died in infancy) to live by the principles of hard work, fair play, and public service. He expected his sons to become lawyers.

Despite his strict demands, Alfonso Taft was a loving, caring father who made certain that his children were not lacking in opportunities to succeed in their endeavors. He urged them to avoid wasting time on frivolous matters. His encouragements were often spiced with criticism. When the children were not at the top of their classes, the father wanted to know why.

William Taft's mother, Louisa Torrey Taft, was Alfonso's second wife. The first wife, Fanny Phelps Taft, died of tuberculosis at 29. Louisa was a strong willed and efficient woman who always referred to her husband as "Mister Taft." William, her second of four children, once joked with his mother that she would be successful in running a railroad company.

William Howard Taft was a round, fat, cherubic baby. When he was seven weeks old, his mother wrote her sister Delia that "he is very large for his age and grows fat every day." Fat—obesity—was something that he had to contend with as long as he lived. He stood tall at six feet, two inches when he was a grown man. He weighed 243 pounds when he graduated from college, and 332 pounds when he was president.

The family dubbed the new baby Willie, but that moniker was changed to Will when he went to school. Will and his brothers liked to skate, swim, and spar with neighborhood boys. He developed a love for baseball, at which he was a good second baseman, a power hitter, but a slow base runner. When he reached high school age, Will's size and physique earned him a formidable reputation as a wrestler and fighter. His father, however, discouraged him from taking an active part in sports at high school and college.

When he was nine years old, Will Taft suffered a slight skull fracture and bad cut on his head when the family horses ran away and overturned the carriage.

Taft's first taste of organized learning was at the Sunday school of the Western Unitarian Conference Church. When he was six years old he entered the Sixteenth District public school in the Mount Auburn section of Cincinnati. He was good at reading and spelling, but he was less able in arithmetic and writing. Twice a week he attended a dancing school. Despite his bulk, he was good dancer.

Will Taft's academic achievements improved greatly when he attended Woodward High School during 1870–1874. He took the college preparatory curriculum, graduating second in his class with a four-year grade average of 91.5. The father was delighted with his son's scholarship and intelligence.

Will Taft followed in his father's footsteps and enrolled at Yale University in 1874; his father had enrolled at Yale in 1829. While he studied and hard and received good grades, he was constantly concerned about pleasing his father.

In a letter to his father, written September 13, 1874, freshman Will Taft outlined his tough study schedule, and complained that he worked long hours and still did not receive any perfect marks. "You expect great things of me," he wrote, "but you mustn't be disappointed if I don't come up to your expectations."

Will Taft was a popular student, but he did not participate in any sports, because his father condemned such activities as a waste of time that would impede his academic studies. He did, however, join the Skull and Bones, a secret society, of which his father was a co-founder in 1832.

Will graduated from Yale on June 27, 1878. He stood second in a class of

William Howard Taft in 1864 (William Howard Taft National Historical Site).

132. His father was pleased. After Yale, Will returned to Cincinnati and enrolled in the Cincinnati Law School, while working part time as a courthouse reporter for the *Cincinnati Commercial*. He passed the Ohio bar examination in May 1880. Principally through his father's connections, Taft became assistant prosecutor of Hamilton County, Ohio, in 1881.

On June 19, 1886, Taft married Helen Herron, whom he had met at a sledding party a few years before.

Taft was appointed judge of the Cincinnati Superior Court in 1887. His goal toward becoming a Supreme Court judge had begun. In 1890 he was appointed U.S. Solicitor General at the Department of Justice.

Taft detoured from his legal goal when President William McKinley appointed him chief administrator in the Philippines. He served there from 1901 to 1904. He was a good administrator, and received much praise for sponsoring land reform, building roads, and establishing schools.

In 1904, his friend Theodore Roosevelt, then president, appointed him secretary of war, a post he held until 1908, when he accepted the Republican Party's nomination as its candidate for president. After his victory in the 1904 presidential election, Theodore Roosevelt had promised publicly not to seek reelection. He later regretted that decision, but felt bound by it, and supported Taft for the presidency.

Taft went on to win the election and became the twenty-seventh president in 1909. He lost the reelection in 1912 to Democrat Woodrow Wilson.

While he played baseball as a youngster, William Howard Taft made baseball history on April 19, 1910, when he opened the game between the Washington Senators and Boston Red Sox by throwing out the first ball. The ball was caught by the Senators' famed pitcher Walter Johnson.

After the presidency, Taft served as professor of Law at Yale University until President Warren Harding appointed him Chief Justice of the United States, a position he held until just before his death on March 8, 1930.

Bibliography

Duffy, Herbert S. *William Howard Taft*. New York: Minton, Balch, 1930.
Pringle, Henry. *The Life and Times of William Howard Taft: A Biography*. Hamden, Conn.: Anchon Books, two volumes, 1964.

Woodrow Wilson

Twenty-eighth President
1913–1921

Woodrow Wilson was a papa's boy.

While he received unrestrained expression of love from both parents, the relationship with his possessive father bordered on overplayed passion. There was a lot of hugging and kissing, and they wrote passionate letters to each other. From the moment that his first son was born, the father was convinced that the child was destined for greatness.

Thomas Woodrow Wilson was born on December 28, 1856, at the Presbyterian manse in Staunton, Virginia. His parents were the Reverend Joseph Ruggles Wilson and Janet "Jessie" Woodrow Wilson, who had been born in England. Their son was named after his maternal grandfather, the Reverend Thomas Woodrow, a Presbyterian minister. He was called "Tommy" by the family, but he dropped the "Tommy" nickname when he entered college.

In the spring of 1858, the Reverend Wilson moved his family to Augusta, Georgia, where he became pastor of the First Presbyterian Church. The Wilson family, who resided in a newly built brick manse, spent the next 12 years in Augusta, through the Civil War and its aftermath.

Woodrow was four years old when the Civil War began. He remembered little of its actual events, but recalled standing by the gate of the family house in 1860 and hearing a passerby saying that Lincoln had been elected and there will be war. During much of the conflict his parents shielded him from the horrors and problems that the war brought to his family and neighbors.

Rather than sending Woodrow to the primitive schools in Augusta, the Reverend Wilson kept Woodrow at home. Suffering from poor eyesight, and sickly during his early childhood, Woodrow made slow progress in his home studies. He did not begin to learn the alphabet until he was nine, and could not read until he was 11. It is generally believed that he suffered from dyslexia, a visual disorder among people who have trouble reading letters and words.

Despite his son's slowness in learning, the Reverend Wilson kept pressing Woodrow to overcome his handicap, often spending hours coaching him in the art of debates. He never permitted his son to use incorrect words, frequently asking Woodrow, "What do you mean by that?" At times the Reverend Wilson would encourage Woodrow to read the works of established authors and to find synonyms to improve their writings. Through this learning process, Woodrow Wilson would eventually become a gifted nonfiction author. He published several important books, including the five-volume "A History of the American People."

Woodrow was 12 years old when he received his first formal schooling, when he enrolled in a small academy established in Augusta by a former Confederate soldier, Professor Joseph T. Derry. The school was held in an old building which also housed a livery stable at the same time. Later the school was moved to better facilities in a cotton warehouse. Derry held classes in Latin and history, while another teacher instructed the students in writing and bookkeeping.

Young Woodrow Wilson was not a good student. He showed little interest in his studies. Once Woodrow and some of the boys skipped school to watch a circus come to town. The stern professor gave Woodrow and his cohorts a thrashing. It was probably the only whipping Woodrow Wilson had ever received.

While growing up in Atlanta, Woodrow Wilson joined with his buddies to form a club they called the "Lightfoot Club." They met in the loft of the Reverend Wilson's barn and formed a baseball team that played against other teams in the area. Woodrow was a good baseball player, but he was more interested in running the youthful organization. His peers gladly elected him their president. He was in his element, making a kind of constitution and requiring all debates to follow certain rules.

In 1870, the Reverend Wilson moved his family to Columbia, South

Carolina, to accept a teaching position at the Columbia Technological Seminary. He also took on the post as minister of the First Presbyterian Church of Columbia. Upon arriving in Columbia, Woodrow Wilson attended a school operated by the family's new neighbor, Professor Charles H. Barnwell. The professor found Woodrow to be a difficult student, lazy and indifferent to his studies.

Despite his lack of scholastic preparation, 17-year-old Woodrow Wilson enrolled in Davidson College, a Presbyterian college in Charlotte, North Carolina. His parents had chosen that school not only because of its sound academic reputation, but because the studies there might also lead him toward the ministry.

In the fall of 1873, when Woodrow entered Davidson College, there were 157 students at the school. Since he was ill prepared for college studies, Woodrow was under heavy pressure to make up his work. He made only average grades; the lowest was in mathematics and the highest were in English and composition.

His real interest was in debating, and he soon became a member of the Eumenean Society. The object of the society was "the acquirement of literary knowledge, the promotion of virtue, and the cultivation of social harmony and friendship." The society always opened its meeting with a prayer, and Woodrow Wilson, although a freshman, was called upon to conduct this religious service.

Wilson was in ill health most of the time he studied at Davidson College. He suffered from headaches, and in May 1874 his indigestion became so severe that in June he left the college and returned to his father's home in Wilmington, North Carolina. The Reverend Wilson had settled there when he accepted the post as minister of the local First Presbyterian Church.

While recuperating at his parents' home, Woodrow Wilson studied Greek and mathematics to prepare him for college. In September 1875, 19-year-old Wilson enrolled at the College of New Jersey, which later changed its name to Princeton University.

While he took the prescribed courses, his interests were literature and history. He was not a particularly bright student in the classroom; he often spent more time on extracurricular activities than on his academic work. He contributed to literary magazines, edited the *Princetonian*, the school paper, participated in various debating clubs, acted in school plays, and served as president of the campus baseball association and secretary of the football association.

On June 3, 1876, Woodrow wrote in his diary that "I have not employed the day to very much advantage except having spent much of my time in loafing." He graduated from Princeton in June 1879. He ranked 38 among 167 students.

Woodrow decided that he wanted to become a lawyer. In October 1879 he enrolled at the University of Virginia Law School in Charlottesville. This move greatly disappointed his father, who had hoped that his son would follow him into the Presbyterian ministry.

Woodrow was a popular student in Charlottesville, but the grind of studying law bored him. His health problems, including headaches, upset stomach, and intense nervousness, further added to his pain and worry. He left the university in December 1890 without a degree, and returned to his parents' home in Wilmington, where he continued to study law.

In the May 1892 Woodrow Wilson formed a partnership with Edward R. Renick, a graduate of the Virginia Law School, and established a legal office in Atlanta, Georgia. Shortly thereafter he passed the Georgia bar examination.

The law firm of Renick & Wilson was not successful. They received few clients, and Wilson, bored with life as an attorney, abandoned the practice. He then enrolled in Johns Hopkins University in Baltimore as a graduate student in history and political science. He earned his doctor of philosophy degree in 1886.

In his last year of graduate school, Wilson, then 28 years old, married Ellen Louise Axson, age 25. A talented artist of strong character, she would exercise substantial influence on her husband, encouraging him to work for the welfare of the poor, and to strive for political and economic reform.

After a teaching career at Bryn Mawr College in Pennsylvania, and at Wesleyan University in Middletown, Connecticut, Woodrow Wilson returned to Princeton in 1890 as professor of jurisprudence and political economy. He served as president of Princeton from 1902 to 1910.

His growing national reputation led Democratic politicians to consider him presidential timber. After serving as governor of New Jersey during 1911–1913, Wilson was nominated for president at the 1912 Democratic convention. He won the ensuing election because of a Republican split. In the election of 1916, he defeated Republican Charles Evans Hughes.

Meanwhile, his wife Ellen had died in 1914. In 1915 he married a widow, Mrs. Edith Bolling Galt.

When World War I began in Europe, Wilson proclaimed American neutrality. In 1917, after German submarines continued to sink American ships, Wilson asked Congress to declare a state of war on Germany. Massive American effort slowly brought the war to an end on November 11, 1918. Wilson went to Paris in attempt to sell his 14 point peace plan, but the Senate failed to support him. President Wilson made a national tour to mobilize public sentiment for the treaty. Exhausted, he suffered a stroke. His wife, Edith, took charge of White House activities, though the American public was little aware of her influence, which included screening matters of state and deciding what should be brought to the attention of the president. For the remainder of his term the ailing president was virtually in seclusion in the White House.

He died at his home in Washington, D.C., on February 3, 1924, and is buried in the National Cathedral.

Bibliography

Baker, Ray Stannard. *Woodrow Wilson: Life and Letters Youth 1856–1890*. Garden City, N.Y.: Doubleday, Page, 1927.

Freud, Sigmund, and William C. Bullitt. *Thomas Woodrow Wilson: A Psychological Study*. Boston, Mass.: Houghton Mifflin, 1966.

Heckscher, August. *Woodrow Wilson*. New York: Charles Scribner's Sons, 1991.

★ 29 ★

Warren G. Harding

Twenty-ninth President
1921–1923

When Warren Gamaliel Harding was born on November 2, 1865, in Corsica (later Blooming Grove), Ohio, his mother wanted him to be named Winfield, but she deferred to her husband's wishes. However, she always referred to her firstborn child as "Winnie."

Warren was named after his great-uncle, the Reverend Warren Gamaliel Bancroft, a Methodist chaplain at the Wisconsin State Prison. His unique middle name, Gamaliel, was a biblical character, a protector and teacher of the apostle Saint Paul.

Warren's father, George Tyron Harding, who was a drummer boy during the Civil War, once met with President Abraham Lincoln. While stationed in Virginia, Tryon Harding and two members of his regiment took furlough in Washington, D.C., where they visited the White House and asked to shake hands with President Lincoln. (At that time there were no restrictions on citizens entering the White House grounds or the president's residence.)

After waiting an hour, the young soldiers met with President Lincoln, who told them that they could return to Ohio satisfied that they had seen "the handsomest man in the United States."

Warren's mother, Phoebe Elizabeth Dickerson Harding, was a deeply religious woman who strongly supported her husband in his various risky endeavors. She bore him eight children, of whom six lived to maturity. When her husband briefly practiced medicine, she assisted him by doing midwifery work. She worked hard keeping a well-ordered house, taking her family to Sunday church services, and giving her children pre-school instruction.

Tryon Harding was an impractical, day-dreaming man who tried just about everything but was seldom successful. His pursuit of happiness led him to try many different jobs. Shying away from hard labor, he would engage in trading, bartering, and land speculating. He tried teaching in a public school, and was practicing medicine and running a small farm when Warren was born. His medical career started after he purchased a set of used medical books and began assisting Blooming Grove physician Dr. Joseph McFarland on his rounds.

Warren was born in a small salt box clapboard cottage that was the family's farm house. In 1867, the father built a larger, two-story frame house with a covered front porch on the site of the original cottage.

Warren's mother taught him to read and write and had him memorizing poems before he entered Blooming Grove's one-room schoolhouse. Under the stern rule of the schoolmaster, James Boggs, the students learned basic reading, writing, arithmetic, history, and geography. Their lessons were enhanced by studying the *Eclectic Readers* books written by educator William Holmes McGuffey.

In the summer of 1873, when Warren was eight years old, Tryon Harding moved his family to the nearby town of Caledonia, where he began a full-time medical practice. He also invested in banks and real estate, but his financial speculations were less successful than his medical practice. In his rural medical rounds, he often had to accept payment in kind—eggs, butter, and other farm produce—instead of monetary payments.

When Warren attended the public school in Caledonia he was able to expand on the poetry recitations his mother had taught him. Every Friday afternoon the school held a declamation contest—a public speaking contest—in which he excelled. He was particularly adept in reciting stories and speeches he found in the McGuffey's *Eclectic Readers* books.

Warren was a good boy; he was always noticed as one who was kind to others, who avoided name calling, and who was charitable to those who were different or less fortunate than he. While he was a strong lad and helped his father with the farm chores, including milking cows and currying horses, he usually tried to avoid hard work. Once, when a farmer offered him a job of shucking corn at 50 cents a day, he quit the job after ten minutes, saying it was too hard.

When Warren was ten years old his father brought home a cornet he obtained in one of his many trading deals. A local harness maker who was also a trombone player taught him how to play the cornet. Soon he became good enough to join the Caledonia Aeolin Band, which performed in the local bandstand on Saturday nights and occasionally performed in neighboring towns.

In the summer of 1875, Tyron Harding acquired ownership of the town's newspaper, the *Caledonia Argus*, a journal that was published whenever its editor was able to pay for paper and ink. Warren and another boy were given jobs as printer's devils—printer apprentices. Their duties were to sweep the floor, run errands, feed the press, wash the rollers, and help the printers with their type blocks. Later Warren became adept at all phases of running a printing press.

In 1880, when Tyron Harding's investments went sour, he lost his home and moved to a 40-acre farm in Marion, Ohio. Somehow he managed to scrape together enough money to send Warren to college. That fall, Warren Harding enrolled in Iberia College (now known as Ohio Central College). The school had a faculty of three; tuition came to seven dollars a term. The student body consisted of about three dozen young men.

He studied the traditional courses such as Latin, mathematics, history, and chemistry, but he did best in debating and composition. He became the editor of the campus newspaper, *Iberia Spectator*. He also played the alto horn in the brass band. Warren graduated from Iberia College in 1882 with a bachelor of science degree. He delivered the commencement address.

After graduation he passed the Marion County school board examination and taught in a one-room school. After one term he gave up the teaching job. He considered entering the legal profession, and studied some old law books that his father had obtained in his trading deals, but he found them boring. He took a job with an insurance company but was fired when he miscalculated the rates.

For a time he worked for the Marion *Mirror* as a reporter, advertising salesman, and delivery boy. He was fired from that job when the newspaper owner charged him with loafing and for hanging around the Republican party headquarters. The newspaper owner was a Democrat.

In 1884, soon after Warren was fired, he joined with two of his old pals from the Caledonia Aeolian Band, Jack Warwick and Johnnie Sickle, and raised $300 to purchase a failing newspaper, the Marion *Star*. Nineteen-year-old Warren Harding became the newspaper's editor, and took full charge in managing his organization, which he named the "Star Publishing Company."

He wrote upbeat editorials, encouraged businessmen to advertise, and hired experienced reporters. During the first struggling months, Warren often slept at his office.

While his publishing venture became a success, his partners, Warwick and Sickle, soon left the organization when they were unable to adjust to the fast pace and turbulence of newspaper publishing. By 1890 the *Star* had arrived. It was a six-page daily with an eight-page Saturday edition. The paper was rated as one of Ohio's most successful small town newspapers.

When Warren Harding was 25 years old when he married Florence "Flossie" Mabel Kling DeWolfe, a divorcee with one son, at his home in Marion. Her managerial skills helped him build his newspaper into a financial success.

Harding was a staunch Republican whose knack for public speaking drew the attention of party leaders. After losing an election for county auditor in 1892, he was elected as a Republican to the Ohio Senate in 1899. In 1902 he was elected to the post of lieutenant governor. During 1915–1920, Harding served as U.S. senator from Ohio.

During the 1920 presidential election, Warren Harding and his running mate, Calvin Coolidge, won more than 60 percent of the popular vote. He was sworn in as the twenty-ninth president of the United States on March 4, 1921. Harding was the first president to ride in an automobile to his inauguration. This inauguration was also the first to be described over radio. Harding's administration was marred by high-level corruption, culminating in the Teapot Dome oil reserve scandal.

In June 1923 Harding was the first president to visit Alaska. While there he became ill, suffering from food poisoning. He returned to San Francisco as his condition worsened. Already weakened by a heart condition, President Harding died of stroke in San Francisco on August 2, 1923.

Bibliography

Downes, Randolph C. *The Rise of Warren Gamaliel Harding, 1865–1920*. Columbus, Ohio: Ohio State University Press, 1970.

Mee, Charles L., Jr. *The Ohio Gang: The World of Warren G. Harding*. New York: M. Evans, 1981.

Russell, Francis. *The Shadow of Blooming Grove: Warren G. Harding in His Times*. New York: McGraw-Hill, 1968.

★ 30 ★

Calvin Coolidge

Thirtieth President
1923–1929

The Fourth of July, Independence Day, was always a special day for Calvin Coolidge. It was his birthday,

Calvin was born July 4, 1872, in Plymouth Notch, Vermont, a small community at the foothills of the Green Mountains. The house in which he was born was attached to his father's general store. He was the first child of John Calvin Coolidge and Victoria Josephine Moor. His sister Abigail died when Calvin was 15 years old.

Calvin was named after his father, John Calvin Coolidge, but was always called Calvin or Cal at home to avoid confusion. He dropped the first name after graduating from college.

The elder Coolidge was an industrious man who ran a successful general store. He managed the post office, sold insurance and real estate, and operated a farm. At times he served as justice of the peace and always had a commission as notary public. He was also a politician, having served in both the Vermont Senate and House of Representatives. Calvin's mother was a frail, sensitive women devoted to her family. She died of tuberculosis when Calvin was 12 years old.

Calvin Coolidge was a shy, undemonstrative, restrained youngster who throughout his lifetime suffered from chronic respiratory and digestive ailments. Calvin was born a redhead, but his hair turned sandy in his youth. He spoke with a New England nasal twang. Calvin started school when he was five years old, but before that he had been introduced to the story-telling of his mother and maternal grandmother. His mother liked to read poetry, and his grandmother read him passages from the Bible and stories about early Vermont settlers. Coolidge remembered that his father had no taste for books, but always read a daily newspaper.

The Plymouth Notch district school that Calvin Coolidge attended was built of field stone from a small quarry nearby. Calvin's class of about 25 students sat on unpainted benches

Calvin Coolidge, 1882 studio portrait (Vermont Historical Society Library).

and desks wide enough to seat two students. Lessons consisted mostly of reading and recitations led by a teacher who had qualified for the position by passing an examination conducted by the town superintendent.

During Calvin Coolidge's youth, children in the Green Mountain area usually attended elementary schools only during the winter months. The rest of the year they helped their parents work the farms. Calvin helped with the haying in the summer and harvesting in the fall. He also helped with the maple tree sugaring. He drained sap from the trees and boiled the sap until it became syrup. It took about 40 gallons of sap to make one gallon of maple syrup.

One of his duties was to make sure that the woodbox was full and that there was plenty of kindling. The wood was needed to heat the house, cook food and heat water. When Calvin was about ten years old, he remembered late one night that he had forgotten to fill the woodbox. So he got out of bed and dressed very quietly. He crept down stairs and filled the woodbox in the middle of the night. The woodbox needed to be near the stove before breakfast the next morning.

Oxens were used on the Coolidge farm. When he was 12 years old, Calvin learned how to drive oxen and to plow with the oxen. He also took care of other animals, including milking cows and taking them out to pasture.

On February 20, 1886, 13-year-old Calvin set off in a sleigh with his father to begin his higher education at the Black River Academy in Ludlow, Vermont. The elder Coolidge had also attended the academy for several terms, but was not a graduate. On the sleigh was a calf that John Coolidge was going to ship to the Boston market. Coolidge lore has it that when they reached Ludlow, the father told his son. "Calvin, if you study hard and are a good boy, maybe sometime you'll go to Boston too, but the calf will get there first."

Black River Academy, also known as B.R.A., was a private boarding school. The fees were $7 a term; room and board were $3 a week. He arrived at the academy with all his belongings tucked into two small handbags. He was excited about new adventure. In his autobiography, Calvin Coolidge noted that "going to the Academy meant a complete break with the past and entering a new and untried field, larger and more alluring than the past, among unknown scenes and unknown people." There were no dormitories, so the students, both male and female, boarded in private houses around town. Calvin lived at different homes during his years at the school.

The student body at Black River Academy numbered about 125. During his stay at B.R.A. Calvin studied English grammar, Latin, Greek, history, mathematics, and literature. In his history studies, he acquired a special interest in the United States Constitution and the workings of the federal government.

Calvin did more than study while at B.R.A.; on Saturdays he worked at the town's carriage shop, where he learned to make toys and baby wagons. Commenting on his first exposure to working in a factory, Calvin Coolidge wrote in his autobiography that "it was a good training. I was beginning to find out what existence meant." During the summer vacations he returned home to Plymouth Notch and helped his father with farm chores.

In the spring of 1890, Calvin graduated in a class of five boys and four girls. Part of the ceremony consisted of brief speeches by each graduate. Calvin presented an address on "Oratory in History." He dealt with the effect of the spoken word in determining human action. During his talk he alluded to the great speeches delivered by such orators as Cicero, Martin Luther, James Otis, Patrick Henry, Daniel Webster and others.

In autumn of 1890, Calvin went to Amherst, Massachusetts, to take the entrance examination for Amherst College. During the trip he caught a cold which got progressively worse by testing time. He was unable to complete the examination and returned home, where the illness persisted into early winter.

In spring 1891, to better prepare himself for another testing session at Amherst, Calvin entered St. Johnsbury Academy, a college preparatory school about 80 miles north of Plymouth Notch. After he completed the spring term, he received a college entrance certificate which qualified him to enter Amherst College.

Just as Calvin was about to enter Amherst College, his father remarried. His new wife, Caroline Athelia Brown, was a schoolteacher who had taught young Calvin at the Plymouth Notch district school. Calvin was pleased with his father's remarriage. In his autobiography he wrote, "After being without a mother nearly seven years I was greatly pleased to find in her all the motherly devotion that she could have given me if I had been her own son."

In September 1891 Calvin Coolidge enrolled as a freshman at Amherst College. Since the two Amherst dormitories had fallen into disrepair, the students were forced to find quarters in private homes. Calvin took a room in a brick house with another student. The room cost him $60 a year and 25 cents a week for service. He had to provide oil for his lamp and his own wood for heating. Later on he boarded down the street at another place for three and a half dollars a week.

Coolidge's grades at Amherst during his first two years were good, although not outstanding, but they improved, especially in his senior year when he was influenced by the teaching of the philosopher Charles E. Garman. The philosophy professor was one of those rare teachers capable of encouraging students to think independently, and to follow the truth wherever it might lead. Garman's teaching influenced Coolidge's social values and encouraged his interest in public service. "We looked upon Garman as a man who walked with God," wrote Coolidge of his college memories.

Coolidge was a shy and quiet fellow who seldom participated in social activities. He found it difficult to make friends. Once he wrote home to his father that "I don't seem to get acquainted very fast." As his grades improved Calvin tried to be more sociable. In his junior year he entered his class's comical "Plug Hat Race," wearing a silk hat. He lost the race, but won applause for his funny speech.

His dry humor won him the dubious honor of being selected as Grove Orator, the graduate picked to deliver a humorous speech—a roast of students and faculty. Calvin delivered his speech with a straight face and a monotone to howls of laughter from his fellow students. While the Grove oration was successful, Calvin was not pleased with his effort. Writing of this in his autobiography, Coolidge took care to note, "While my effort was not without some success, I very soon learned that making fun of people in a public way was not a good method to secure friends, or likely to lead to much advancement, and I have scrupulously avoided it."

For his senior essay, "The Principles Fought for in the American Revolution," Coolidge won first prize, a $150 gold medal, in a national contest sponsored by the Sons of the American Revolution. Coolidge graduated cum laude from Amherst College on June 26, 1895.

Instead of entering law school he applied for a job with the law firm of Hammond and Field at Northampton, Massachusetts, so that he could study under professionals. He was admitted to the bar in 1897, opened a practice in Northampton, and became active in local Republican affairs. In 1905 he wed Grace Anna Goodhue.

After holding several minor political posts, Coolidge served as Massachusetts state senator during 1912–1915; as lieutenant governor of Massachusetts, 1916–1918; and as the state's governor 1919–1920. Coolidge was a candidate for the Replication presidential nomination in 1920, but lost to Warren G. Harding. The party then picked him for the vice presidential spot.

On the morning of August 3, 1923, Vice President Calvin Coolidge was in Plymouth Notch visiting his father when the news of President Harding's death reached him. Since the elder Coolidge did not have a telephone, members of the vice president's staff, who stayed at the neighboring town of Bridgewater, brought the words of Harding's death. They aroused Calvin's father, who then awoke his son with the dramatic news.

Calvin Coolidge went to a general store that had a telephone and contacted Secretary of State Charles Evans Hughes, who urged Coolidge to take the presidential oath immediately. It should be done before a notary, he advised. Calvin then realized that his father, a justice of the peace and notary public, could swear him in. So, at 2:47 in the morning, John Coolidge administered the oath that made his son Calvin the thirtieth president of the United States.

Calvin Coolidge was a popular president; people saw him as a symbol of the prosperous times. He was admired for his old-fashioned virtues of thrift and common sense. Coolidge chose not to run for reelection, and after leaving the White House he retired to his home in Northampton. He wrote articles for newspapers and published his autobiography. On January 5, 1933, he died suddenly of a heart attack.

Bibliography

Coolidge, Calvin. *The Autobiography of Calvin Coolidge.* Rutland, Vt.: Academy Books, 1972. (This is a reproduction of the original 1929 first edition published by the Cosmopolitan Book Corporation of New York.)

Ferrell, Robert H. *The Presidency of Calvin Coolidge.* Lawrence: University Press of Kansas, 1998.

McCoy, Donald R. *Calvin Coolidge: The Quiet President.* Lawrence: University Press of Kansas, 1988. (Originally published in 1967 by Macmillan of New York.)

Sobel, Robert. *Coolidge: An American Enigma.* Washington, D.C.: Regnery, 1998.

★ 31 ★

Herbert Hoover

Thirty-first President
1929–1933

Life began hard for Herbert Hoover. His father died when he was six years old, and his mother passed away when he was nine. Fortunately, a compassionate uncle guided the orphan boy through his youth while his older brother Theodore and younger sister Mary were raised by other family members.

The future president was born about midnight on August 10, 1874, in a small, two-room cottage in West Branch, Iowa. The front room, measuring about 14 by 20 feet, served as the parlor, kitchen and dining area. The rear room, 14 by 7 feet in size, was the family's bedroom. At the rear of their small home, the Hoovers kept a small flock of chickens which provided fresh eggs for the household. They also maintained a vegetable garden. Out of season, the vegetables were stored in a cellar near the front porch.

Herbert's parents were Quakers, members of the Society of Friends, a church known for its pacifism, humanitarianism, and emphasis on inner quiet. They lived in a Quaker community in which a simple life and religious adherence was practiced daily.

Herbert's father, Jesse Clark Hoover, who built the family home, was the town's blacksmith. He also sold farming equipment and served as the town's assessor and councilman. After his daughter was born, he sold the small cottage and built a roomy two-story house nearby. He died of a heart attack at the age of 34.

The future president's mother, Hulda Minthorn Hoover, a native of Canada, was living on a farm near West Branch when she married Jesse Hoover. She had attended the University of Iowa and taught school briefly before her marriage. Later she became a Quaker minister. After her husband died she took in sewing, carefully saving his $1,000 insurance money for the education of her children. She died of pneumonia at the age of 35.

Though named Herbert Clark Hoover, from early childhood the young- ster was known as Bert, or Bertie, to family and friends. He was a husky boy who loved to play outdoors and swim in swimming hole near the railroad tracks. In the winter he joined with his playmates to slide down the hills on homemade sleds. In his youth he developed a lifelong passion for fishing. He trapped rabbits and shot pigeons and prairie chickens with bow and arrow. At age five, Herbert learned the fundamentals at the West Branch Free School. One of his teachers remembered him as being an "industries and determined" student.

It wasn't all fun and play for Herbert. He had chores to do around the home and on the farm. He helped with planting corn, hoeing the garden, milking the cows, sawing wood, and various other jobs that needed attention. Herbert didn't complain about the hard work. It made him grow strong. In his memoirs Hoover noted that he approved of such work for young boys—"I can speak for the strong and healthy bodies which came from it all."

After the death of his father, Herbert from time to time was sent to stay with relatives in order to ease the burden on his mother. An uncle, Major Laban Miles, United States Indian agent to the Osage Nation, had Herbert live with him on the Indian reservation at Pawhuska, Arkansas, for eight months. During his stay with Uncle Miles, Herbert learned to appreciate the Indians' way of life. He also attended their Sunday school, which was con- ducted in English.

In 1885, Herbert went to live with his uncle Henry John Minthorn, who was a doctor in the Quaker settlement in Newberg, Oregon. Henry John and Laura Minthorn had recently lost a son, and they thought that having another boy in the house might ease their grief. The Minthorns arranged for Herbert to travel to Oregon in caravan of new settlers who were traveling west. An immigrant family named Hammil agreed to look after Herbert during the seven day westward trek.

Herbert Hoover (right) at age 14, with brother Theodore and sister Mary (Herbert Hoover Library).

145

When Herbert arrived at Newberg, he found Aunt Laura Minthorn and her daughters busy boiling pear butter for their winter supply. He was asked to stir the butter and urged to eat as many pears as he liked. Never having tasted the fruit before, he proceeded to gorge himself. "I liked them. But after two days of [an] almost exclusively pear diet I did not eat pears again for years," Hoover reminisced about the incident in his memoirs.

Herbert found Uncle Minthorn to be a fascinating, unorthodox Quaker who did not hold to extreme pacifism. As a youngster the uncle had helped slaves escape through the "Underground Railroad," fought with the Union Army during the Civil War, and served as a Unites States Indian agent in Oregon.

Uncle Minthorn put Herbert to work taking care of his horses, tending to and milking the cows, splitting firewood, and helping clear tracts of a fir forest. One summer Herbert got a summer job weeding onions at a Newberg farm. The job lasted about two months, and Herbert earned $30, which he considered a great sum.

Dr. Minthorn also placed Herbert in the Friends Pacific Academy, a Quaker school of which he was the superintendent. He also taught history and literature. Herbert received average marks, but he excelled in mathematics.

In 1889, when Herbert was 15 years old, Uncle Minthorn moved his family to Salem, the capital of Oregon, where he and several partners established the Oregon Land Company, a real estate business. Herbert went along and was offered an office job at 15 dollars a month. Later he received a five dollar raise. He learned bookkeeping, and he also helped draft advertisements, blueprint plots and roadways of housing projects. With the help of the secretary, he learned how to use the typewriter.

A chance meeting with an engineer named Robert Brown in his uncle's office gave Herbert Hoover the idea that he wanted to become an engineer. During their conversation, Brown discussed the advantages of a college education for a profession and described the importance of engineering. Young Hoover was impressed. "For a year I mulled over it, talking to all who would listen," he wrote in his memoirs. "I haunted the little foundry and sawmill and the repair shops of the town. I collected catalogues and information on engineering universities. I was determined to become an engineer."

When a business school was opened in Salem, young Hoover promptly enrolled in the evening classes. One of the teachers who specialized in mathematics was delighted to discover that Herbert had a natural aptitude for the subject. The teacher offered him free lessons in algebra and geometry outside of regular school hours.

Herbert Hoover's early education was lacking in the studies of history and literature. That was to change when Miss Jennie Gray, a school teacher, walked into the office of the Oregon Land Company and announced that she was there to advise young working boys about their schooling.

Miss Gray asked Herbert if he was interested in reading books. When she learned that his reading had been limited to required Bible reading, the encyclopedia, text books, and newspapers, she invited him to go with her to the small lending library in town. She borrowed a copy of *Ivanhoe* and gave it to him to read, which he did at the office between chores and in the evenings. The story fascinated him, and he remembered that "suddenly I began to see books as living things and was ready for more of them.... They broadened my scope and made me feel a part of the mighty stream of humanity."

When he learned that a new, free university founded by California Senator Leland Stanford would be opened in California, Herbert went to Portland, Oregon, where entrance examinations were being held. He did well in mathematics, but since he had never attended high school, he failed the entrance examination. One of the examiners, a Quaker educator, impressed with Herbert's eagerness and general intelligence, suggested that he go to the university three months early, hire a tutor and take some subjects over again.

Herbert then quit his job with the Oregon Land Company, gathered up is belongings, which included two suits and a bicycle, and with $600 savings in his pocket, left for Palo Alto in the summer of 1891. The Minthorn family added $50 and put him on the train with their blessings and a large package of food.

Luck was with Herbert at the beginning of his journey. He traveled with another Salem boy, Fred Williams, whose father, a local banker, insisted on paying Herbert's fare in consideration for some tutoring in mathematics for his son.

Upon arrival at Palo Alto, Herbert and Fred were assigned quarters in the men's dormitory. Herbert began immediately the required tutoring service, and he passed the entrance examination, just barely, with a few "conditions"; one of them being English. The condition was removed in his senior year. In reality, the examiners were less concerned about the applicants' initial academic records than their potential for learning. The misfits would be weeded out later.

Stanford University officially opened on October 1, 1891. Herbert Hoover was then 17 years old. The need to make a living turned Herbert into a university entrepreneur. He started a newspaper route, and a laundry service which he later sold to another student. Since he could type, he landed a job in the university office at $5 a week. Later he would secure a similar job with one of the professors for $30 a month. He also became manager of the university's baseball team, which made him responsible for arranging games, collecting the gate money, and finding cash for equipment and uniforms.

The baseball activities brought Hoover in contact with former president Benjamin Harrison, who had delivered lectures at the university. President Harrison was a baseball fan and frequently attended the Stanford baseball games. Stanford had no enclosed baseball field, so Hoover had gate collectors stationed at various areas. One afternoon President Harrison came to the game. Either he ignored the collector or the collector was overcome with shyness. Informed that Harrison had not paid his 25 cent fee, Herbert Hoover respectfully asked the former president for the fee, which he cheerfully paid. Harrison also purchased a ticket for the following week's game.

During his first summer vacation, Herbert Hoover worked with the Geological Survey of Arkansas. He was assigned to help map rock formations and rock deposits on the north side of the Ozarks. The next summer vacation he was hired by the United States Geological Survey to assist Dr. Waldemar Lindgren, a ranking geologist who worked in the High Sierra, the deserts of Nevada, and in various mining camps. Much of the exploration was done on horseback, which was not to Herbert's liking, but he had earned $200 towards his sophomore expenses.

When the maps of the survey were published by the Government Printing Office, Hoover's name appeared beside Dr. Lindgren's in the credit line. That was the first public recognition to come to Hoover in his chosen field of endeavor. During his senior year at Sanford Herbert Hoover met his future wife, Lou Henry. She was also a geology student whose love of fishing and the outdoors paralleled that of Herbert's.

In May 1895 Hoover graduated from Stanford with a degree in geology. Failing to find a decent job after graduation, he pushed ore carts 70 hours a week at gold mine near Nevada City, California. However, he soon landed a job as a typist for a San Francisco engineering firm. The head of the firm, Louis Janin, promoted Hoover to engineering jobs and in 1896 Hoover was hired by an English mining firm, Bewick, Moreing and Company, as a mining engineer in Australia. Transferred to China in 1899, he served as China's mining engineer in the Chihli and Jehol provinces.

Meanwhile, he had become well known as a financier, promoter, geologist, engineer, and metallurgist. In 1908 Hoover left the Bewick, Moreing firm to set up his own engineering firm. He financed new projects and speculated in mining projects.

In August 1914, the Hoovers were in London when war broke out in Europe. Thousands of American tourists fled to London trying to book passage back to the United States. The embassy in London asked Hoover to help. He formed a committee that helped over 120,000 Americans get passage on ships back America, and food and shelter in England.

When the invading German troops prevented Belgian civilians from getting food, Hoover headed the American Relief Committee which distributed 34 million tons of American food to the starving country. Through four years of war, the Hoover group fed 11 million people in Belgium and northern France. When the United States declared war on Germany on April 6, 1917, President Wilson called Herbert Hoover home to take charge of food organization in America. Hoover exhorted the nation to observe wheatless and meatless days to conserve food for the war effort.

Having supported Warren G. Harding for president in 1920, Hoover was appointed secretary of commerce and stayed in that position during President Calvin Coolidge's administration. The Republican Party nominated Herbert Hoover for president in 1928, and in the election he defeated the Democratic Party's nominee, Alfred E. Smith. Hoover was defeated for reelection in 1932, losing a bitter contest to Democrat Franklin D. Roosevelt.

After the election, Hoover retired to his home in Palo Alto, California. Throughout the years he kept a strong interest in government activities. Herbert Hoover died on October 20, 1964, in New York City, following a long illness.

Bibliography

Hoover, Herbert. *The Memoirs of Herbert Hoover: Years of Adventure, 1874–1920.* New York: Macmillan, 1952.

_____. *On Growing Up.* New York: William Morrow, 1962.

Lyons, Eugene. *Herbert Hoover: A Biography.* Garden City, N.Y.: Doubleday, 1964.

★ 32 ★

Franklin D. Roosevelt

Thirty-second President
1933–1945

Until he was 14 years old, Franklin Delano Roosevelt had never attended school. He had been taught at home by governesses and tutors. Growing up as the only child of loving and doting rich parents, Franklin's childhood was filled with all the comforts that money could buy.

His parents were James Roosevelt, a lawyer and financier of Hyde Park, New York. His mother was Sara Delano Roosevelt, the daughter of a Newburgh, New York, sea captain who made his fortune in trade with China. James was a widower when he married Sara. She was 26; he was 52 and had a son as old as she. When their son was born on January 30, 1882, the happy father wrote, "At quarter till nine my Sallie had a splendid large baby boy. He weighs 10 lbs., without clothes."

Franklin Delano Roosevelt was born in a two-story home called Springwood, the center of activities on the 60 acres of farmland that his father owned in Hyde Park. The home was located on magnificent grounds that overlooked the Hudson River. During his lifetime, Franklin would spend as much time as possible at his historic home.

Franklin's adoring, strong-willed mother dominated his upbringing and supervised every detail of his daily life. Even when he became an adult, she attempted to meddle in his work. She taught him how to read and write before he was six. Then he was educated by tutors who instructed him in Latin, French, German, history, geography, science, and arithmetic. He was also given lessons in drawing, and for several years, piano.

The tutors went along whenever the Roosevelts traveled abroad. Franklin's first voyage abroad was at age three. Before he was 15, Franklin had accompanied his parents on eight European trips, each of several months' duration. During the summer, he would enjoy the pleasant surroundings of the summer home his father had built on Campobello Island, Canada, in the Bay of Fundy off the coast of Maine.

Franklin's early childhood was rather regimented. He would arise at seven, eat breakfast at eight, and have his lessons from nine to twelve. Lunch was a one o'clock, followed by more studies. Sara let his hair grow so she could enjoy his blond curls, and she had him wear dresses long after he had outgrown babyhood. He was almost eight before he was permitted to wear long pants. Once she wanted him to wear Scottish kilts, but he balked, calling them "skirts." They struck a compromise; he would wear sailor suits, she recalled in her book, *My Boy, Franklin*, written after her son became president. Franklin usually did what his mother told him to do, but at times he would try to get his own way without rebelling openly. When he wanted to skip a piano lesson, he told his music teacher that his hand hurt. Having a big headache was an excuse for not attending church services, or for skipping a day of home schooling.

As a boy, Franklin's social world was limited to his home in Hyde Park, where he kept company with grown-ups—his parents, relatives and business associates of his father. Most of the kids he played with were children of his father's friends or rich neighbors. His mother did not allow him to mingle with other children in Hyde Park.

James Roosevelt was a devoted father, whom young Franklin affectionately called "Popsie." The elder Roosevelt took great interest in nature and transmitted this interest to his son. Franklin learned to identify and care for the various trees on the Hyde Park estate. He learned how to recognize the various birds of the area, and to make a collection of them.

While staying at the summer cottage on Campobello Island, Franklin learned to sail his father's cutter, the *Half Moon*, and during the winters when the Hudson River was frozen solidly from shore to shore, Franklin gleefully enjoyed skating and sailboating on the river.

From his mother, Franklin learned about the seafaring exploits of his

Delano relatives. At the age of eight, with her mother and other family members, Sara Delano had sailed to Hong Kong on one of her father's clipper ships. Her stories stirred his interest in nautical subjects, and he began collecting books on naval history. As a girl, Franklin's mother had collected stamps of foreign countries. She gave Franklin her collection when he was ten years old. He then began his own stamp collection that would absorb him throughout his life.

In the fall of 1896, Franklin Roosevelt left the comforts of Hyde Park to enter the Groton School for Boys at Groton, about 35 miles north of Boston, Massachusetts. This was his first experience of living and studying with a large group of boys away from home. A boy was suppose to enter Groton at the age of 12, but Franklin entered when he was 14. His mother kept him at home, partly because she couldn't bear to part with him and partly because she thought a boy of 12 was too young to be sent away from home.

Franklin D. Roosevelt, photograph taken 1895 (Franklin D. Roosevelt Library).

Franklin had no problems with getting adjusted to his new life. At Groton, each boy had a small room partitioned off from the others by a curtain, which opened to a common corridor. The students' day began at seven, when they took a cold shower. They marched to breakfast and to morning chapel services conducted by the school's headmaster, an Episcopal minister. Their classes included Greek, French, algebra, literature, and religious studies until three, with a break at noon for the main meal of the day.

At three o'clock in the afternoon, the boys were required to participate in sports events. Franklin tried his luck in several sports, including baseball and football, and track and field events. He was a good mixer and made many friends; some of them served with him in his adult political career. After supper, the students attended chapel services, then studied alone. At ten o'clock the boys walked in line to the headmaster's cottage, where they shook his hand and wished him good night.

At commencement in June 1900, Franklin won the all-school Latin prize. He also was cited for "punctuality" and "neatness."

With his love for sea lore and a desire to follow in the footsteps of his seagoing Delano relatives, Franklin wanted to attend the U.S. Naval Academy at Annapolis, Maryland, after he graduated from Groton. His father took a dim view of a naval career for his son, noting that he would have better career opportunities if he attended Harvard University. James Roosevelt had gone to Union College in Schenectady, New York, and had completed his education at Harvard Law School. He wanted his son to go to Harvard, earn his degree, then stay there and study law.

The eager son did not go against his aging father's wishes. In September 1900, 18-year-old Franklin D. Roosevelt arrived at Cambridge, Massachusetts, to begin his studies as a freshman at Harvard University. Franklin majored in history and government, with English and public speaking as minors. Franklin was not a great student. Classes bored him and as a result his grades were usually C's. His favorite activity was as editor of the *Harvard Crimson*, the university's newspaper. He graduated in June 1904.

During Franklin's freshman year, his father died. James Roosevelt, who was 72, bequeathed to his son an annual income of $6,000. His mother received Springwood and the rest of the estate.

While attending Harvard, Franklin became engaged to his fifth cousin, Anna Eleanor Roosevelt. They married in New York City on March 17, 1905. Her father being dead, President Theodore Roosevelt gave his niece away. Franklin's mother was unhappy about their marriage and interfered in their housekeeping matters for years.

After graduating from Harvard, Roosevelt attended the law school at Columbia University, New York. He was a poor student who appeared to have little interest in the law. His grades ranged from B to F. While be became eligible to complete the requirements for a law degree, he quit the school in the spring of 1907 after taking and passing the New York state bar examination. He then took an unpaid job with the Wall Street firm of Carter, Leyard, and Milburn. He would receive basic entry pay after a year of apprenticeship. Much of the firm's practice was in corporate law. Roosevelt found the work tedious, and again quit his job. By 1910 he was 28 years old, restless, and unfulfilled.

Franklin Roosevelt wanted to enter politics. The Democratic Party supported him, and he was elected to serve as a New York state senator from 1911 to 1913. As an early supporter of President Woodrow Wilson for the 1912 Democratic presidential nomination, Roosevelt was rewarded with the appointment of assistant secretary of the Navy in 1914.

In 1920, Roosevelt was nominated as the Democratic candidate for vice president on a ticket with James Cox. Although they did not win, Roosevelt's spirited campaigning won him a strong following in the Democratic Party. While vacationing at Campobello Island in the summer of 1921, Roosevelt contracted poliomyelitis. Despite courageous efforts to overcome his crippling illness, he never regained the use of his legs.

After serving as governor of New York from 1929 to 1933, Roosevelt won the Democratic nomination for president in 1932. In the November election, he soundly defeated Republican Herbert Hoover to become the thirty-second president. He was reelected three times, becoming the first U.S. president to serve four consecutive terms.

When the Japanese attacked Pearl Harbor on December 7, 1941, Roosevelt directed organization of the nation's manpower and resources for a global war. As the war drew to an end, Roosevelt's health deteriorated, and on April 12, 1945, while in Warm Springs, Georgia, he died of a cerebral hemorrhage. Franklin D. Roosevelt is buried in the garden of his home at Hyde Park.

Bibliography

Devaney, John. *Franklin Delano Roosevelt, President.* New York: Walker, 1987.

Freedman, Russell. *Franklin Delano Roosevelt.* New York: Clarion Books, 1990.

Hickok, Lorena A. *The Road to the White House: FDR, the Pre-Presidential Years.* New York: Scholastic Book Services, 1962.

Israel, Fred L. *Franklin Delano Roosevelt.* New York: Chelsea House, 1985.

Morgan, Ted. *FDR: A Biography.* New York: Simon & Schuster, 1985.

Weingast, David E. *Franklin D. Roosevelt: Man of Destiny.* New York: Julian Messner, 1952.

★ 33 ★

Harry S. Truman

Thirty-third President
1945–1953

When biographer Merle Miller asked President Harry S. Truman about his childhood, he cheerfully answered, "I had just about the happiest childhood that could be imagined." Harry Truman did have a happy childhood, but it wasn't all fun and play. The future president, whose father was a mule trader, worked hard alongside his father on the family farm.

Harry S. Truman was born on May 8, 1884, in the farm village of Lamar, Missouri, 120 miles south of Kansas City. His parents, John Anderson Truman and Martha Ellen Young Truman, named him Harry after his uncle, Harrison Young. The middle initial, S, would represent both of his grandfathers, Anderson Shippe Truman and Solomon Young. (His name sometimes appears with no period after the S but Harry himself preferred the "S." form.) To celebrate Harry's birth, his father planted a pine seedling in his front yard.

John Anderson Truman was a small man but a feisty one who, in his younger days would not hesitate to fight bigger men. His temper did not extend to his family, whom he treated with kindness and respect. While he prospered as a farmer and livestock trader, he suffered large losses when he speculated in commodities futures in 1901.

Harry's mother, Martha Ellen Young Truman, had studied art and music at the Baptist Female School in Lexington, Missouri, before her marriage.

She taught Harry to read and write by the age of five, and instilled in him a lifelong appreciation for books. Harry was the oldest of three Truman children. His brother, John Vivian, was born in 1884, and his sister, Mary Jane, in 1889. His brother was always referred to as Vivian, not John.

The Truman family moved from Lamar in 1885 and took up residence in several other towns. In 1887, John Truman moved his family to Grandview, Missouri, where they lived on the farm owned by Harry's maternal grandfather, Solomon Young. Harry had two pet animals—a Maltese gray cat named Bob and a little dog named Tandy because of his black-and-tan color. The two animals followed Harry and Vivian everywhere they went on the farm.

Bob, the cat, got his name after a freak accident. The cat was asleep in front of the fireplace when a piece of coal popped out and lit the end of the cat's tail, burning off about one inch of it. Now looking like a stubby-tailed bobcat, Harry's cat was aptly named Bob.

His father bought him a black Shetland pony and a little saddle. They would ride together over the farm, the father on his big horse and the son on his pony. One day as the two riders approached the farmhouse, Harry fell off the pony and had to walk about a half a mile to the house. John Truman told his son that a boy who was not able to stay on a pony at a walk ought to walk himself. Recalling that incident many years later, Truman said. "Mamma thought I was badly mistreated but I wasn't, in spite of my crying all the way to the house, I learned a lesson."

On the Fourth of July, 1889, the Truman family attended Independence Day celebrations in Grandview. The day ended with a series of fireworks, sizzling rockets that exploded clusters of stars into the sky. Harry jumped when the rockets exploded, but he couldn't see the shiny showers of the fireworks. His mother had for some time worried about Harry's eyesight, noting that when she pointed out distant objects, such as a horse and wagon coming down the road, or calling attention to a cow or horse at the end of the pasture, Harry did not see them.

Martha Truman decided to take her son to an eye doctor. While her husband was away on business, she hitched up a team of horses to a wagon and drove 15 miles to Kansas City to have Harry examined by an ophthalmologist. The doctor diagnosed Harry as having "flat eyeballs," nearsightedness of an unusual sort, and prescribed a pair of thick glasses. The boy was ordered to avoid playing sports and rough games to keep the glasses from breaking and injuring his eyes.

In December 1890, when Harry was six, the Truman family moved to Independence, Missouri, because his mother was eager for her children to be educated in a good school. His father bought a large house on South Chrisler Street with several acres of land. At the same time, he was operating a farm southeast of the city, and restarted his livestock trading business.

The Truman house in Independence had a special attraction. It was lighted by gas, the first time the Trumans had experienced such modern convenience. In 1896, John Truman sold the house and bought a larger home located on Waldo Street.

In his memoirs, Harry Truman wrote about a happy event from his days at the Chrisler Street home. In the fall of 1892 Grover Cleveland was reelected president, defeating Benjamin Harrison, who had beaten Cleveland in 1888. Harry's father was very much elated by Cleveland's victory. To celebrate Cleveland's win, John Truman rode his beautiful gray horse in a torchlight parade and decorated the weather wane—a gilded rooster—on the corner of the house with a flag and bunting. Harry's first participation in any major political activity took place in 1900, when he worked as a page at the Democratic national convention in Kansas City.

Having been taught at home by his mother, Harry Truman was well prepared for entering the public school system. He entered his first elementary school, the Noland School, in 1893. He was a good student. His first term grades included 95 in spelling, 96 in reading, 92 in writing, 99 in language, 90 in arithmetic, and 95 in deportment.

In January 1894, during his second year at Noland School, Harry and his brother Vivian had bad cases of diphtheria. There were no antitoxins in those days, so the brothers were given ipecac

Harry S. Truman at age 13, 1897 (Harry S. Truman Library).

syrup and whiskey. "I hated the smell of both ever since," Harry would recall in his memoirs. Vivian made a rapid recovery from the illness, but Harry had difficulties. His legs, arms, and throat were paralyzed for some months.

After attending the Noland and Columbian grade schools in Independence, Harry Truman attended Independence High School, from which he graduated in May 1901. He was a hardworking though not brilliant student whose favorite subject was history. "Reading history, to me, was more than a romantic adventure. It was solid instruction and wise teaching which I somehow felt that I wanted and needed," Truman wrote in his memoirs. "Even as a youth I felt that I ought to know the facts about the system of government under which I was living, and how it came to be.... I know of no surer way to get a solid foundation in political science and public administration than to study the histories of past administrations of the world's most successful system of government."

In 1898, the Truman family bought an upright piano, which his talented mother taught Harry to play. Later he studied with Mrs. E.C. White in Kansas City. She had studied music in Vienna. Once she took Harry to a concert by Ignace Paderewski. After the concert she introduced Harry to the famed pianist, who spent 15 minutes giving him instructions on how to play the maestro's *Minuet in G.*

During his last year at Independence High School, Harry worked with three other students to publish a school magazine called *The Gleam*, after Alfred Tennyson's poem, *Merlin and the Gleam*. One of the students was Charlie Ross, who later became President Truman's press secretary in the White House.

After school Harry spent a great deal of time in the Independence Public Library, which was in the high school building. In later years he would claim that he had read all the books in the library before he graduated from high school. His mother provided him with more reading material when she bought a four volume set of biographical sketches of famous people from a door-to-door salesman.

Harry's first paying job was opening a drugstore in Independence at 6:30 in the morning. Harry had to mop the floor, sweep the sidewalk, and have medicine bottles and other items ready for the customers. His first week's wages were three silver dollars.

In the fall of 1901, after graduating from high school, Harry enrolled in the Spaulding Commercial College in Kansas City. He took a year of instruction in bookkeeping, shorthand, and typing. He commuted daily from Independence to Kansas City by streetcar.

During his studies at the Spaulding college, it became clear to Harry Truman that he was not going to get a real college education since his father had lost a great amount of money speculating in grain futures. He then tried to obtain an appointment to a military academy, West Point or Annapolis, but was turned down because of his poor eyesight.

Harry's first paying job after he graduated from high school was as time-keeper for a railroad construction contractor, who was building a double track for the Santa Fe Railroad from Eton to Sheffield, a suburb of Kansas City. Harry worked ten hours a day for $35 a month and board. He kept the job until the contract was finished, living in railroad tent camps along the Missouri River where the Santa Fe ran. He then worked briefly in the mailing room of the *Kansas City Star*, stuffing one section of the newspaper into another as fast as possible then stacking the papers and tying them together in bundles for shipping. He earned seven dollars a week at the *Star*.

When his father moved to Kansas City, Harry took a job with the National Bank of Commerce, where he handled the transit checks that came through the bank as a clearinghouse. The job paid $35 a month, but soon he was promoted to personal filing clerk for the president and cashier of the bank at a salary of $40 per month. Another move came when he went to the Union National Bank for $60 a month as a bookkeeper. By 1905 Truman was getting $100 a month.

In 1904 Harry's father moved back to Grandview to work the farm of Solomon Young. In 1906 Harry quit his bank job and joined his father in Grandview. He continued doing farmwork until 1917, when he was ordered to fulfill his National Guard duties. Truman had joined the Missouri National Guard in 1905. At the outbreak of World War I, he helped organize the 2nd Regiment of Missouri Field Artillery, which was quickly called into federal service as the 129th Field Artillery and sent to France. Truman was promoted to captain and given command of the regiment's battery D. His unit saw action in several important battle areas.

Once discharged from the army, Truman returned to Independence on some important business: to claim the hand of his childhood sweetheart, Bess Wallace. They were married in Independence on June 28, 1919.

Later, Truman returned to Kansas City, where he and a wartime buddy ran a men's clothing store. The store failed in the postwar recession. Truman was elected in 1922 to be one of three judges of the Jackson County Court in Kansas. His duties were administrative rather than judicial, and he built a reputation for honest and efficiency in the management of the county affairs.

In 1934, Truman was elected to the United States Senate, and in July 1944, he was nominated to run for vice president with President Franklin D. Roosevelt. On January 20, 1945, he took the vice presidential oath, and after President Roosevelt's death only 82 days later on April 12, 1945, he was sworn in as the thirty-third president.

As president, Truman made some of the most crucial decisions in history. Soon after allied victory in Europe during World War II, Truman ordered the dropping of two atomic bombs on Japan, forcing Japan to surrender on August 14, 1945. In 1948, Truman won reelection. He left the presidency and retired to Independence in January 1953. Harry S. Truman died on December 26, 1972.

Bibliography

Farley, Karin Clafford. *Harry S. Truman: The Man from Independence.* Englewood Cliffs, N.J.: Julian Messner, 1989.

Ferrell, Robert H. *Harry S. Truman: A Life.* Columbia: University of Missouri Press, 1994.

_____, ed. *The Autobiography of Harry S. Truman.* Boulder, Colorado: Colorado Associated University Press, 1980.

Hamby, Alonzo L. *Man of the People: A Life of Harry S. Truman.* New York: Oxford University Press, 1995.

Miller, Merle. *Plain Speaking: An Oral Biography of Harry S. Truman.* New York: Berkley Publishing, 1973.

Truman, Harry S. *Memoirs by Harry S. Truman: Year of Decisions*, Vol. 1. Garden City, N.Y.: Doubleday, 1955.

★ 34 ★

Dwight D. Eisenhower

Thirty-fourth President
1953–1961

When Dwight David Eisenhower graduated from Abilene High School (Texas) in 1909, the class prophecy predicted that he would "wind up as a professor of history at Yale." Eisenhower didn't make it to Yale, but he did become president of Columbia University after leading allied forces to victory over Germany in World War II. Young Eisenhower was not only greatly interested in history, but went on to make history himself, including becoming the thirty-fourth president of the United States.

Dwight David Eisenhower was born on October 14, 1890, in a modest two-story house his parents had rented in Denison, Texas. His father, David Jacob Eisenhower, was then working for a railroad as an engine viper. His mother, Ida Elizabeth Stover Eisenhower, was a deeply religious woman who ran a tightly organized household for her large family. The parents had met when they were both students at the Lane University, a church-supported school in Kansas.

Dwight David was the third of seven sons born to the Eisenhowers; one had died in infancy. They had no daughters. He was originally named David Dwight, and was never known as David. His mother decided that he should be referred to as Dwight to avoid any confusion with his father's name and make sure that nobody called her son Dave. She hated the use of nicknames, even when her son became known throughout the world as "Ike."

Dwight Eisenhower's parents worked hard to provide for their growing family. They belonged to the River Brethren faith, a fundamentalist Christian sect. The Eisenhower family conducted daily prayers and Bible readings, which the boys were required to attend.

In the spring of 1891, after he failed in business, David Eisenhower's father arranged for him to get a job as a mechanic at the Belle Springs Creamery in Abilene. The creamery was owned by the River Brethrens. David Eisenhower then rented a small house, which had a garden that enabled the family to grow vegetables. In 1898, David Eisenhower purchased a larger house with three acres of land and a large barn. The Eisenhowers raised almost all their own food, selling surplus for cash.

Work was a necessary and natural fact for Dwight Eisenhower and his brothers. To encourage the boys to take on work loads, their father allotted each boy a bit of ground on the land surrounding the family's homes. Each could raise any kind of vegetable he chose and to sell them. Dwight chose to grow sweet corn and cucumbers. He had made inquiries and decided that these were the most popular vegetables.

Each morning before school, the boys had certain chores to perform, such as milking cows, feeding chickens and horses, and cleaning the stalls and chicken houses. When Dwight grew older, he worked nights at the Belle Springs Creamery, pulling ice from the delivery dock, firing up the coal burning boilers, and other jobs assigned to him.

David and Ida Eisenhower were against quarreling and fighting, and they deplored bad manners. Nevertheless, the six Eisenhower boys often fought among themselves, and they were always ready to take on any outsiders who dared to challenge any of the brothers. Dwight had a temper when he was young, but he learned to control it as he grew older.

When Dwight was ten years old, his mother gave permission to Arthur and Edgar, the oldest Eisenhower boys, to go out with a group for Halloween trick or treating. Dwight became quite upset when his father and mother told him that he was too young to go along. Dwight threw a tantrum, ran out into the yard, and attacked an apple tree, hitting it until his fists were raw and bloody, screaming in anger. His father grabbed him and shook him back into consciousness, then spanked him and ordered him to bed.

Later his mother came into his bedroom, wiped the dirt from his bruised hands, applied some salve and wrapped them in bandages. She talked about temper and how easy it is to lose one's temper sometimes, but it was never right to hate anyone. Years later, Dwight Eisenhower would remember that conversation "as one of the most valuable moments in my life."

Dwight began his education when he first attended the Lincoln elementary school, located directly across the street from his home, in grades one through six. Next he attended the Garfield school for grades seven and eight and Abilene High School, which he entered in September 1904.

High school studies came easy to Dwight. He earned the equivalent of an A in English, history and geometry. In composition, algebra, and physical geography his grades were somewhat lower. His favorite subject was history, especially ancient military history. His first military hero was Hannibal. When he began studying American history, George Washington excited his imagination. He admired Washington's stamina and patience in adversity, and his courage and daring.

During his first semester Dwight nearly lost a leg. Playing one evening with some of his friends, he fell and scraped one knee. There was no bleeding, only a raw, red spot on his knee. There was no ill effect, and he went to school the next day. The following day he became ill with high fever and lost consciousness. A doctor determined that Dwight had developed blood poisoning, and when treatment failed to heal the damaged knee, the doctor recommended amputation.

When Dwight, in a semi-conscious state, heard of the doctor's recommendation, he pleaded with his brother Edgar to make sure that under no circumstances would his leg be amputated. After consulting with another physician, his doctor decided that the leg could be saved by painting a belt of carbolic acid around Dwight's body. The process of the disease was stopped, but he remained seriously ill for so long that he stayed out of school the rest of the spring and had to repeat that school year. The result was that he did not graduate until 1909.

While attending Abilene High School, Dwight Eisenhower played both baseball and football. He played center field on the baseball team and was viewed as a heavy hitter. On the football team, Dwight, at 140 pounds, played right end on offense and wherever he was needed in defensive positions.

Abeline school officials took little interest in athletics, leaving the matter to student initiatives. So Dwight and his friends organized the Abilene High School Athletic Association to promote sports and encourage the citizenry to support school teams. In his senior year he was elected president of the association.

Throughout his high school years, Dwight worked at odd jobs. Upon graduation from Abeline High School, he went to work full time as the second engineer at the creamery's ice plant. He felt his salary was "impressive"—90 dollars a month. Dwight might have stayed with that job for a long time, had it not been for a new challenge set forth by Everett "Swede" Hazlett, a school chum from the days they attended the Garfield grade school in Abeline.

A son of a doctor, Hazlett had attended a private military school in Wisconsin and had done well enough to secure a congressional appointment to the Naval Academy in Annapolis, Md. He urged Dwight to apply for an Annapolis appointment. Dwight Eisenhower jumped at the opportunity with gusto. "It was not difficult to persuade me that this was a good move—first, because of my long interest in military history, and secondly, because I realized

Dwight D. Eisenhower, Abilene High School graduate (Dwight D. Eisenhower Library).

that my own college education would not be achieved without considerable delay while I tried to accumulate money," he wrote in his memoirs.

In October 1910, he participated in a competitive examination for aspirants to West Point and Annapolis. He received an overall score of 87.5, which was good enough for him to place second among eight candidates. Dwight then learned that at age 20 he would be too old to enter the Naval Academy. When Senator Joseph Bristow offered him an appointment to the U.S. Military Academy at West Point, N.Y., Dwight gladly accepted the offer, telling his buddy Swede Hazzlet that he could not "look a gift horse in the mouth." While Dwight was happy about getting the appointment to West Point, his pacifist parents were not, but they did not try to prevent him from going.

Dwight D. Eisenhower entered the U.S. Military Academy on June 14, 1911. He was an above average student whose first love was athletics. When a knee injury ended his football career, he almost dropped out. Encouraged by his classmates to continue, Eisenhower graduated in the top third of his class and was commissioned an infantry officer with the class of 1915. He was a lieutenant in the army when he married Mary "Mamie" Geneva Doud in Denver, Colorado, in 1916.

During his early Army career, he excelled in staff assignments, and after the Japanese attack on Pearl Harbor, General George Marshall called him to Washington for a war plans assignment. He commanded the Allied Forces' landing in North Africa in November 1942; on D-Day, June 6, 1944, he led the invasion of France that led to the final phase of the European war. Germany surrendered 11 months later in May 1945.

After the war, Eisenhower became president of Columbia University, then took leave to assume supreme command over the new NATO forces being assembled in 1951. In 1952, the Republican Party nominated him for president, and he defeated the Democratic candidate, Adlai E. Stevenson, receiving 55 percent of the popular vote. He was reelected in the 1956 election, again defeating Democrat Stevenson.

During his presidency, Eisenhower concentrated on maintaining world peace. Before he left office in January 1961, he espoused the necessity of maintaining adequate military strength, but cautioned that vast, long-continued military expenditures could breed potential danger to the American way of life. Eisenhower died, after a long illness, on March 28, 1969.

Bibliography

Ambrose, Stephen E. *Eisenhower: Soldier, General of the Army, President-elect, 1890–1952.* Vol. 1. New York: Simon & Schuster, 1983.

D'Este, Carlo. *Eisenhower: A Soldier's Life.* New York: Henry Holt, 2002.

Eisenhower, Dwight D. *In Review: Pictures I've Kept.* Garden City, N.Y.: Doubleday, 1969.

Morin, Relman. *Dwight D. Eisenhower: A Gauge of Greatness.* New York: Simon & Schuster, 1969.

Perret, Geoffrey. *Eisenhower.* New York: Random House, 1999.

John F. Kennedy

Thirty-fifth President
1961–1963

John F. Kennedy was not a very good student in school. He did not always pay attention to the teachers. John was never very healthy, always suffering from one ailment or another. Yet, he was fiercely competitive, always seeking to outdo his older and stronger brother Joseph, who bested him in friendly family contests.

The competitive spirit was driven into him by his father, Joseph P. Kennedy, who held his children to high standards and expected them to put forth their best in every game and endeavor. Loser received no praise, not even sympathy. To do less than one's best was a disgrace.

John Fitzgerald Kennedy was born May 29, 1917, at 83 Beals Street in Brookline, a suburb of Boston, Mass. (The home is now a historic site administered by the National Park Service.) His parents were Joseph Patrick Kennedy, a multimillionaire businessman, and Rose Fitzgerald Kennedy, an activist for charitable causes who devoted herself to raising a family of nine children. John, her second son, was named after her father, John Francis Fitzgerald, a colorful Boston politician nicknamed "Honey Fitz." Young John was usually referred to as Jack by family members and friends.

Joseph P. Kennedy saw politics as a means of attaining great success. As architect of his children's lives, he decided that his first son, Joseph, Jr., would become a politician and eventually the president of the United States. When Joseph, Jr. was killed in July 1944 while flying a Navy plane across the British Channel, this task was then transferred to the second son, John F. Kennedy.

Although the Kennedys were wealthy parents, they did not spoil their children with money. Their allowances were modest, never any more than those of the neighborhood children. The parents wanted the children to know the value of money and not to spend it foolishly. The children's initial allowance was 10 cents a week. When John Kennedy was ten years old, his allowance went up to 40 cents a week. The parents were determined that their children understood the value of money and the importance of earning it through dignified work.

While Joseph Kennedy, Sr., impressed upon his children the importance of working hard to earn money and to invest it wisely, he generously provided for their future by setting up a million dollar trust fund for each one when they reached age 21. Each child would also receive an additional one thousand dollars if they did not take up smoking before they were 21; another thousand dollars if they refrained from drinking. The "overwhelmingly" favorite drink in the Kennedy household was milk, Rose Kennedy noted in her memoirs.

John's Kennedy's schooling began in 1921 after the growing Kennedy family moved to a larger, three-story home in Brookline. While living there, John and his elder brother Joseph, Jr., attended the Edward Devotion School, then the Lower Noble and Greenough School, which later became the Dexter School.

At Dexter, a private all-male school in Brookline, the Kennedy boys learned the harshness of snobbery and prejudice. Most of their classmates were Protestants and at times they would taunt the Kennedy brothers for being Irish and Catholics. The ethnic slurs usually resulted in fist fights, in which the Kennedy brothers displayed their superior fighting talent.

John and Joseph Kennedy could be quite combative when playing with each other. Once when racing with their bicycles they crashed head-on. Joseph emerged unscathed, but John had to have 28 stitches to mend his cuts and bruises.

The teaching staff at Dexter worked hard to uphold the school's motto, "Today our best, tomorrow better." The teachers drilled the students in mathematics, English, and history, which was John Kennedy's favorite subject. The students were also taught the art of effective public speaking by reciting notable parts of famous speeches and excerpts from the writings of well-known authors.

John F. Kennedy at about eight years old, circa 1925 (John Fitzgerald Kennedy Library).

In the fall of 1927, the Kennedy family moved from Brookline to Riverdale, New York City, just north of Manhattan. Here John attended the Riverdale Country Day School in fourth through sixth grades. He did reasonably well, receiving a B average for his studies. In the sixth grade, he got a 97 in history and won the school's essay contest.

In the fall of 1930, 13-year-old John Kennedy left home for the first time to join the ranks of boarding school students. He enrolled in the Canterbury School, a Catholic college preparatory school in New Milford, Connecticut. While John was homesick at first, he did well scholastically, receiving good marks in English, although his spelling was bad and his paragraphing clumsy. While he struggled with Latin, he did well in other subjects, especially history. He kept up with current events and asked his father to send him the *Literary Digest*, a political magazine of the early thirties.

During the spring term in May 1931 John Kennedy was stricken with appendicitis. His appendix was removed in a hospital in Danbury, Connecticut. He did not return to school after the operation, spending the summer recovering at the family's new large home at Hyannisport, Cape Cod, Massachusetts.

While John recuperated at Hyannisport, his parents hired a tutor to help him prepare for the entrance examinations for the Choate School, a college preparatory school in Wallingford, Connecticut. In the fall of 1931, John joined his brother Joseph, Jr. at Choate.

Joseph, Jr., was two years ahead of John at Choate. He was an excellent student and a top athlete, a very popular man on the campus. John, although lighter and smaller, played with tiger-like ferocity against his competitors in intramural sports.

John Kennedy's time at Choate was marked with health problems and poor work habits that often got him in trouble with his teachers. One teacher complained that he paid little attention to his study assignments, and that he failed to bring his books, pencils, and paper. He did poorly in Latin, biology, and chemistry, but received above average grades in English and history. He bought *The New York Times* in order to keep up with important economic and political events. John F. Kennedy graduated from the Choate School in 1935 when he was 18. Scholastically he ranked 64th in a class of 112.

To the surprise and disappointment of his father, John Kennedy chose not to go to his father's alma mater, Harvard College, but to Princeton University in New Jersey. His father accepted the decision, but suggested that

John first study under socialist economist Harold Laski at the London School of Economics in London, England. Joseph P. Kennedy was not a supporter of socialism, but he wanted John to learn from the famed liberal thinker.

Obediently, John sailed for England in early 1935, but soon after arriving, he came down with jaundice, a liver ailment, and had to return home. After spending months recuperating he entered Princeton University, only to be struck down again by jaundice. When he recovered from his illness, he dropped the idea of attending Princeton University, opting instead to enroll at Harvard University in Cambridge, Massachusetts, as a freshman in the fall of 1936.

When he entered Harvard, his primary interests was sports; studies were secondary. He went out for football, golf, and swimming. During a hard football scrimmage, he suffered a back injury, a ruptured disc, which would plague him for the rest of his life. Harvard professors found John Kennedy to be a bright student, but his grades were seldom higher than C in his first two years. He majored in political science with emphasis on international relations. When his father was appointed ambassador to Britain's Court of St. James's in 1938, John asked Harvard to let him to spend his spring semester of 1939 overseas, working on a fact-finding tour for his father. This request was granted, and he spent several months checking trouble spots throughout Europe. John was in Europe at the outbreak of World War II, which began on September 1, 1939.

The events in Europe had sharpened his intellectual interest. He returned to Harvard a more serious student. His grades improved, and he used his observations from the European work on behalf of his father to write his thesis, which later became the basis for the best-selling book *Why England Slept*. It was his explanation of the inaction of democratic nations in the face of the early threats of war from Nazi Germany. The book sold 80,000 copies in the United States and England. He graduated from Harvard cum laude in 1940.

After Harvard, Kennedy spent some months studying at the Stanford University Graduate School of Business in California, and visiting several countries in Latin America. In October 1941, shortly before the United States became a combatant in World War II, Kennedy was appointed an ensign in the U.S. Naval Reserve. In January 1943, then a lieutenant, junior grade, he was assigned to a motor torpedo boat squadron. On August 2, 1943, the boat he commanded—PT 109—was rammed and sunk by a Japanese destroyer near the Solomon Islands. Kennedy performed heroically in rescuing his crew, but aggravated his old back injury and contracted malaria. He was discharged from the Navy in early 1945.

After the war, he became interested in politics and, in 1946, as a Democrat, won a seat in the U.S. House of Representatives, serving the constituents of Massachusetts's eleventh district. After serving as a U.S. representative from 1947 to 1953, Kennedy was elected to the U.S. Senate, serving there from 1953 to 1961.

It was during his term in the Senate that he married Jacqueline L. Bouvier on September 12, 1953.

In 1960, as the Democratic Party's presidential nominee he went on to defeat Republican candidate Richard M. Nixon. John F. Kennedy was sworn in as the thirty-fifth president of the United States on January 20, 1961. His inaugural address offered this memorable statement: "Ask not what your country can do for you—ask what you can do for your country."

On November 22, 1963, while riding in an automobile procession during a reelection campaign tour in Dallas, Texas, John F. Kennedy was shot and killed by a gun fired by an assassin. Kennedy was buried at the Arlington National Cemetery.

Bibliography

Anderson, Lois E. *John Kennedy*. Stamford, Conn.: Longmeadow Press, 1992.

Carr, William H. A. *JFK: A Complete Biography, 1917–1963*. New York: Lancer Books, 1968.

Cooper, Ilene. *Jack: The Early Years*. New York: Dutton Children's Books, 2003.

Kennedy, Rose Fitzgerald. *Times to Remember*. Garden City, N.Y.: Doubleday, 1974.

Lee, Bruce. *Boy's Life of John F. Kennedy*. New York: Sterling Publishing, 1965.

Wood, James Playsted. *The Life and Words of John F. Kennedy*. New York: Scholastic Book Services, 1965.

★ 36 ★

Lyndon B. Johnson

Thirty-sixth President
1963–1969

Lyndon B. Johnson was a determined, competitive boy who scratched his way out of near poverty to become the thirty-sixth president of the United States. His parents, although struggling to make a living, had high hopes for their son.

His parents were Sam Ealy Johnson, Jr., a farmer, trader, and politician who was a member of the Texas House of Representatives. His mother, Rebekah Baines Johnson, a graduate of Baylor University, was a former teacher and editor of a small town newspaper.

When the first of their five children was born on August 27, 1908, Sam and Rebekah Johnson lived in a three-room farmhouse on the Pedernales River between Stonewall and Johnson City, Texas. The farmhouse had been the home of Sam's parents before they moved to a larger home in Johnson City, the town that was named after Lyndon's grandfather, Sam Ealy Johnson, Sr., a cattleman who established a ranch on the Pedernales River.

The home of Sam and Rebekah Johnson had no electricity; kerosene lamps were used for illumination and there was no indoor plumbing. Johnson's farming was minimal. He kept some livestock, including a cow, several mules, and a few chickens on his land. He also grew some vegetables.

The baby boy was not given a name until three months had gone by. He was just called "Baby," until one day his mother refused to prepare breakfast for her husband unless he made up his mind to give the child a name. After rejecting several of his suggestions, she agreed to have the child named after her husband's lawyer friend, W. C. Linden, but on the condition that she could change the spelling. She wanted it spelled "Lyndon," with the middle name Baines, after her family name. He agreed and had his breakfast.

Rebekah Johnson was determined that her son was going to be well educated. Lyndon was hardly out of infancy when she began reading him stories and have him learn the alphabet with A-B-C blocks. Lyndon showed himself to be a gifted child. He had learned the alphabet by the time he was two, and by the age of three he could do simple spelling. She read him stories from the Bible, history, and mythology. Fascinated by the tales, he would end each storytelling session with a loud demand: "Is that true, Mama? Did that really happen?"

Later, as he grew older, his father, using a cruder and more direct way of teaching, would shake the boy awake in the morning with a cry, "Son. Get up! Every boy in town has a two-hour start on you."

When Lyndon was four years old his mother took him to the nearby Junction School, where Miss Kate Deadrich taught all the grades from first through seventh. The teacher soon discovered she had a problem child in her classroom. When called upon to read Lyndon would stand still and refuse to read. His mother then suggested that the teacher allow him to sit on her lap while reading. Miss Deadrich tried and the tactic succeeded. The strange reading session ended after three months, when Lyndon contracted whooping cough and had to stay home for the remainder of the school year.

In 1913, when Lyndon was five, the Johnsons moved to a six-room frame house in Johnson City, which had a population of slightly more than 300 people, a bank, a café, and a school. Although Sam had bought her one of the finest houses in town, Rebekah learned that moving to Johnson City was no solution to her problems. She still lacked the amenities of indoor plumbing and electricity that would have made it easier for her to raise her rambunctious and growing family.

In 1913 Lyndon was the youngest student in his grade when he entered his new elementary school in Johnson City. Due to his talent and intelligence, as well as his mother's close supervision of his schoolwork, he received high marks. Although bright, he disliked schoolwork, and was often disciplined for misbehavior. At the end of the first year, the teacher had her best girl and boy student recite a poem to their classmates and parents. The poem Lyndon chose was "I'd Rather Be Mamma's Boy." His selection of the poem reflected the close relationship he had with his mother, although she often irritated him with her close supervision of his schoolwork. Lyndon's relationship with his father was tense. His father was a strict disciplinarian who would show his temper by beating Lyndon with a razor strap.

When Lyndon was a toddler Rebekah Johnson let his curly hair grow long. One Sunday, when she was in church, his father took a large pair of scissors and cut off all of Lyndon's hair. When Lyndon balked at his mother's attempts to have him take violin and dancing lessons, she would ignore him, walking around the house pretending that he was not there.

After the first year in grammar school, Lyndon failed to live up to his capabilities. He had problems with certain subjects, especially arithmetic, and an overwhelming desire to be outdoors instead of in the schoolroom. He liked to call attention to himself by acting as a show-off and a big tease to the girls. To contain his energy, his teacher assigned him special duties such as cleaning the blackboard, removing chalk dust from the erasers, and bringing in firewood.

In 1918, when Lyndon was ten, his father began taking him to the state legislature, where he sat in the gallery watching all the activity on the floor. At times he would come on the House floor, and though not an official page, would run errands for his father and other legislators.

Whenever Lyndon Johnson wanted spending money, he had to earn it. Lyndon found work picking cotton, building fences, and herding goats at farms and ranches nearby. At age ten he operated a shoe shining business.

While all the Johnson children were assigned daily chores by their parents, Lyndon would at times cajole his siblings into doing his duties while he enjoyed playing and hanging out with his buddies. Somehow he believed that he was entitled to the same rights and privileges as his father.

Lyndon's brother Sam Houston Johnson had strong affection for his older brother even though Lyndon would at times refuse to do certain chores around the house, passing them off to his siblings. When he was nine years old, Sam Houston earned $11.20 by shining shoes, sweeping out the church, and working in a restaurant. Lyndon then approached his brother with a business deal. They would form a partnership and use the money to buy a secondhand bicycle. Sam agreed to be the senior partner.

On his first attempt to ride the bike Sam's feet couldn't reach the pedals;

he lost his balance, overturned the bicycle and fell
into a nearby ditch. When
his father learned about
Sam Houston's accident
and the boys' partnership
deal, he became angry
with Lyndon, demanding
that he return the money
to Sam, and admonishing
him never to make any
deals like that again. Sam
had his money returned,
and his father bought him
a new, small bicycle.

As a teenager Lyn-
don developed the ability
to ingratiate himself with
young and old alike. In
high school he often con-
vinced the girls in his class
to do his math and En-
glish homework for him.
He was quite adept in
making older men and
women like him. He vis-

Lyndon B. Johnson wearing cowboy hat, circa 1915 (LBJ Library by unknown photographer).

ited the elderly when they were sick, and often sought out the advice of the
older men.

When Lyndon was 15, he smashed up his father's car. Frightened at what
he had done and too scared to face his father, he ran away to his uncle. His
father tracked him down on the telephone and ordered his son to come home.
The father then told Lyndon that he had bought a new car and wondered if
he could pick it up and drive it home. Then he told Lyndon to drive the car
slowly, at least 50 times, around the courthouse so that people could see who
the driver was.

"You see there's talk around town this morning that my son is a coward,
that he couldn't face up to what he'd done, and that he ran away from home.

Now I don't want anyone thinking I produced a yellow son," father Sam said to Lyndon. "So I want you to show up here in that car and show everyone how much courage you've really got."

In May 1924, Lyndon Johnson graduated from Johnson City High School with more units than he needed for a diploma. He was the president and youngest member of the six member senior class. He was on the school's two-man debating team that won the county title during his final year.

His parents were eager for him to attend college, but he did not share their feeling. Instead he joined with five friends and together they bought a used car and drove to California, where they lived a vagabond life, surviving by picking fruits and vegetables, working in all-night diners, and doing odd jobs wherever they find someone to hire them.

After a year, when his money dried up completely, Lyndon found a clerical job with a Los Angeles lawyer who was a cousin of his mother. There he stayed for another year, until August 1928, when hitchhiked his way back to Texas.

After he came home, he worked briefly with a road construction crew. In 1927, borrowing $75, he enrolled in the Southwest Texas State Teachers College in San Marcos, Texas. He graduated in 1930 and went on to teach at several schools in Pearsall and Houston, Texas. In 1934 he married Claudia Alta "Lady Bird" Taylor.

Johnson quit education to become secretary to Democratic Representative Richard M. Kleberg of Texas during 1931–1934. This was his introduction to national politics. In 1937 he was elected to the House of Representatives. During World War II, he served briefly in the Navy as a lieutenant. After six terms in the House, Johnson was elected to the Senate in 1948.

In the 1960 presidential election campaign, Johnson, as John F. Kennedy's running mate, was elected vice president. On November 22, 1963, when Kennedy was assassinated, Johnson was sworn in as president. After attending the inauguration in 1969 of his successor, Richard M. Nixon, Lyndon Johnson retired to his LBJ ranch in Texas. He died of a heart attack on January 22, 1973.

Bibliography

Dallek, Robert. *Lone Star Rising: Lyndon Johnson and His Times. 1908–1960.* New York: Oxford University Press, 1991.

Johnson, Sam Houston. *My Brother Lyndon.* New York: Cowles Book, 1970.

Kearns, Doris. *Lyndon Johnson and the American Dream.* New York: Harper & Row, 1976.

Steinberg, Alfred. *Sam Johnson's Boy: A Close-up of the President from Texas.* New York: Macmillan, 1968.

Unger, Irwin and Debi. *LBJ: A Life.* New York: John Wiley & Sons, 1999.

★ 37 ★

Richard M. Nixon

Thirty-seventh President
1969–1974

When Richard Nixon was growing up in Yorba Linda, California, the romance of trains—seeing the smoke from their steam engines and hearing the sound of their whistles—made him dream of the far-away places he wanted to visit someday. All through grade school his ambition was to become a railroad engineer. His early hero was a Santa Fe Railroad engineer who lived in his town.

Yorba Linda was a small farming community about 30 miles from Los Angeles. One of the town's farmers was Richard's father, Francis A. "Frank" Nixon, who built the house in which Richard was born on January 13, 1913. The house cost $800 and was assembled from a do-it-yourself house-building kit purchased from the Sears Roebuck department store.

Frank Nixon was a lemon grower at Yorba Linda at the time of Richard's birth. He had held a variety of jobs, including trolley operator with Pacific Electric. He was quick-tempered, loud, demanding, and often argumentative, but he was never heard to have said a cross word to his wife. Richard's mother, Hannah Milhous Nixon, was raised as a devout Quaker, and had been a student at Whittier College, California, before her marriage to Frank Nixon.

The second of five children, Richard had four brothers, Harold, (Francis) Donald, Arthur, and Edward. Arthur died of tuberculosis at the age of seven; Harold would die of the same disease in 1933. The setting in the Nixon household was simple, an ordinary rectangular interior with a living room, kitchen, and small bedroom. The first three boys, Richard, Harold, and Donald, slept in a second bedroom Frank Nixon had added to the rear of the house.

Richard Nixon's first memory of his childhood was an accident which almost killed him. One day in 1916, his mother prepared a horse and buggy to take her sister to the train in Placenta. She had asked a neighbor girl to ride along to help her with Richard while she held on to Donald.

Richard would not sit still. He squirmed away from the his young guardian and stood up in the buggy. As the horse went around a short corner, the boy toppled over, and a wheel ran over his head, cutting his scalp. Blood spurted from a large gash that stretched across the top of his head. His mother held the gash together until they could get to a doctor, who stitched the wound together. To hide the ugly scar, Richard Nixon always parted his hair on the right.

Despite the economic difficulties and emotional tension of the Nixon household, young Richard survived the temper tantrums and leather strap lashings that his father unleashed on his sons. His mother never physically punished the boys; she would talk to them and explain the problems of their transgressions. When Richard came home with handful of grapes he had picked from a neighbor's vine without permission, his mother made him return them and take five cents of his allowance to pay for what he had eaten. When the neighbor at first declined take the money, Richard adamantly demanded that she take the pennies.

Frank and Hannah Nixon were eager for their boys to be educated. Hannah read them poems and stories every night, and she had taught Richard to read when he was five years old. Richard began school in the autumn of 1919, entering the second grade in the Yorba Linda grammar school. Since his mother had taught him how to read at home, he skipped first grade. Shortly after school began, Hannah Nixon visited Richard's teacher and implored her not to call her son Dick. "I named him Richard," she said. She had no use for nicknames, especially for her children.

Richard was an attentive, serious, well-behaved student who received good marks. A quick learner, his ability set him apart from the other students. He skipped second grade and was advanced to third grade. Richard's father taught Sunday school; at the age of five Richard began attending regularly. When he was six, he won a children's recitation contest held at the Quaker church, defeating his older brother Harold and other older children.

Richard took an early interest in reading books and magazines. After homework and chores, Richard would often sit by the fireplace or in the kitchen, immersed in a book or magazine. The Nixons took the *Los Angeles Times, Saturday Evening Post*, and the *Ladies Home Journal*. His aunt Olive and her husband Oscar Marshburn, who lived in nearby Whittier, subscribed to *National Geographic* magazine. Richard would borrow a copy of the magazine whenever he visited them.

When Richard was seven years old, he began taking piano lessons at home after school. His first piano teacher was his uncle, Griffith Milhous, who also taught him the fundamentals of the violin. Later he took six months of piano lessons from his aunt, Jane Beeson, in Lindsay, California. An accomplished musician, she had studied piano at the Metropolitan School of Music in Indianapolis.

In 1919 oil deposits were found near the Nixon home in Yorba Linda. Speculators offered Frank Nixon $45,000 for his property, but he turned them down, hoping to make more money later. The oil boom he had hoped for never happened. When Richard was nine years old his father gave up the lemon grove and opened a gas station and general store in Whittier, about 15 miles north of Yorba Linda. The family residence was above the store. Later they moved to a single family home on East Whittier Boulevard.

Operating the store became a family affair. The boys worked in the store when they were not in school, and Hannah Nixon baked cookies and angel food cakes, which sold for 35 cents apiece. When he became older, Richard helped his father with the fresh fruit and vegetable buying. Each morning they arose at four o'clock, drove to a Los Angeles market and purchased fruits and vegetables. Then they drove back to East Whittier to wash, sort, and arrange the produce in the store. By eight o'clock Richard set off for school. Richard would keep that schedule throughout his high school years and on into college.

In 1926, when Richard was 13 years old, he entered Fullerton High School, where he received high grades in most of his studies. He achieved a high level of competence in English, Latin, history, mathematics, physics and chemistry. He took the nationally used Otis intelligence test in his freshman year, and scored 143 out of 160, far above the norm of 117.

With the aid of his English teacher, Richard honed his skills in debating and public speaking. He was on the school's debating team, and as a sophomore won the Constitutional Oratorical Contest. In 1928, when he transferred to Whittier High School, he continued to excel in debates and public speaking. In the spring of 1929, he entered an area-wide oratorical contest sponsored by the Kiwanis Club. He won the contest for his speech titled "Our Privileges Under the Constitution." Later, in other debating contests, he would successfully use the U.S. Constitution as his theme.

He graduated from Whittier High School in 1930 and was presented the California Interscholastic Federation Gold Seal Award for scholarship and the Harvard Award for being the best all around student. Richard dreamed about going to college in the east, perhaps Harvard or Yale, but that was ruled out because of family expenses and the reduced income his father suffered during the national depression. He had no choice but to live at home and attend a local college.

Richard M. Nixon, senior at Whittier High School, about 17 years old (National Archives and Records Administration).

In September 1930, 17-year-old Richard Nixon enrolled at Whittier College, named after John Greenleaf Whittier, prominent Quaker, poet, and leader in the abolitionist movement. Though it continues to honor its Quaker heritage, the college has been a secular institution since the 1940s.

At Whittier he was a dedicated student, a history major who received good grades. He was very interested in politics. In his freshmen year he was elected to the student council. He was elected president of the student body during his senior year. He ran on a platform of promising "A Dance a Month." The college had banned dancing, but Nixon convinced the administrators that campus dances might keep the students away from second rate dance halls in Los Angeles.

Nixon was a member of the Whittier debating team. During his senior year he won the intercollegiate extemporaneous speaking contest for Southern California. These debates increased his interest in international trade and politics.

He graduated from Whittier College second of 85 students in the class of 1934. He applied for and received a $200 scholarship to the Duke University

Law School in Durham, North Carolina. To keep the scholarship he was required to maintain a B average. During his first year he had an A average so the scholarship was renewed in full. His scholarship covered only tuition, but he was able to supplement his income by working in the law library at 35 cents an hour, under a grant offered by the National Youth Administration. He also received an allowance of $35 a month from his family. Nixon graduated from Duke Law School in 1937, placing third in a class of 35 students. After graduation, Nixon returned home to Whittier, passed the California bar examination in November 1937, and joined the town's oldest legal firm, Wingert and Bewley. As a good trial lawyer, he became a partner in the firm in 1939. On June 21, 1940, he married Thelma Catherine "Pat" Ryan.

In 1942 Nixon worked briefly for the Office of Price Administration in Washington, D.C., before joining the U.S. Navy as a lieutenant junior grade. During World War II he served for a time as supply officer at Bougainville, in the Solomon Islands. He left the Navy in 1945 as a lieutenant commander.

In 1946 Nixon ran to become U.S. representative from California's twelfth congressional district, which included Whittier and parts of Los Angeles. He defeated the Democratic incumbent in smear tactic campaign in which he accused his opponent of supporting communist causes. He was to use this theme in other election campaigns.

In 1950 Nixon was elected to the U.S. Senate, and in 1952 he was nominated to become the vice president on the Republican presidential ticket headed by Dwight D. Eisenhower. In 1960 he lost a close election for the presidency to John F. Kennedy.

In 1968 he won the presidential election, defeating the Democratic candidate, Vice President Hubert H. Humphrey. He followed that with a triumphant reelection landslide over George S. McGovern in 1972.

As the result of scandals in Maryland, Vice President Spiro T. Agnew resigned in 1973. Nixon nominated, and Congress approved, House Minority Leader Gerald R. Ford as vice president.

Nixon's second term was cut short by the so-called Watergate scandal, stemming from a break-in at the offices of the Democratic National Committee during the 1972 campaign. The break-in was traced to the president's reelection committee. A number of administration officials resigned; some were later convicted of offenses connected with efforts to cover up the crime. Nixon denied any personal involvement, but when faced with impeachment and almost certain conviction, he resigned from the presidency on August 9, 1974.

He was succeeded by Vice President Gerald R. Ford, who later would pardon him for any crimes that he may have committed as president. Nixon accepted the pardon.

During his retirement, Nixon wrote several books on his experience in public life and on foreign policy. He died on April 22, 1994, and was buried at the Nixon Presidential Library in Yorba Linda, California.

Bibliography

Aitken, Johnathan. *Nixon: A Life.* Washington, D.C.: Regnery, 1993.

Ambrose, Stephen E. *Nixon: The Education of a Politician, 1913–1962.* New York: Simon & Schuster, 1987.

Mazo, Earl Mazo, and Stephen Hess. *Nixon: A Political Portrait.* New York: Harper & Row, 1968.

Morris, Roger. *Richard Milhous Nixon: The Rise of an American Politician.* New York: Henry Holt, 1990.

Nixon, Richard. *The Memoirs of Richard Nixon.* New York: Grosset & Dunlap, 1978.

★ 38 ★

Gerald R. Ford

Thirty-eighth President
1974–1977

Gerald Rudolph Ford was born on July 14, 1913, in a basement apartment in Omaha, Nebraska. Named Leslie Lynch King at birth, he was the son of Dorothy Gardner King and Leslie King, a wool trader.

The Kings lived a tempestuous marriage. Leslie King, the son of a wealthy family, was a temperamental, mean-spirited husband who often berated and beat his wife, not only at home but also in public places. About a year after Gerald's birth, the three-year stormy marriage of his parents ended. Fearing for her and her son's safety, Dorothy King took Leslie and fled to her parents' home in Grand Rapids, Michigan. She divorced King in 1915.

While living with her parents, Dorothy Gardner met a young paint salesman named Gerald Rudolf Ford. He was man of good character and good temper. She found him to be genial and dependable.

The elder Ford had a rough life as a child. His father was killed when the boy was only 14, forcing him to quit school and help support his mother and three sisters. He had worked for the electric railroad company and a wood finishing company in Grand Rapids before becoming a paint salesman.

After almost a year of courting, Dorothy King and Gerald Ford were married on February 1, 1916. Dorothy immediately named her son Gerald Rudolf Ford. Her husband did not adopt Gerald after their marriage, probably of the belief in those times that it would be harmful to an adopted child to know that he was adopted. However, Ford took out formal adoption papers on December 3, 1935, and named his son Gerald Rudolf Ford, Jr. Gerald did not know until 1930 that Gerald Ford, Sr., was not his biological father. The son would later change the spelling of his middle name to Rudolph.

The marriage of Gerald and Dorothy Ford would produce three half-brothers for Gerald: Thomas G. Ford, born in 1918; Richard A. Ford, born in 1924; and James F. Ford, born in 1927.

For the first three years of their marriage, the Fords lived in a rented two-story house in Grand Rapids. In 1918, when Gerald was five years old, he developed a terrible stomach ache. His parents rushed him to a hospital, where the doctors diagnosed his problem as appendicitis and decided to operate as soon as possible. When it turned out his appendix had not been infected, his parents were furious.

In 1919, the family moved to East Grand Rapids and bought a two-story house. It was here that Gerald Ford's formative years were shaped. As a child, Gerald Ford had a temper, which his mother tried to curb. Afraid that he might have inherited his quick temper from his real father, she tried to reason with him and made faces at him to show how ridiculous he looked when mad. She also used to twist his ear. Other times she would send him upstairs to his room with orders to stay there until he was ready to discuss rationally what he had done wrong. One time she gave him the poem "If" by Rudyard Kipling. "Read this and profit from it," she said. "It will help you control that temper of yours."

"Despite all discipline, I never doubted her love," Gerald Ford wrote in his book, *A Time to Heal*.

Although Gerald's stepfather didn't show his emotions quite as openly, Gerald was well aware of his feelings. As a disciplinarian, he was every bit a strict as his wife. He drilled into Gerald and his half-brothers the importance of honesty and hard work. While a serious-minded person, the stepfather enjoyed playing games and sports with his sons.

During his first year in Madison Elementary School Gerald began stuttering. Certain words would not come out. Eventually, when he was about ten, the stuttering problem ended. Gerald Ford taught the stuttering was relating to his ambidexterity. Years later he would explain that he was left-handed when sitting down and right-handed when standing up. He threw a football with his right hand and wrote with his left. While it seemed perfectly natural to him, his parents and teachers tried without success to make him use his right hand all the time.

As a toddler, Gerald's mother called him Junie, short for Junior. First he was Junie King, then Junie Ford, but from high school on he was called Jerry. As an adult, Ford signs his name "Jerry," except when a formal signature is required. His friends call him Jerry.

When Gerald was 12 years old he became a Boy Scout, joining Troop 15, sponsored by the Trinity United Methodist Church in Grand Rapids. During the summer months, Gerald worked at the troop's training camp and became the first scout from Grand Rapids to be in the Governor's Honor Guard at the summer capital on Mackinac Island, Michigan. The Michigan governor makes Mackinac Island his home from June to September. Tradition is that Indians called the island the place of the Great Dancing Spirits— the loveliest spot in creation. When he left the troop in 1930, Gerald had attained the rank of Eagle Scout with 26 merit badges.

As the oldest boy in the family, Gerald had to help with various household chores. In the winter, he not only helped with snow shoveling, but it was his job to shovel coal into the furnace and empty out the ashes. During the summer he cut the lawn and helped clean out the garage. All of the boys had to make their own beds and take turns cleaning up the kitchen and washing dishes after every meal.

Life in the Ford family was not all chores. During the summer, his stepfather would put the family in his touring car and drive off on exciting sightseeing trips. Other times he would take Gerald on camping and fishing trips.

In 1929, when the Great Depression struck the nation, the Ford family lost their home when the bank foreclosed on the mortgage. The family was forced to move to a rented home on Union Avenue in Grand Rapids. The stock market crash nearly wiped out Ford Senior's newly formed Ford Paint and Varnish Company. Fortunately, since he had an impeccable reputation for paying his bills, the DuPont Corporation extended him credit. None of his employees lost their jobs, but took temporary pay cuts until the economy improved. To show his sincerity, Ford Senior also took a pay cut until he could afford to pay his workers more.

The rented home had a two-story garage in which Gerald and his playmates established their private social club, where they learned how to play penny-ante poker and other games. It was a great hideaway until his stepfather caught the boys red-handed and reprimanded them severely.

When Gerald was a teenager he took summer jobs, cutting lawns for neighbors, handling concessions at a local amusement park, and frying hamburgers in Bill Skougis' restaurant, across the street from the South High School. It was at the restaurant that Gerald Ford Junior learned that Gerald Ford Senior was not his real father. A man approached him at the counter and said, "I'm Leslie King, your father. Can we have lunch?" Gerald was stunned, but remained calm. Bill Skougis freed him from his duties and he joined King at another restaurant, where King explained how he had located Gerald by checking all the high schools in Grand Rapids for a "Junior Ford." Their talk over lunch was superficial, Gerald Ford recalled. After lunch, King gave him twenty-five dollars, and then waved goodbye.

That night was one of the most difficult times of his life. After he told his parents about meeting King, they comforted him, and told him the whole story of his adoption. His stepfather assured him he loved him as much as he loved his own three sons. When he went to bed that night, Gerald broke down and cried.

In 1927, Gerald Ford enrolled in Grand Rapids South High School, where he excelled in history and government. He also performed well in math and sciences and became a member of the National Honor Society. He joined the school's football team, playing center on offense. At that time football players played both offensive and defensive positions. On defense Ford was a roving linebacker. In 1930, the South High football team won the state championship.

After his graduation from South High School in June 1931, Gerald Ford's football record attracted the attention of some of the country's leading universities. He won a scholarship to the University of Michigan and enrolled as a pre-law student majoring in economics and political science.

At the University of Michigan, Ford was a center on Michigan's undefeated championship teams of 1932 and 1933. He was voted the team's most valuable player in 1934, and in 1935 he was selected as a College All-Star. When Ford graduated with a liberal arts degree in 1935, he refused offers from the Green Bay Packers and the Detroit Lions to play professional football. He decided instead to accept a job as a boxing coach at Yale University, where he qualified for admittance to its law school. Ford received his law degree in January 1941 and was admitted to the Michigan bar in June. He practiced law for a short time before joining the U.S. Navy in April 1942. During his naval service, from 1942 to 1946, he spent much of his service aboard the aircraft carrier USS *Monterey* as an assistant navigator, gunnery officer, and athletic officer.

187

Gerald R. Ford posing in his Grand Rapids South High School football uniform, 1930 (Gerald R. Ford Library).

Returning to Grand Rapids after the end of the war, Ford joined the law firm of Butterfield, Keeney, and Amberg in Grand Rapids. In 1948, the incumbent congressman of the Fifth Congressional District in Michigan was an isolationist Republican. With the support of his stepfather, who was county Republican chairman, Gerald Ford, Jr., challenged and soundly defeated the incumbent congressman. That same year, Gerald Ford married Elizabeth Ann ("Betty") Bloomer of Grand Rapids.

Gerald Ford served in the House of Representatives from January 1, 1949, to December 6, 1973, being reelected 12 times with more than 60 percent of the vote.

When Vice President Spiro Agnew resigned during the autumn of 1973, President Richard M. Nixon appointed Ford his vice president. Eight months later, on August 9, 1974, Nixon resigned, and Gerald R. Ford was inaugurated as the thirty-eighth president of the United States.

As president, Ford tried to calm the nation's political turmoil by granting former Nixon a full pardon for any crimes that he may have committed as president. Ford won the Republican nomination for the presidency in 1976, but lost the election to his Democratic opponent, former Governor Jimmy Carter of Georgia.

After leaving the White House, President Ford retired to Rancho Mirage, California. He continues to participate in the political process and to speak out on important political issues.

Bibliography

Cannon, James. *Time and Change: Gerald Ford's Appointment with History.* New York: HarperCollins, 1994.

Ford, Gerald R. *A Time to Heal.* New York: Berkley Publishing, 1980.

terHorst, Jerald F. *Gerald Ford and the Future of the Presidency.* New York: Joseph Okpaka Publishing, 1974.

★ 39 ★

James E. Carter, Jr.

Thirty-ninth President
1977–1981

When he was five years old, and flashing a toothy grin, James Earl Carter, Jr., sold boiled peanuts on the streets of Plains, Georgia. His father at first called him "Hot," as in "Hot Shot," but he is best known as Jimmy. He signs his name, "Jimmy Carter."

Jimmy, the oldest of the four children of James Earl Carter, Sr., and Lillian Gordy Carter, was born on October 1, 1924, at the Wise Hospital in Plains where his mother worked as registered nurse. Jimmy would later have two sisters, Gloria and Ruth; and a brother, Billy.

Carter Senior, who went by the name Earl Carter, or "Mr. Earl," as most townspeople called him, was a stern disciplinarian who punished Jimmy severely when he misbehaved. The punishment was administered with a peach tree switch. Once, when attending Sunday school as a five year old, Jimmy's father gave him a penny to put in the collection plate. Instead of donating the penny, Jimmy removed a penny from the plate. When Carter Senior discovered that his son had stolen a penny, he whipped his errant son immediately after the church service. "That was the last money I ever stole," Jimmy Carter wrote in his autobiography.

His mother, Bessie Lillian Gordy Carter, who went by her middle name, was a liberal who was always willing to adopt new ways. She advocated racial equality before it was acceptable in the South. As a nurse she served as a mid-wife to black sharecropper mothers who could not afford a doctor. She encouraged Jimmy to read and instilled in him the value of a good education. When she was 68 years old, she volunteered for the Peace Corps, spending two years in India disseminating birth control information.

Earl Carter's family settled in Plains in 1904 when he was ten years old. When he was 17 he left Plains and worked as a cowboy in Texas for two years. After a brief stint in the Army during World War I, he returned to Plains and invested his savings in business enterprises. After clerking in his brother's store, he invested in an ice house, a laundry and cleaning business, and a small grocery store. He also became a commodity broker, buying peanut futures on contract from local farmers and selling to an oil mill. He sold seeds and fertilizer to farmers.

In 1928 Earl Carter moved his family from their house in Plains to a 350-acre farm in Archery, a rural community and train stop about three miles west of Plains. The Carters and the family of a railroad worker were the only two white families living in Archery. There were about 25 black families in the community. During the Carters' stay in Archery, most of Jimmy's friends and playmates were the children from these black families. Realizing that there was prosperity to be found in agriculture, Earl Carter began investing in farm property. As an austere landowner and merchant, he would eventually own 4,000 acres, which were farmed by 200 black tenant farmers.

It was an exciting day when the Carter family moved into their new home in 1928. The front door was locked, and Earl discovered that he had forgotten the key. He tried to raise one of the windows that opened onto the front porch, but a wooden bar prevented the window from opening fully. He lifted four-year-old Jimmy so he could crawl through the partially open window to open the door from the inside.

The house was set back about 50 feet from the dirt road. It had broad front porch, and a screened porch that extended across the back of the house. The home was heated by fireplaces and wood stoves and did not have running water or electricity until 1938.

As a small boy, Jimmy Carter was required to help with the farm work. He carried water from a nearby spring to the men who worked the fields. He learned handle the mules and to plow. Farm work was heavy and a year-round job. As he became older and entered school, Jimmy still had chores to do on the farm. He helped with the planting and harvesting of peanuts and cotton.

Other produce from the Carter farm included sweet potatoes, watermelons, sugar cane syrup named "Plains Maid," and various fruits and vegetables. Earl Carter sold such goods at his general store in Plains.

Farm life wasn't all work. There were many opportunities for games and fun, fishing and hunting, and searching for Indian arrowheads in the fields. Earl Carter, a good athlete and a pitcher on the local baseball team, had installed a dirt tennis court on his farm. Jimmy remembers that he could play well against his high school buddies, but he could never beat his father playing tennis.

One day Jimmy tried to ride the farm's billy goat, named Old Gene Talmadge after the state governor. He quickly learned that goats are not like horses. The goat didn't try to throw him off like a bucking bronco, instead it ran head-on into a barbed-wire fence. The goat stopped but Jimmy didn't. He still has a two-inch scar on his right thigh as a permanent reminder of the goat-riding incident.

Earl and Lillian Carter wanted their children to be well educated. Reading was an important part of their daily lives. Earl Carter usually limited his reading to the daily and weekly newspapers and farm journals, but he also owned a small library, which contained mostly travel and adventure books. Lillian Carter was an avid reader who encouraged her children to read whenever they had an opportunity to do so. While talking at the dinner table was forbidden, it was acceptable to bring a book or magazine to read while eating. Jimmy became interested in books at an early age.

When Jimmy was about four years old, his godmother, Gussie Abrams, asked him what he wanted for Christmas. "Books," he replied. The godmother, apparently not knowledgeable about literature, gave him a set of the complete works of Guy de Maupassant. It would be years before he was able to read the books by the great French storyteller and novelist.

In 1930, when he was six years old, Jimmy Carter began school at the Plains School. The building housed the grammar school in its east wing and the high school in the north and west wings. The all-white school served students from first through eleventh grade. The school day began in the auditorium. Students sang patriotic songs, announcements were made, and on special occasions students performed plays on the stage for the student body.

Eager to learn, Jimmy was a good student. He enjoyed reading and from time to time would receive a silver star for every five books he read and a gold star for ten book reports. When he won a prize for reading most books in the third grade, his teacher invited him to her house for lunch. Sauerkraut, which Jimmy had never tasted, was served. He found the sauerkraut to be strange and vile and he believed that some terrible mistake had been made in the kitchen. Having been taught by his parents to clean his plate, he struggled to finish his strange meal.

Julia Coleman, the school principal and a seventh grade English teacher, was "the best teacher I ever had," Jimmy Carter wrote in his 2001 memoirs about his boyhood. "I thought ... that I was one of her pets ... but later learned that many others in my class had the same impression about themselves."

Miss Coleman encouraged Jimmy to learn about music, art, and especially literature. Every student in her classroom was required to debate, to memorize and recite poems and chapters from the Bible, and to participate in spelling bees and other cultural activities.

When Jimmy was 12 years old, Miss Coleman told him that he was ready to read *War and Peace*. Jimmy was happy with the title, because he thought that Miss Coleman had chosen for him a book about cowboys and Indians. He was appalled to learn that the book she had chosen was Leo Tolstoy's voluminous classic about the Napoleonic invasion of Russia.

Jimmy Carter's interest was not only in cowboys and Indians; he was very interested in the U.S. Navy, hoping some day to attend the United States Naval Academy in Annapolis, Maryland. His deep interest in the Navy can be traced to his early hero, Tom Watson Gordy, his mother's youngest brother.

Jimmy Carter and his dog Bozo, 1937 photograph (Jimmy Carter Library).

Uncle Tom, a Navy radioman, sent Jimmy small mementos, photographs, and letters telling him about his experiences in foreign lands. He was also lightweight boxing champion of the Pacific fleet.

Uncle Tom was stationed on the island of Guam when World War II started. He was captured a few days after the Japanese attack on Pearl Harbor, when the Japanese invaded Guam. Tom was first reported dead, but he was found to be alive, having been a prisoner in Japan during the war.

While in grammar school, Jimmy wrote to the Naval Academy and without revealing his age, asked for the entrance examination requirements. When the catalogue arrived, he almost memorized its content, making plans for his future naval career.

While an ensign at the Naval Academy, Jimmy Carter married Rosalynn Smith, his childhood sweetheart. They were wed on July 7, 1946, in Plains.

After Jimmy graduated from Plains High School in 1941 he enrolled at Georgia Southwestern College, a two-year school in Americus. He concentrated on subjects that were recommended in the Annapolis guidebook for prospective midshipmen. Then followed a year of engineering studies at the Georgia Institute of Technology, where he was a member of the Navy Reserve Officer Training Corps. The ROTC training qualified him for appointment to the U.S. Naval Academy, where he graduated in 1946. In the Navy he became a submariner, serving in both the Atlantic and Pacific fleets, and rising to the rank of lieutenant.

When his father died in 1953, Jimmy Carter resigned from the Navy and returned to Plains to run the family business. Soon after his return to Plains, he became involved in community activities. In 1962, he was elected to the Georgia Senate, and in 1971 became the governor of Georgia.

Carter announced his candidacy for president in December 1974 and began a two-year campaign that gradually gained momentum. At the Democratic convention in 1976, he was nominated on the first ballot. He chose Senator Walter F. Mondale of Minnesota as his running mate. He was elected president on November 2, 1976, defeating Republican President Gerald R. Ford by a popular vote of 50.06 percent to 48 percent. He served as president from January 20, 1977, to January 20, 1981.

After the presidency Jimmy Carter retired to Plains. He takes part in a variety of international political and humanitarian activities. He is active in Habitat for Humanity, a non-profit organization that helps build homes for the needy in the United States and in underdeveloped countries.

In 2002, the Norwegian Nobel Committee awarded Jimmy Carter the Nobel Peace Prize "for his decades of untiring effort to find peaceful solutions to international conflicts, to advance democracy and human rights, and to promote economic and social development."

Bibliography

Bourne, Peter G. *Jimmy Carter: A Comprehensive Biography from Plains to Postpresidency.* New York: Scribner, 1997.

Carter, Jimmy. *An Hour Before Daylight: Memoirs of a Rural Boyhood.* New York: Simon & Schuster, 2001.

_____. *An Outdoor Journal: Adventures and Reflections.* New York: Banta Books, 1988.

_____. *Why Not the Best?* Nashville, Tenn.: Broadman Press, 1975.

Morris, Kenneth E. *Jimmy Carter, American Moralist.* Athens: University of Georgia Press, 1996.

Wooten, James. *Dasher: The Roots and the Rising of Jimmy Carter.* New York: Summit Books, 1978.

Ronald W. Reagan

Ronald Wilson Reagan was born in the early hours of February 6, 1911, in an apartment above a bakery on Main Street in Tampico, Illinois. He was delivered by a doctor and midwife who braved a ten inch snowstorm to reach the Reagan apartment. When the father, John Edward "Jack" Reagan, first saw his son, he quipped that the ten pound baby was making a lot of noise like a fat Dutchman. He nicknamed his son "Dutch."

Jack Reagan, of Irish ancestry, was a shoe salesman, eking a modest living selling shoes in small Illinois towns. Reagan's problem with drinking kept him from holding well paying jobs. At the time of Ronald's birth, he was employed by the H.C. Pitney General Store. Ronald's mother, Nelle Wilson Reagan, was of Scot-English ancestry. She was named Nellie at birth, but called herself Nelle after her marriage to Jack. She was a warm-hearted, generous woman who often helped the needy and organized local drama recitals.

Ronald had a brother two years older, John Neil Reagan, who went by his middle name but was nicknamed "Moon" after a comic-strip character.

The Reagans' five-room apartment above the bakery on Main Street had no toilet facilities. The family had to use an outdoor toilet, and an outside pump supplied water. The apartment was heated by a coal-burning stove.

Three month's after Ronald's birth, the family moved to an old bungalow that had an indoor toilet and modern plumbing. The bungalow was located across a park that featured a Civil War cannon and pyramided cannon balls. The house was also near the railroad depot.

One day when Ronald was about 18 months old, he and Neil crawled through a stopped freight train to retrieve some ice chips from the train's ice wagon. Just as the train began to pull out of the station, Nelle Reagan saw the boys as they crawled out from between the cars to head back home. She was horrified at what she had seen, but happy that they were alive to receive a spanking when they arrived home.

During Ronald Reagan's early childhood, his father was constantly searching for a better and more secure job. When Ronald was two years old, the family moved to Chicago, where his father had gotten a job selling shoes at the Marshall Field's Department Store. The family lived in a small apartment that was lighted by a gas jet which provided light only if a quarter was deposited in the meter down the hall.

The Reagans had been in Chicago less than two years when Jack was offered a job with O.T. Johnson, a department store in Galesburg, about 140 miles to west of Chicago. Ronald was five years old at that time. Since the Galesburg school had no kindergarten, Nelle Reagan taught Ronald how to read by sitting with him every evening and having him follow her finger as she read. One day the father came home from work to find Ronald on the living room floor with a newspaper in front of him. "What are you doing?" he asked. "Reading the paper," Ronald replied.

"Okay, read something to me," the father said, and when Ronald did, he stunned both his parents. Young Ronald Reagan had demonstrated his extraordinary power of retention, a trait that would enhance his future careers.

Ronald was enrolled in the first grade of Silas Willard School in Galesburg in February 1916. His schooling was interrupted in 1918 when his father lost another job and the family was forced to move to Monmouth, Illinois, where Jack Reagan found a new job selling shoes at the E.B. Colwell Department Store.

At Monmouth Ronald entered Central School, where he impressed his third grade teacher with his amazing memory and his speed at multiplication and division. The nationwide flu epidemic which struck the nation in 1918 hit Monmouth in October, forcing the schools to close temporarily. Before the winter of 1918 ended, Ronald had contracted pneumonia and his mother nearly died from the flu. A short time later, a truck hit Neil and ran over his leg. Fortunately, the leg healed without complications.

During the summer of 1919, the Reagan family moved back to Tampico when H.C. Pitney offered Jack better pay and a chance to become a partner if he managed the H.C. Pitney General Store. Jack quickly accepted the offer, and the Reagans left Monmouth in August. This time they moved into an apartment above the Pitney store on Main Street.

The family's stay in Tampico was short. In 1920 Pitney decided to open a new store called the Fashion Boot Shop in Dixon, about 25 miles from Tampico. Pitney offered Jack Reagan a partnership. Reagan accepted the offer and borrowed money for his share of the partnership. Once again the Reagan family moved. Ronald was nine years old at that time, and from then on he considered Dixon his hometown.

In December 1920 the Reagan family moved into a two-story frame house located at 816 South Hennepin Avenue in Dixon. This would be the first of five homes Ronald Reagan lived in while in Dixon. Ronald and Neil shared one bedroom, the parents another, and the third was Nelle's sewing room.

After the family settled in their new home, the boys were enrolled in South Central Grammar School; Ronald entered fifth grade and Neil in the seventh grade. Personable Ronald had no trouble convincing fellow students to refer to the Reagan boys by their nicknames, Dutch and Moon.

Ronald Reagan had poor eyesight, which gave him trouble reading the blackboard even from a front seat in the classroom. Since he had excellent retention qualities, he bluffed his lessons, receiving good marks despite his handicap. When he participated in sports, he chose football over baseball. His poor eyesight made it difficult for him to catch and hit the baseball. However, he was an excellent football player.

Not long after his thirteenth birthday, the Reagans went for a Sunday afternoon automobile ride. Riding in the back seat, Ronald noticed his mother's reading glasses. On an impulse, he put them on. For the first time in his life he saw the scenery about him clearly. He was delighted to be fitted with horn-rimmed glasses, even though some of his classmates started calling him "Four Eyes." Nonetheless, the new glasses made his reading more pleasurable; he had more fun watching the Saturday matinee movies, and was able to catch and hit a baseball.

Dixon had two high schools. In September 1924, Ronald entered the North Dixon High School, which stressed culture in its courses. Neil was then attending South Dixon High School, which emphasized manual training. Ronald graduated from his high school in 1928. In sports the two schools fielded single teams in baseball and football.

Ronald Reagan at Dixon, Illinois, at the age of 12 or 13 (the White House).

After he had passed a lifesaving course at the YMCA, Ronald Reagan spent six summers—1927 through 1932—working as a lifeguard at Lowell Park on the Rock River. He was also responsible for suppling the park's concessions with ice and food. He worked seven days a week, 10 to 12 hours a day; first at $15, then $20 a week. He saved most of the money for his college education.

Reagan saved 77 lives during his six years as a lifeguard, a feat that made him a local hero. However, few of the swimmers whose lives he saved thanked him for his deed. Most of them argued that they weren't in any trouble, and didn't need to be saved. Only one person, a blind man, thanked him for saving his life. Once he was rewarded; a swimmer lost his dental plate. Ronald dove into the water and retrieved it. The swimmer gave him $10 for his effort.

Ronald Reagan was a low-B student at North Dixon High School. An indifferent student, he was concerned only with making the grades needed to remain eligible for football and other activities. A charismatic youngster, Ronald was a popular student who became president of the student body, wrote for the yearbook, and appeared in school plays.

B.J. Frazer, a new English teacher at North Dixon High School, wanted his students to be original and creative. The school's English teachers until then had graded student essays solely for spelling and grammar. Frazer announced that he was going to base his grades in part on the originality of their essays. Frazer discovered that Ronald was quite interested in literature and English. He found Ronald's essay so entertaining that he encouraged him to read them before the class. Frazer also staged plays in which Ronald was an eager participant. Frazer believed that Ronald could make a good actor.

Ronald Reagan graduated from North Dixon High School in 1928 and immediately enrolled at Eureka College, a small Disciples of Christ school near Peoria, Illinois. After plunking down the $200 he had saved from his lifesaving job, Ronald immediately applied for a needy student scholarship to cover the cost his savings would not afford. The college took a chance on the energetic young man and granted him the scholarship and a campus job to pay for his meals.

While Ronald Reagan majored economics at Eureka, he was fortunate to have an English professor, Ellen Marie Johnson, who had a talent for teaching dramatics. She helped him develop his theatrical skills, and by the time he graduated from Eureka in 1932, he was determined to establish himself as an actor. In 1937, after an initial career as a radio sportscaster, Reagan took a screen test at Warner Brothers Studio, which led to a seven-year contract.

Hollywood cast him as the All-American boy, a role he played many times. He eventually appeared in more than 50 feature films.

Reagan was married twice. He married actress Jane Wyman on January 26, 1940. After their divorce, he married actress Nancy Davis on March 4, 1952.

Reagan became involved in politics in the 1960s. During 1967–1975, he served as governor of California. Reagan won the Republican presidential nomination in 1980 and chose as his running mate former Texas congressman and United Nations Ambassador George Bush. In the election, Reagan defeated Jimmy Carter by 489 to 49 electoral votes.

On January 20, 1981, Reagan took office. Only 69 days later he was shot by a would-be assassin, but quickly recovered. Reagan and Bush were reelected in 1984. President Ronald Reagan died June 5, 2004, after a long illness.

Bibliography

Boyarsky, Bill. *Ronald Reagan: His Life and Rise to the Presidency*. New York: Random House, 1981.

Cannon, Lou. *Reagan*. New York: Perigee Books, Putnam, 1982.

Edwards, Anne. *Early Reagan*. New York: William Morrow, 1987.

Reagan, Ronald. *An American Life*. New York: Pocket Books, a division of Simon & Schuster, 1990.

Wills, Gary. *Reagan's America: Innocents at Home*. Garden City, N.Y.: Doubleday, 1981.

★ 41 ★

George H. W. Bush

Forty-first President
1989–1993

George Herbert Walker Bush was born June 12, 1924, in a makeshift delivery room of the family's Victorian mansion on Adams Street in Milton, Massachusetts. His birthplace may be of importance to those who believe in omens. Adams Street was named to honor President John Adams and his son, President John Quincy Adams. President George Herbert Walker Bush, born on Adams Street, sired another president, George Walker Bush.

George's parents were Prescott S. Bush and Dorothy Walker Bush. His father was a Wall Street investment banker and later served as a U.S. senator from Connecticut. His mother, an athletic woman and superb tennis player, was a devout Christian who emphasized self-discipline and good habits.

Because of his affluence, Prescott Bush was able to raise his children in an environment of wealth and privilege. However, George and his one sister and three brothers had to obey his demands and strict rules of behavior. While he showed much interest in his children's activities, they feared letting him down.

In a correspondence with this author, President George Bush wrote, "From my Dad I learned about service to country and service to others. Because of his example I became involved in community service and in service to our country in uniform. He was the true "Point of Light" and he epitomized the view that I later talked about, 'There can be no definition of a successful life that does not include service to others.'"

From his mother, President Bush learned the following: "Do not brag. Give the other guy credit. Be kind and help the ones that are teased and hurt by others. Tell the truth. Help those less fortunate than yourself. Be a good sport."

Despite the strict rules laid down by their father, the Bush children were happy. When they were taught to do something, they were also given the reason or purpose. Religion was an important part of the Bush family's daily life. The father would read a lesson from the Bible before breakfast on weekdays. On Sundays the family made regular visits to church.

George Bush was named after his mother's father, George Herbert Walker, whom she called Pop. George was called Poppy—little Pop, but the nickname faded away when George reached adulthood.

In 1925, Prescott Bush joined the United States Rubber Company based in New York and moved his family to the affluent neighborhood of Greenwich, Connecticut. At their comfortable eight-bedroom home in Greenwich, the family was served by three maids and a chauffeur who would drive the father to and from work and the children to and from school.

George Bush's best friend and favorite playmate was his brother, Prescott Junior—Pres—who was two years older. Pres and George shared a large bedroom. In 1931, when the family moved to a larger eight-bedroom house in Greenwich, their mother offered the brothers separate bedrooms. After a trial period, the boys decided that they liked to be together, and returned to their joint bedroom. They shared their toys, Matchbox toy cars, baseball cards and stamp collections.

The Bush family engaged heartily in athletics and games. Tradition was not just to play, but play to win. Each of the Bushes were expected to win. Occasionally, in his eagerness to win, George would abandon good sportsmanship. As a ten-year-old tennis player, he once ordered an aunt off the tennis court for making too much noise. When he complained to his mother that he lost a tennis match because his game was off, his feisty mother retorted, "You don't have a game."

Summer vacations for George and his siblings meant having fun at Walker's Point in Kennebunkport, Maine. Walker's Point, a ten-acre spit of rocks and land that reaches into the Atlantic Ocean, was purchased by his grandfather, George Herbert Walker, in 1902. At Walker's Point, George learned how to sail his grandfather's lobster boat, *Tomboy*, and fish for mackerel and pollack. He purchased the property shortly after becoming vice president.

In 1930, when he was six years old, George Bush entered the Greenwich Country Day School, a kind of prep school that prepared its students for real preparatory schools. Students attended first through ninth grade. George was a good student, with a particular flair for spelling and handwriting. He developed an interest in history and current events.

Every year, the students in the upper classes were required to deliver a memorized speech to the assembled school. Each student had two minutes to deliver his speech; if words failed him he had to stay on the podium until the time had passed. A long period of silence could be quite embarrassing, but George was never at loss for words. His two-minute talks were always humorous and interesting.

In the fall of 1937, 13-year-old George Bush was sent to the Phillips Academy in Andover, Massachusetts. Phillips Academy, better known as Andover, is one of the finest preparatory schools in the country. George plunged into the regimens of Andover with gusto. He was an industrious student, an all around athlete, and an eager participant in extracurricular activities. He was captain of the school's baseball and soccer teams and president of the senior class.

George developed a nearly fatal health problem during his junior year at Andover. A staph infection settled under his right arm, and with no sulfa drug to repel the germs, he spent several weeks in Massachusetts General Hospital. He had to stay at Andover for an extra term to make up for lost studies.

George Bush was six months away from his Andover graduation when Japan attacked Pearl Harbor on December 7, 1941. After Andover, George was scheduled to attend Yale University. However, he chose to delay his college education and, on June 12, 1942, his eighteenth birthday, he enlisted in the Navy as a seaman second class.

Since he wanted to be an aviator, the Navy sent him to flight school. He received his wings and commission in June 1943, thus becoming the youngest pilot in the Navy at that time. After flight training, Bush was assigned to a torpedo bomber squadron, taking part in 58 combat missions.

In September 1944, while on a bombing mission against a Japanese radio center in the Bonin Islands, his plane was struck by enemy gunfire. Two of his crewmen were killed. Forced to bail out from the stricken aircraft, Bush strug-

George Bush at age 13, July 13, 1937 (the White House).

gled in the water for more than three hours before he was rescued by the submarine Finback. For his service in the Navy, George Bush was awarded the Distinguished Flying Cross and three Air Medals.

After World War II ended, George Bush began his education at Yale University, where he pursued a degree in economics and served as captain of the varsity baseball team. He graduated Phi Beta Kappa in 1948. After graduation, he and his wife, Barbara, whom he had married in 1945, moved to Texas, where he worked in the oil fields, eventually heading a major off shore oil drilling company.

Having settled in Houston, Bush became active in Republican Party politics. He served in the House of Representatives during 1967–1971. In 1980, Ronald Reagan picked Bush to be his running mate. He served two terms as vice president. In 1988, George Bush became his party's nominee and in the general election, he and his vice presidential running mate, J. Danforth Quayle of Indiana, easily defeated the Democratic candidates, Michael Dukakis and Lloyd Bentsen, Jr. The Bush-Quayle ticket won 54 percent of the popular vote.

George Bush served as president of the United States from 1989 to 1993. After his presidency, Bush retired to his home in Houston, Texas.

Bibliography

Buckman, Dian Dincin. *Our 41st President, George Bush.* New York: Scholastic, 1989.

Bush, George, with Victor Gold. *Looking Forward.* New York: Doubleday, 1987.

Green, Fitzhugh. *George Bush: An Intimate Portrait.* New York: Hippocrene Books, 1989.

King, Nicholas. *George Bush: A Biography.* New York: Dodd, Mead, 1980.

Parmet, Herbert S. *George Bush: The Life of a Lone Star Yankee.* New York: A Lisa Drew Book/Scribner, 1997.

★ 42 ★

William J. Clinton

Forty-second President
1993–2001

William Jefferson Clinton, best known as Bill Clinton, had a difficult beginning. His father was killed in a car accident before he was born. His widowed mother remarried, but her marriage was troublesome; her alcoholic husband frequently beat and abused her. As a teenager he tried to keep peace in the family while protecting his mother and younger brother. Despite these difficulties, he excelled in school, becoming a student leader at an early age.

Bill Clinton was born early in the morning on August 19, 1946, under a cloudy sky after a violent summer storm to a widowed mother in the Julia Chester Hospital in Hope, Arkansas. His mother, Virginia Dell Cassidy Blythe, named the six and a half pound baby William Jefferson Blythe IV after his father, who had died in an automobile accident three months earlier.

When Bill was two years old, his mother left him with her parents, Eldridge and Edith Cassidy, and moved to New Orleans where she underwent training to become a nurse anesthetist. Grandmother Edith Cassidy took good care of Bill. She doted on him and fed him well because she liked fat babies. When he was two years old, she made flash cards with letters and numbers on them and taught him the rudiments of reading while he sat in a high chair. At least once a day, she would read him stories from children's books. Other times, when she was busy, Grandfather Eldridge Cassidy would bring

Bill to his small grocery store, where he came in contact with grown-ups. Since most of his customers were blacks who often brought their children to the store, Bill Clinton's early playmates were African American children.

Bill Clinton broke a leg when he was a four-year-old student in kindergarten. Dressed in a cowboy outfit, one of his boots got caught in a rope during recess. He fell and broke his leg above the knee. Since he was growing fast, the doctor was reluctant to place him in a cast. Instead, the doctor placed Bill's leg in traction. For the next two months he lay in a hospital bed with his leg elevated.

Another misfortune took place when Bill Clinton lived briefly on a farm in Hot Springs, Arkansas. Among the farm animals was a mean ram that he tried to avoid, but one day the ram spotted him and charged at Bill and his playmate, Karla, the daughter of one of his stepfather's friends. Karla ran fast and escaped over the fence. Bill stumbled over a rock and fell, then tried to escape from the ram by running around a tree until help came. Soon the ram caught up with Bill, knocked him down several times and butted him in the stomach and head until he started bleeding. Bill was rescued by an uncle, but the encounter with the angry ram left him with a scar on the forehead near the scalp.

After a year in New Orleans, Bill's mother returned home to Hope eager to put her anesthesia training into practice, and elated to be reunited with her son. She worked at several area hospitals before she landed a steady job at a hospital in Hot Springs, Arkansas.

Bill's mother met Roger Clinton, a shifty but charming car dealer, during the time she studied nursing in New Orleans. She knew nothing about him; still, she decided to marry him, to the dismay of her family. Her mother, Edith Cassidy, threatened to seek custody of her son. Clinton's reputation was not the best; he was known to be a heavy drinker, a gambler, and a womanizer. When Virginia Cassidy Blythe married Roger Clinton in Hot Springs on June 19, 1950, her parents and her four-year-old son were not at the ceremony.

The new family moved into a small wooden bungalow in Hot Springs. Roger Clinton tried to be a good father to Bill, but he never legally adopted his stepson. Soon Bill began calling his stepfather Daddy, and called himself Bill, or Billy, Clinton. During the 1951-1952 school year Bill Clinton attended Miss Marie Purkins' School for Little Folks kindergarten in Hope. The school was run by two sisters, Mary and Nannie Purkins. He then spent another year in Hope attending first grade at the Brookwood School.

In 1952, when Bill Clinton was seven years old, his mother enrolled him in the second grade at St. John's Catholic School in Hot Springs. The family belonged to a Baptist church, but Virginia Clinton believed that Bill would be better educated at the Catholic school than in a small rural school.

Bill received good grades at St. John's, except that he got low marks in conduct. His teacher explained to his mother that Bill was so intelligent and alert that he answered before the other children could raise their hands. She gave him a D grade in conduct, hoping that it would curb his over-enthusiastic behavior. Bill got the message and learned to give his classmates an equal chance.

In fourth grade he was transferred to Ramble Elementary School, the public elementary school in Hot Springs. From the first moment he attended Ramble he made friends with fellow students. When he got excited about something he used a catch phrase, "hot dog." Within a week most everyone in the school was saying "hot dog." Hot Springs had a school band composed of students from all the city's elementary schools. Bill Clinton joined the band, first playing the clarinet, then switching to tenor saxophone because the band needed a sax player.

Bill started the 1958-1959 school year at Central Junior High School in Hot Springs. His interest in music grew, and he enjoyed playing and marching at football games, in Christmas parades, and at regional and state band festivals. With the encouragement by his band directors he attended a summer band camp at the University of Arkansas campus in Fayetteville. He continued to attend the summer music camp during his high school years.

The Clinton family increased in July 1956 when his mother gave birth to a boy, Roger Cassidy Clinton. The new family member was born on the birthday of his father, who celebrated the event by getting drunk. Roger Clinton, Sr., was an alcoholic given to unbridled rage. Once Bill found his stepfather, raging drunk, brandishing scissors at his mother's throat while pinning her over the washing machine. Another time, when she fled the house to escape his angry outburst, he fired a gun near her.

Bill Clinton entered ninth grade at Hot Springs High School in 1960. His scholastic work was frequently hampered by his stepfather's alcoholism and violent abuse of his mother. The tumult created by his stepfather's excesses erupted into a serious confrontation one night when his stepfather started screaming at his mother, then hitting her in their bedroom.

Fourteen-year-old Bill Clinton, afraid that his mother was being hurt, grabbed a golf club and threw open the door. There he found his mother on the floor being beaten by her husband. Bill yelled to his stepfather to stop, and if he didn't, he would beat him with the golf club. The confrontation ended with the stepfather being arrested and taken to jail.

In 1962, Bill's mother divorced her husband and bought a brick ranch-style house on Scully Street in Hot Springs. As he had done several times before, Roger Clinton promised to change, and the couple were remarried later that year.

Bill Clinton was not happy about his parents' remarriage; however, shortly thereafter he went to the Garland County Courthouse and had his name legally changed from William Jefferson Blythe to William Jefferson Clinton. His mother agreed to the name change. Bill offered various reasons for the name change, but in his autobiography, *My Life*, he explained, "I wanted the same name as the rest of my family."

At Hot Springs High School, Bill Clinton was an outstanding student who participated in a variety of activities. He was especially interested in music, playing saxophone in several school bands, including the All-State Band. He also formed his own jazz combo, "The Three Blind Mice." He was a National Merit Scholarship semifinalist. He graduated fourth of the 323 students of the class of 1964.

During the summer of his junior year at high school, Bill Clinton attended a week-long camp sponsored by the American Legion Boys State program. At the end of the camp, Bill was one of two participants elected to go to the Boys Nation program held at the University of Maryland in College Park. On July 24, 1963, the boys were invited to the White House to meet President John F. Kennedy in the Rose Garden. After accepting a Boys Nation T-shirt, President Kennedy walked among the youths and began shaking hands. Bill Clinton nudged his way to the front and was delighted to have his hero shake his hand.

His meeting with President Kennedy fortified his interest in national and international affairs and set him on the road to a political career. Upon his graduation from high school, Bill Clinton enrolled in Georgetown University in Washington. He chose that university because of its excellent foreign service studies and because it was in the nation's capital.

During his spare time at Georgetown he worked in the office of Senator J. William Fulbright of Arkansas. Upon his graduation from Georgetown with a degree in international affairs in 1968, he won a two-year Rhodes scholar-

Bill Clinton gets ready to graduate from high school in 1964 (Clinton-Gore 1992 campaign).

ship to Oxford University in England. He returned to the United States in 1970 to study law at Yale University. At Yale he met fellow law student Hillary Rodham, whom he married on October 11, 1975. He received his law degree in 1973, and entered politics in Arkansas.

Clinton was elected Arkansas attorney general in 1976, and won the governorship in 1978. He lost his bid for reelection, but made a comeback to become governor of Arkansas during 1983–1992. The Democratic Party picked him to be its presidential candidate in the 1992 election. With Senator Albert Gore of Tennessee as his running mate, Bill Clinton won the national election, defeating his Republican opponent, President George Bush, by 370 to 168 electoral votes.

In 1998, as the result of issues surrounding personal indiscretion with a young female White House intern, Clinton was the second U.S. president to be impeached by the House of Representatives. He was tried in the Senate and found not guilty of the charges brought against him. He apologized to the nation for his actions and continued to have unprecedented popular approval ratings for his job as president.

William Jefferson Clinton served as president of the United States from 1993 to 2001. After the presidency, Clinton has remained in demand as a speaker and Democratic fundraiser. In 2001 he set up an office in Harlem in New York City. In 2004, Clinton published his autobiography, *My Life*. That same year, he successfully underwent quadruple heart bypass surgery.

Bibliography

Allen, Charles E., and Jonathan Portis. *The Comeback Kid: The Life and Career of Bill Clinton*. New York: A Birch Lane Book/Carol Publishing Group, 1992.

Clinton, Bill. *My Life*. New York: Alfred A. Knopf, 2004.

Kelley, Virginia, with James Morgan. *Leading with My Heart*. New York: Simon & Schuster, 1994.

Levin, Robert E. *Bill Clinton: The Inside Story*. New York: S.P.I. BOOKS/Shapolsky Publishers, 1992.

Maraniss, David. *First in His Class: A Biography of Bill Clinton*. New York: Simon & Schuster, 1995.

Oakley, Meredith L. *On the Make: The Rise of Bill Clinton*. Washington, D.C.: Regnery, 1994.

★ 43 ★

George W. Bush

Forty-third President
2001–

George Walker Bush was born at 12:30 a.m. on July 6, 1946, at the New Haven Hospital. His mother, Barbara Pierce Bush, was quick to tell family members to call him Georgie or Little George, but never refer to him as George Junior or George Bush II. Today he is referred to as George W., but at times misidentified as Junior. His father, former U.S. president George Herbert Walker Bush, a heroic Navy flier during World War II, was then a student at Yale University.

George and Barbara Bush lived in a small apartment in New Haven while George finished his degree at Yale. After his graduation in 1948, George accepted a job as a drilling equipment clerk with the International Derrick and Equipment Corporation in Odessa, Texas. The Bushes first purchased a small bungalow in nearby Midland. In 1955, after several moves, the family settled in the large brick home where George W. and his siblings grew up. George W. Bush has three brothers, John E. "Jeb," Neil M., and Marvin P., and a sister, Dorothy W. Another sister, Robin, died in 1953 of leukemia at age four.

Seven-year-old George W. was greatly saddened by the death of his sister. He cried and couldn't understand why his parents had not told him about his sister's illness. He asked questions, but his parents had no words to soften the pain. Some time later, when Little George was watching a high school football game with his father, the son looked up at the sky and said: "I wish that I was Robin." There was an awkward silence, and finally his father asked him why. "Because I bet she can see the game better from up there than we can here," explained Little George.

While the Bush family lived in Midland, George W. attended the Sam Houston Elementary School and San Jacinto Junior High School. He was an active youngster, riding his bicycle, and playing football and baseball, his favorite sport. He had a passion for baseball statistics and kept a large collection of baseball cards. His baseball idol was Willie Mays, star slugger and center fielder for the New York Giants. Scrappy and fearless, George W. played catcher for the Little League team, the Midland Cubs.

George W. did well at Sam Houston Elementary School and San Jacinto Junior High School, both academically and socially. He maintained decent grades, but being quick with smart remarks and foolish actions, he would at times get himself in trouble with his teachers. Once, during recess at the elementary school, he threw a football through a window. He created a disturbance in the fourth grade music class when, using a ball point pen, he marked his face to look like Elvis Presley. His teacher ordered him to the principal's office, where he was warned and sent to the washroom to scrub his face.

By the end of 1958 George Bush's oil business took him to Houston. The family moved to their new home in Houston in 1959, and George W. was enrolled in the Kincaid School, one of the most exclusive private schools in Texas. He studied at the Kincaid School during eighth and ninth grade. The effervescent boy quickly made friends and played football and other sports. He was fair student with a special interest in history. The school held speech and debate tournaments in which George W. scored well.

Kincaid was a stepping stone for more intense education. In 1961, after he had been at Kincaid for two years, his parents informed him that he had been accepted at the elite Phillips Academy in Andover, Massachusetts. When his buddies learned of him going to the New England boarding school, they jokingly asked what he had done wrong. In those days, Texas boys who were in trouble with their parents usually were shipped off to far away schools. In George W.'s case, it was a family tradition. George W. would follow in the footsteps of his father. His parent was eager for him to learn not only the academics but also how to thrive on his own.

When George W. arrived at Andover in the fall of 1961, he found him-

George W. Bush with his dog in Midland, Texas, February 11, 1954 (George Bush Library).

self in a regimented atmosphere. Life at Andover was a continual round of classes, athletics, required daily chapel attendance, and very little free time. The headmaster, a retired Army colonel, had established strict rules. Demerits were handed out to anyone who was even a few minutes late to chapel, classes or assemblies.

George W. was a popular student. He was head cheerleader for the football team and played baseball and basketball. In academics George W. was an average student who worried that he would not live up to his father's expectations. The elder Bush had been an outstanding student when he attended Andover.

One of the younger Bush's favorite subjects at Andover was history. George W. had been interested in history since he attended elementary and junior high school in Texas. The history of Texas was taught in fourth grade and then again in seventh grade. At Andover, history teacher Tom Lyons's description of events that shaped America's political history captured his imagination. Recognizing the importance of history, George W. decided that he would major in history when he went to college.

When George W. left home for Andover, his mother gave him a copy of the *Roget's Thesaurus*. He found use for it when his English teacher assigned the class to write a story about an emotionally powerful moment. George W. decided to write about his sister Robin's death. Trying to impress the instructor, George W. leafed through the thesaurus seeking a synonym for "tears." Finding his substitute word, he wrote, "And the lacerates ran down my cheeks." The paper came back marked "zero" with a note, "See me immediately." So much for trying to be smart.

George W. graduated from Andover in June 1964 and then enrolled at Yale University, where he majored in history. Before classes started at Yale, George W. returned to Texas to help with his father's first congressional campaign. The father lost the election, but George W. learned much that would help him in his own political career.

George W. Bush attended Yale from 1964 to 1968, graduating with a degree in history. In May 1968, just prior to his graduation from Yale, he enlisted as an airman in the Texas Air National Guard. He earned his pilot wings in December 1969; the following year he completed combat crew training and was certified as a fighter pilot. He flew with the Texas Air National Guard until 1973, when he resigned from the service in order to enter Harvard Business School.

George W. married Laura Welch, a librarian, on November 5, 1977, in Midland, Texas. They first met at a backyard barbecue at the home of a mutual friend, and were married three months later.

After working on his father's successful 1988 presidential campaign, George W. Bush assembled a group of partners who purchased the Texas Rangers baseball franchise. He later entered politics in Texas, and in 1994, was elected governor.

Bush's victory in Texas opened the way for the Republican Party's presidential nomination in 2000. With former Wyoming congressman Richard Cheney as his vice presidential running mate, Bush defeated Democrat Albert A. Gore in the 2000 presidential election. George W. Bush was sworn in as the forty-third president of the United States on January 20, 2001. He was reelected in 2004.

Bibliography

Bush, George W. *A Charge to Keep*. New York: William Morrow, 1999.
Minutaglio, Bill. *First Son: George W. Bush and the Bush Family Dynasty*. New York: Times Books/Random House, 1999.
Mitchell, Elizabeth. *Revenge of the Bush Dynasty*. New York: Hyperion, 2000.
Wukovits, John F. *George W. Bush*. San Diego, Calif.: Lucent Books, 2000.

Further Reading

Angelo, Bonnie. *First Mothers: The Women Who Shaped the Presidents*. New York: William Morrow, 2000.
Beschloss, Michael, ed. *American Heritage: The Presidents*. New York: iBooks. 2003.
DeGregorio. William A. *The Complete Book of U.S. Presidents*. New York: Gramercy Books, 2001.
Faber, Doris. *The Mothers of American Presidents*. New York: The New American Library, 1968.
Gullan, Harold I. *First Fathers: The Men Who Inspired Our Presidents*. Hoboken, N.J.: John Wiley & Sons, 2004.
Kane, Joseph Nathan. *Presidential Fact Book*. New York: Random House, 1998.
Kunhardt, Philip B., Jr., Philip B. Kunhardt, III, and Peter W. Kunhardt. *The American President*. New York: Riverhead Books (Penguin Putnam), 1999.
Whitney, David C., and Robin Vaughn Whitney. *American Presidents*. Garden City, N.Y.: Doubleday Book & Music Clubs, 1993. Published by The Reader's Digest Association, 1993.
Young, Jeff C. *The Fathers of American Presidents*. Jefferson, N.C.: McFarland, 1997.

Index